THE ONLY WAY TO...
LEARN
ASTROLOGY
VOLUME I

BASIC PRINCIPLES

THE ONLY WAY TO...

LEARN ASTROLOGY

VOLUME I

BASIC PRINCIPLES

BY MARION D. MARCH & JOAN McEVERS

International Standard Book Number 0-917086-00-7

Printed in the United States of America

Published by ACS Publications, Inc.
P.O. Box 16430
San Diego, CA 92116-0430

First printing, January 1980
Second printing, July, 1981
Third printing, December, 1982
Fourth printing, December, 1983
Fifth printing, April, 1985

We dedicate this book with many thanks to our students, whose urging and encouragement made it a reality, and with love to our husbands, Dean McEvers and Nico March, who spent many a long evening alone and neglected.

Contents

Foreword

Astrology is so profound and diverse that teaching it is a complex art. Too many teachers surrender to the difficulties and end up repeating the stereotyped lore and methods that have come down to us from earlier and far different times.

Not so Marion March and Joan McEvers. This book is the result of several years of experimentation, paying special attention to the needs of the beginning student. These are by no means the same as the needs of the beginner studying a more conventional and less controversial subject. Each lesson is carefully worked out with test questions at the end to assure that the student really understands what has been covered. (Many texts tend to go too fast and too superficially.) It should therefore prove a boon to those who live in out-of-the-way places or cannot find a teacher and must therefore teach themselves from books.

An unusual feature of the March-McEvers method is that it postpones teaching chart casting until after the student learns the rudiments of interpretation. As the authors explain, it is all too common for the student to cast the charts of everyone he or she knows and to be far from modest in interpreting them, before learning the meanings of the signs, planets and aspects. And the beginner does indeed have a tendency to zero in on disaster, often with unfortunate psychological results.

There is no subject that demands more tolerance and patience of the practitioner than astrology. This book is a step forward because it strives to develop these difficult virtues from the beginning.

Barbara H. Watters
Washington, D.C.
July 1976

Preface

We have written this book because we believe that the teaching outline, which we have developed over the last ten years is easy, logical and the best. We have taught hundreds of students and over forty percent have either gone on to become professional astrologers or stayed with us through the intermediate and advanced courses. But more important than this unusually low dropout percentage is the fact that the ones who stayed with it are all excellent astrologers. We can't even say that this is because we are great teachers. Our group, under the auspices of Aquarius Workshops, Inc., has many other teachers who use this same teaching outline, and their results are as good as ours.

What really convinced us to write this book were the many students who came to us from other schools and/or teaching methods, who urged us repeatedly to put our course outline into book form so that others could benefit from it.

Now you know the why. Before we show you the how, here are a few important facts and suggestions. Astrology, like any new field, takes time and application. You might compare it to learning a new language. Only practice brings mastery.

For every lesson in this book (and they are truly "lessons" not chapters), you should spend at least two hours on review and homework. The more you practice, the quicker astrology will sink into your subconscious. At the end of the book you should be totally familiar with all of the new words and symbols. You will have learned about the signs of the zodiac, the planets, the houses and the relationships they all have to each other. In the first part of this book we give you keywords to help you remember the basic qualities assigned to each sign, planet and house. In the second part, we go into more detail.

It is quite normal, at first, to feel overwhelmed by this mass of new material, but don't get discouraged. Many others have felt the same way. Throughout the book we repeat and repeat and repeat again, until it all begins to sink in and becomes crystal clear. Because this book was adapted from our teaching material, we already know the questions new students will ask, the areas of frustration and the stumbling blocks, and we have learned how to handle them.

Everyone learns differently. Yet we know that if we use more than one approach, the learning process will be quicker. Reading is just one part of learning; therefore, it is very important that you do the assigned homework, which will involve writing, another approach.

Do try to read this book from beginning to end, rather than jumping from lesson to lesson and gleaning some information here and there without a proper foundation. The order of the lessons is based on a definite sequence, one that we've found leads to an easier and better understanding of basic astrology.

We hope that you will enjoy this book, but more than that, we hope that astrology will open up new horizons of understanding and broaden and enrich your scope of life.

We have each been actively involved with astrology for many years, and during this time we have had some marvelous teachers to whom we owe a lot. To mention a few: Ruth Hale

Oliver, Kiyo, Irma Norman and Zipporah Dobyns. Some of their thinking and philosophy is obviously incorporated into this book. To each of them our deepest thanks.

Joan McEvers and Marion March
Los Angeles, California
January 1980

Part I

Lesson 1: Introduction

What is Astrology?

Astrology is the science that explores the action of celestial bodies upon animate and inanimate objects, and their reactions to such influences. Astrology has its place among the earliest records of human learning. It is the parent of astronomy; for many years they were one science. Now, astronomy is a science of distances, magnitudes, masses, motions, speeds, locations, and so on, based upon observations made with instruments like the telescope. Astronomy may therefore be termed an "objective" science, while astrology must be termed a "subjective" science. Thus, the charting of the horoscope is really an astronomical process; the judgment or delineation of the horoscope is an astrological process.

Astrology also deals with angles between the planets and

their observed effect upon humanity. The signs are a way of dividing the heavens; so are the houses, but they are based upon the place of birth. The sign may be considered the field of action; the house is the place where the action occurs, and the planet is the motivating power or force.

Astrology teaches us that there is harmony and symmetry in the universe and that everyone is part of the whole. Thus, you should try to understand astrology as a philosophy which helps to explain life, and not as a predictive art or science. The purpose of astrology is not to blame the planets for what happens to us, but, on the contrary, to learn about ourselves by planetary indication. When we see ourselves clearly we can discover within ourselves new qualities, and thus our lives can become more fulfilled, purposeful and productive.

Originally, astrology was divided into four parts:

Natural or *physical:* the action of the planets on the tides, weather, atmosphere and seasons.

Mundane or *judicial:* the astrology of nations, their economic and political cycles.

Natal or *genethliacal:* the astrology of individuals and the study of their birth charts.

Horary: the study of some particular question that occurs at some moment in time and place.

In this book we will be concerned with *natal astrology*.

There are two kinds of astrology practiced in the west. One is called *tropical* astrology; the other, *sidereal*. Tropical astrology gives the position of a planet by sign. Sidereal astrology gives the position by constellation. To understand the difference between the two, we must understand the difference between the signs and the constellations. Both have the same names, which can cause considerable confusion to beginners. Approximately 4,000 years ago, when on the vernal equinox, the first day of spring, the Sun was in the constellation of Aries, there was no difference. The signs and the constellations coincided. Now, because of precession, the slow wobble of the Earth about its axis, the Sun enters the vernal equinox in the sign of Aries but in the constellation of Pisces.

The signs are divisions of space along a circle called the ecliptic. The ecliptic is the path through the heavens that all of the planets appear to follow. There are 360 degrees in a circle, and there are twelve signs, each occupying a segment of exactly thirty degrees. $30 \times 12 = 360$. Aries is the name given to the first thirty-degree sector of space that begins with the vernal equinox.

Thus signs are calculated from what astrologers call the *Aries ingress*, or the point at which the Sun reaches 0° Aries. This point is now located in the constellation Pisces. We mention this here, right at the beginning, because you will meet people who are familiar with astronomy or sidereal astrology who may attempt to undermine your confidence by insisting that if you think your Sun is, for example, in Aries, you were really born with your Sun in the constellation of Pisces. You are both right, so there is no need to argue about it. Sidereal and tropical astrology are based upon different principles, and both are valid. In this book, we will be teaching you *tropical astrology.*

What is a Horoscope?

The word *horoscope* means "hour pointer." It is a map or diagram of the heavens erected to determine the potentials and characteristics of a person born at a specific time and place upon the planet Earth. This diagram is also called a *natal chart,* a *radical chart* or a *nativity.* In order to construct an accurate horoscope, it is essential to have the exact birthtime and the exact latitude and longitude of the birthplace. It is wise to remember, right from the beginning, not to erect a horoscope unless the data can be verified from official records. Your mother's testimony that you were born at a certain time is probably inaccurate. It may lead to hours of wasted time and effort, and finally to doubting the validity of astrology, because the horoscope and the person won't seem to match.

To erect a birth chart is relatively easy for anyone who can add, subtract, and multiply. However, the reading or delineation of a chart calls for judgment and the ability to deduce what is likely to happen under certain astrological conditions. The intricacies of astrology take considerable learning, time, practice and, most of all, serious reflection and application.

In this book we will teach you the meanings of the signs, planets, houses and aspects. After you have acquired some knowledge of these basic elements of astrology and learned how to read a natal horoscope, then you will be ready to

Figure 1: The Alphabet of the Astrologer Here are the basic astrological glyphs (symbols). It is important that you become familiar with these symbols and memorize them.

The Planets

☽ Moon

☿ Mercury

♀ Venus

☉ Sun

♂ Mars

♃ Jupiter

♄ Saturn

♅ Uranus

♆ Neptune

♇ Pluto

⊕ Earth

☊ North Node

☋ South Node

The Signs

♈ Aries

♉ Taurus

♊ Gemini

♋ Cancer

♌ Leo

♍ Virgo

♎ Libra

♏ Scorpio

♐ Sagittarius

♑ Capricorn

♒ Aquarius

♓ Pisces

calculate one. Keep in mind that you are really learning a new kind of symbolic language, and only by rote and application will you become fluent in it.

The astrology you learn will enable you to view the events that occur in your life and in the lives of others more intelligently. This is because you will be able to see and understand what forces are operating, and you will learn to see how these forces correspond to what is happening. However, always remember that your free will and your attitude will determine how much or how little use you make of the talents and potentials you were born with. The choice is yours.

The Natural or Flat Wheel

On page 7 you will find what astrologers call a *natural* or *flat wheel*. In order to familiarize yourself with the construction of the natal horoscope, you will now learn where the twelve signs belong in the natural horoscope. You can either write in the book, or if you prefer, you can draw your own wheel.

Start by placing the symbol for Aries in its correct position on the eastern point of the chart. This point is the boundary line between the twelfth and first houses. This line is called the first house cusp, and it is given a very special name, the *Ascendant* or *rising sign*. Put the symbol for Aries near the point where the cusp meets the circle.

Next, move down counterclockwise to the cusp of the second house, the line dividing the first and second houses. At the point at which this cusp meets the circle, place the symbol for Taurus.

Again, move counterclockwise to the cusp of the third house and place the symbol for Gemini in its proper place.

Continue around the circle until you have inserted the symbol for each sign (as given in the chart on page 4) in its proper place in the chart. You should finish with the sign Pisces on the cusp of the twelfth house. You may check your work by comparing it with the completed chart in the Appendix (see page 282).

The Elements

We sort the twelve signs of the zodiac into groups with certain common characteristics. One way to do this is by temperament. This grouping is said to be by *element* or *triplicity*, and is as follows:

Fire signs: Aries, Leo and Sagittarius. These signs are fiery, ardent, enthusiastic, spontaneous, self-sufficient and romantic. Misused, they can be bossy and too forceful.

Earth signs: Taurus, Virgo and Capricorn. These signs are practical, earthy, dependable, conservative and sensual. They love material comforts and have good recuperative powers. Misused, they can be dull and too materialistic.

Air signs: Gemini, Libra and Aquarius. These signs can communicate well; they tend to be intellectual, and they are able to handle abstract reasoning. They are logical, broad-minded, objective, idealistic and unprejudiced. Misused, they can be cold and impractical.

Water signs: Cancer, Scorpio and Pisces. These signs are feeling, sustaining and receptive. They are emotional, intuitive, responsive, sensitive and deep. They tend to be susceptible to moods, and are easily influenced by the environment. Remember that water is found in three forms: liquid (water), frozen (ice) and gaseous (steam). Cancer is the liquid form; Scorpio is the frozen form, and Pisces is the gaseous form. Misused, these signs can be self-indulgent, self-pitying and wavering.

Using your flat wheel you will now place the proper elements with their correct signs. In order to do this you must first understand that the sign on the cusp of each house is the sign that has precedence in that house. Place the word "fire" in the three houses that are related to the fire signs. To do this, you will place the word "fire" in the first house (Aries), in the fifth house (Leo), and in the ninth house (Sagittarius). Continue to do this with the three other elements until each house contains the name of one element. For example, the sixth house should contain the word "earth", the eleventh house the word "air", etc. You may check your work against the completed chart in the Appendix (page 282).

The Qualities

We can also divide the twelve signs of the zodiac into three groups of four signs each; the signs in each group have certain *qualities* in common. Each group has a distinct mode of operating in life. The qualities or *quadruplicities* are:

Figure 2: Natural or Flat Wheel This is the wheel of the twelve houses of the zodiac showing the directions (east, west, north, and south) and the meridian and horizon lines. As you proceed with lesson 1, you will put the information that we give you into the proper houses on the chart. You may want to draw your own chart. You can do this by drawing a circle and dividing it into twelve sections, numbering the houses as below, and writing in the words "Ascendant," and so on, as we have done here.

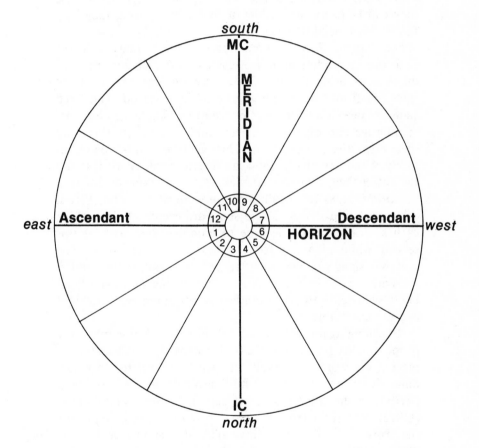

Cardinal signs: Aries, Cancer, Libra and Capricorn. These signs are the four cardinal points of the compass: east, west, north and south. Aries is east; Libra is west; Cancer is north, and Capricorn is south. These signs are called cardinal because they govern the change of the seasons: Aries, spring; Cancer, summer; Libra, fall; and Capricorn, winter. Cardinal signs are initiatory, active, ardent, ambitious, enthusiastic and independent. Their minds are quick and insatiable. Used negatively, they can be hasty, inconsiderate and domineering; they may fail to finish what they start.

Fixed signs: Taurus, Leo, Scorpio and Aquarius. These signs are the middle month of each season. Whereas the cardinal signs bring the transition between seasons, the fixed signs are firmly set in the middle of each season. The fixed signs are determined, able to concentrate, stable, resolute, accumulative and dignified. Their minds are penetrating, and their memories are excellent. They achieve results slowly but surely. Used negatively, they can be stubborn, egotistical and too entrenched in their particular ways of looking at things.

Mutable signs (also called *common signs*): Gemini, Virgo, Sagittarius and Pisces. These signs are the closing month of each season. This is the time to complete the work of this season while planning for the new season to come. The mutable signs are versatile, adaptable, changeable, subtle, sympathetic and intuitive. Their minds are ingenious and flexible. Used negatively, they can be deceptive, crafty, inconstant and undependable.

Returning again to your flat wheel you will now insert the proper quality for each of the twelve signs. To do this, start by placing the word "cardinal" in each house related to a cardinal sign: thus, you will write "cardinal" in the first house (Aries), in the fourth house (Cancer), in the seventh house (Libra), and in the tenth house (Capricorn). Continue placing the words "fixed" and "mutable" in the proper houses. Again, check the accuracy of your work against the completed flat wheel in the Appendix.

Rulerships

Each sign of the zodiac has a planetary *ruler,* a planet that is harmonious in temperament with the sign it rules. The sign rulerships are as follows:

Sign		*Ruler*	
♈	Aries	♂	Mars
♉	Taurus	♀	Venus
♊	Gemini	☿	Mercury
♋	Cancer	☽	Moon
♌	Leo	☉	Sun
♍	Virgo	☿	Mercury
♎	Libra	♀	Venus
♏	Scorpio	♇	Pluto
♐	Sagittarius	♃	Jupiter
♑	Capricorn	♄	Saturn
♒	Aquarius	♅	Uranus
♓	Pisces	♆	Neptune

On the flat wheel insert the proper planetary symbol in the house that corresponds to the sign of that house. For example, insert the symbol for Mars in the first house (Aries); the symbol for Venus in the second house (Taurus), and so on until there is a planetary symbol in each of the twelve houses.

The Houses

The houses can also be classified into three groups of four houses each; these correspond to the qualities of the signs previously discussed. Each house group shares characteristics in common, which we shall discuss in detail later in this book. The houses are grouped as follows:

The angular houses: first, fourth, seventh and tenth.
The succedent houses: second, fifth, eighth and eleventh.
The cadent houses: third, sixth, ninth and twelfth.

On your flat wheel, place the word "angular" in the first, fourth, seventh and tenth houses; the word "succedent" in the second, fifth, eighth and eleventh houses and the word "cadent" in the third, sixth, ninth and twelfth houses.

In astrology, each house has a meaning, which will be fully explained in lesson 4. To help you understand the significance of each of the houses, at this point we will give you one keyword for each house to insert on the flat wheel. Note that opposite houses have opposite keywords.

First house: I or me (the person whose chart it is)
Seventh house: you (the other person)

Second house: mine (what belongs to me)
Eighth house: yours (possessions of others)

Third house: here (my immediate environment)
Ninth house: there (more distant places)

Fourth house: private (my private life)
Tenth house: public (my public life)

Fifth house: love given (the love I give)
Eleventh house: love received (the love I receive)

Sixth house: physical health (the state of my body)
Twelfth house: mental health (the state of my mind)

On the flat wheel write each keyword in the appropriate house.

All functions and energies in nature follow the positive/negative principle. Astrology is no exception. The signs of the zodiac are divided into positive and negative, or in astrological terms, *active* and *passive* signs, also called *masculine* and *feminine*. All odd-numbered signs (the fire and air signs) are considered active. All even-numbered signs (the earth and water signs) are considered passive. Please write the words "active" and "passive" in the appropriate houses on the flat wheel.

Summary

You have now completed your flat wheel and have been introduced to some of the basic elements of a horoscope. Every profession has its tools: the carpenter works with a saw and hammer, the surveyor with a transit and the astrologer with a horoscope. In order to become proficient a person must learn to handle the tools of that profession well. In this lesson, you have taken the first step in learning how to use the horoscope. In the next few lessons, we shall study each of these basic elements in detail to learn more about them.

Before proceeding to lesson 2 you should memorize the symbols given on page 4. Write each symbol until you feel comfortable writing it and until you know what each symbol means automatically. Then you will have the basic alphabet of astrology.

Lesson 2: The Signs

Introduction

In lesson 1 you learned that there are twelve signs in the zodiac, and that each of these signs has a natural planetary ruler. You also learned that there are different ways of grouping these signs. We pointed out that each sign is a field of action in which the planetary forces operate. Each sign has a full range of possibilities, and the individual has the option of using what the sign indicates in a positive or beneficial manner, on the one hand, or in a negative or abusive manner on the other.

In this lesson we will focus our attention only on the signs. How each planet operates in a particular sign and what that means will be discussed in later lessons. What you learn here you can later apply to any planet found in any sign. For example, you will discover that Aries is bold and dynamic. The

Moon represents the emotions, and when the Moon is in Aries we would expect that person to express emotions in a bold and dynamic manner. If Mercury is in Aries, we would expect the individual to reason and think boldly and dynamically. First, however, it is necessary to learn these basic modes of expression for each of the signs.

As you learn the basic qualities of each sign and then discover where each of your own planets is located, you may begin to express each of your planetary energies in accordance with the positive qualities and traits of that sign.

♈ ARIES (the ram)

quality	cardinal	glyph	ram's horns
element	fire		
principle	active	natural sign of	first house
ruler	Mars ♂	opposite sign	Libra ♎
anatomy	head, face, brain, upper teeth		
key phrase	*I am*	keyword	*activity*

positive characteristics		negative characteristics	
	pioneering		domineering
	executive		quick-tempered
	competitive		violent
	impulsive		intolerant
	eager		hasty
	courageous		arrogant
	independent		"me first"
	dynamic		brusque
	lives in present		lacks follow-
	quick		through

♉ TAURUS (the bull)

quality	fixed	glyph	bull's head and horns
element	earth		
principle	passive	natural sign of	second house
ruler	Venus ♀	opposite sign	Scorpio ♏
anatomy	throat, neck, ears, vocal chords, thyroid, tongue, mouth, tonsils, lower teeth		
key phrase	*I have*	keyword	*stability*

positive characteristics	negative characteristics
patient	self-indulgent
conservative	stubborn
domestic	slow-moving
sensual	argumentative
thorough	short-tempered
stable	possessive
dependable	greedy
practical	materialistic
artistic	
loyal	

♊ GEMINI (the twins)

quality	mutable	glyph	Roman numeral 2
element	air		
principle	active	natural sign of	third house
ruler	Mercury ☿	opposite sign	Sagittarius ♐
anatomy	lungs, collar bone, hands, arms, shoulders, nervous system		
key phrase	*I think*	keyword	*versatility*

positive characteristics	negative characteristics
dual	changeable
congenial	ungrateful
curious	scatterbrained
adaptable	restless
expressive	scheming
quick-witted	lacking in concentration
literary	lacking in follow-through
inventive	
dextrous	
clever	

♋ CANCER (the crab)

quality	cardinal	glyph	crab's claws
element	water		
principle	passive	natural sign of	fourth house
ruler	Moon ☽	opposite sign	Capricorn ♑
anatomy	breast, stomach, upper lobes of liver		
key phrase	*I feel*	keyword	*devotion*

positive characteristics	negative characteristics
tenacious	brooding
intuitive	touchy
maternal	too easily hurt
domestic	negative
sensitive	manipulative
retentive	too cautious
helpful	lazy
sympathetic	selfish
emotional	sorry for self
patriotic	
good memory	
traditional	

♌ LEO (the lion)

quality	fixed	glyph	lion's tail
element	fire		
principle	active	natural sign of	fifth house
ruler	Sun ☉	opposite sign	Aquarius ♒
anatomy	heart, sides, upper back		
key phrase	*I will*	keyword	*magnetism*

positive characteristics	negative characteristics
dramatic	vain
idealistic	status conscious
proud	childish
ambitious	overbearing
creative	fears ridicule
dignified	cruel
romantic	boastful
generous	pretentious
self-assured	autocratic
optimistic	

♍ VIRGO (the virgin)

quality	mutable	glyph	spelling of Greek word for "virgin"
element	earth		
principle	passive	natural sign of	sixth house
ruler	Mercury ☿	opposite sign	Pisces ♓
anatomy	intestines, liver, pancreas, gall bladder, lower plexus, upper bowel		
key phrase	*I analyze*	keyword	*practicality*

positive characteristics	negative characteristics
industrious	critical
studious	petty
scientific	melancholy
methodical	self-centered
discriminating	fears disease and
fact-finding	poverty
exacting	picky
clean	pedantic
humane	skeptical
seeks perfection	sloppy

♎ LIBRA (the scales)

quality	cardinal	glyph	the scales
element	air		
principle	active	natural sign of	seventh house
ruler	Venus ♀	opposite sign	Aries ♈
anatomy	kidneys, lower back, adrenal glands, appendix		
key phrase	*I balance*	keyword	*harmony*

positive characteristics	negative characteristics
cooperative	fickle
persuasive	apathetic
companionable	loves intrigue
peace-loving	peace at any price
refined	pouting
judicial	indecisive
artistic	easily deterred
diplomatic	
sociable	
suave	

♏ SCORPIO (the scorpion)

quality	fixed	glyph	scorpion's tail and its sting
element	water		
principle	passive	natural sign of	eighth house
ruler	Pluto ♀	opposite sign	Taurus ♉
anatomy	the genitals, bladder, rectum,		reproductive organs
key phrase	*I desire*	keyword	*intensity*

positive characteristics	negative characteristics
motivated	vengeful
penetrating	temperamental
executive	secretive
resourceful	overbearing
determined	violent
scientific	sarcastic
investigative	suspicious
probing	jealous
passionate	intolerant
aware	

♐ SAGITTARIUS (the archer)

quality	mutable	glyph	archer's arrow
element	fire		
principle	active	natural sign of	ninth house
ruler	Jupiter ♃	opposite sign	Gemini ♊
anatomy	hips, thighs, upper leg		
key phrase	*I understand*	keyword	*visualization*

positive characteristics	negative characteristics
straightforward	argumentative
philosophical	exaggerative
freedom-loving	talkative
broadminded	procrastinating
athletic	self-indulgent
generous	blunt
optimistic	impatient
just	a gambler
religious	pushy
scholarly	hot-headed
enthusiastic	

♑ CAPRICORN (the seagoat)

quality	cardinal	glyph	seagoat's horn and tail
element	earth		
principle	passive	natural sign of	tenth house
ruler	Saturn ♄	opposite sign	Cancer ♋
anatomy	knees and lower leg		
key phrase	*I use*	keyword	*ambition*

positive characteristics	negative characteristics
cautious	egotistic
responsible	domineering
scrupulous	unforgiving
conventional	fatalistic
businesslike	the mind rules the heart
perfectionist	
traditional	stubborn
practical	brooding
hardworking	inhibited
economical	status-seeking
serious	

♒ AQUARIUS (the water-bearer)

quality	fixed	glyph	waves of water or electricity
element	air		
principle	active	natural sign of	eleventh house
ruler	Uranus ♅	opposite sign	Leo ♌
anatomy	the ankles		
key phrase	*I know*	keyword	*imagination*

positive characteristics	negative characteristics
independent	unpredictable
inventive	temperamental
tolerant	bored by detail
individualistic	cold
progressive	too fixed in opinions
artistic	
scientific	shy
logical	eccentric
humane	radical
intellectual	impersonal
altruistic	rebellious

♓ PISCES (the fish)

quality	mutable	glyph	two fish tied together
element	water		
principle	passive	natural sign of	twelfth house
ruler	Neptune ♆	opposite sign	Virgo ♍
anatomy	the feet		
key phrase	*I believe*	keyword	*understanding*

positive characteristics	negative characteristics
compassionate	procrastinating
charitable	over-talkative
sympathetic	melancholy
emotional	pessimistic
sacrificing	emotionally
intuitive	inhibited
introspective	timid
musical	impractical
artistic	indolent
	often feels misunderstood

Dual Planetary Rulerships of Signs

Reading the preceding description of the signs, you probably noticed that both Taurus and Libra are ruled by Venus, and both Gemini and Virgo are ruled by Mercury. Originally, when only the Sun, Moon and five planets, Mercury, Venus, Mars, Jupiter and Saturn, were known, each was given the rulership over two signs. While the Sun and Moon are technically known as *luminaries,* they are commonly referred to as planets. The Sun ruled only Leo, and the Moon ruled only Cancer. However, Mars ruled both Aries and Scorpio; Jupiter ruled both Sagittarius and Pisces; and Saturn ruled both Capricorn and Aquarius.

As the outer planets (Uranus, Neptune and Pluto) were discovered, they were given the rulership of Aquarius, Pisces, and Scorpio respectively after careful observation and study. However, to this day, Jupiter is considered to be a sub-ruler of Pisces, Saturn a sub-ruler of Aquarius, and Mars a co-ruler of Scorpio. In the future, if astronomers discover two more planets (as many astrologers predict they will), we will probably have a planetary ruler for each sign.

There is a school of thought that says that the Earth (⊕) is the ruler of Taurus. Keep this in mind as a possibility to be explored further.

Quiz 1

To test your basic understanding of the material on the signs that you have studied in this lesson, here is a short quiz. Match the name of the famous person in the left column with the combination of signs and planets in the right column that best fits the famous person. You'll find the correct answers to this quiz in the Appendix on page 281.

1. William Shakespeare (writer)   A. ☉ ♉ ♀ ♋
2. Florence Nightingale (nurse)   B. ☉ ♉ ♀ ♊
3. Robert Peary (explorer)   C. ☉ ♉ ♀ ♉
4. Leonardo Da Vinci (artist)   D. ☉ ♉ ♀ ♈

Quiz 2

As a further test, to make sure that you have absorbed the materials in lessons 1 and 2, please do the following true-false test. The answers to these questions will be found in the Appendix on page 283.

1. Aries: I think
2. Cancer: ruled by Venus
3. Virgo: rules the intestines
4. Scorpio: intensity
5. Pisces: eleventh sign
6. Taurus: I believe
7. Aquarius: I know
8. Leo: I am
9. Cancer: rules the knees
10. Capricorn: I use
11. Libra: rules the kidneys
12. Virgo: I analyze
13. Gemini: ruled by Mercury
14. Sagittarius: the archer
15. Pisces: understanding
16. Aries: activity
17. Aquarius: harmony

18. Taurus: ruled by Jupiter
19. Capricorn: ambition
20. Gemini: I understand
21. Libra: I feel
22. Cancer: fourth sign
23. Aries: rules the feet
24. Capricorn: imagination
25. Aquarius: versatility
26. Leo: rules the heart
27. Scorpio: seventh sign
28. Taurus: I have
29. Sagittarius: I balance
30. Pisces: ruled by Saturn
31. Aries: ruled by Pluto
32. Scorpio: I desire
33. Virgo: rules the thighs
34. Libra: opposite of Taurus
35. Capricorn: practical

See if you can provide the correct answer for every question that you have marked false. The correct answers will be found in the Appendix on page 283.

Lesson 3: The Planets

Introduction

In this lesson we shall consider the planets. The Sun (☉) and the Moon (☽) are properly referred to as the luminaries, but for the sake of simplicity, most astrologers refer to them as planets, along with Mercury (☿), Venus (♀), Mars (♂), Jupiter (♃), Saturn (♄), Uranus (♅), Neptune (♆), and Pluto (♇). These planets are present in every horoscope and their influences act in everyone's life.

Students often ask, "Does the discovery of new planets upset the principles of astrology?" The answer is no. Astrologers from ancient times have known that there were more planets influencing our life on Earth than they were aware of. The transuranium metals did not upset chemistry when they were first discovered. In like fashion astrology was not upset with the discovery of Uranus in 1781 coincidental with the industrial revolution and the harnessing of electricity, nor by the discovery of Neptune in 1846, heralding a time of metaphysics and the birth of psychoanalysis, nor by the discovery of Pluto in 1930, just prior to the beginnings of the atomic age, the rise of dictatorships and the rebirth of underworld crime.

Keeping the possible discovery of newer planets in mind, let us study those planets discovered thus far. Taking the planets in the order of their speed, not necessarily the importance they assume in the horoscope, they are as follows:

Moon	Takes 28 days to complete one cycle.
Mercury	Takes 88 days to complete one orbit of the Sun.
Venus	Takes 224½ days for one orbit of the Sun.
Sun	Takes one year to complete the cycle of the zodiac.
Mars	Takes 22 months, almost 2 years to complete one cycle of the zodiac.
Jupiter	Takes about 12 years for one cycle (about one sign per year).
Saturn	Takes 28-30 years for one cycle.
Uranus	Takes 84 years for one cycle.
Neptune	Takes 165 years for one cycle.
Pluto	Takes 248 years for one cycle (estimated).

When visualizing the travel of these planets through the twelve signs of the zodiac, please keep in mind that we are referring to the movement of the planets around the Sun, calculated in Earth time, with the exception of the Moon which travels around the Earth. As previously mentioned, the Moon is really not a planet.

Each planet is strong in the sign that it rules; this is the sign of its *dignity*. Every planet also has one sign, apart from the one it rules, where it expresses itself harmoniously; this is the sign of its *exaltation*. When a planet is in the sign opposite to the one it rules, it is in the sign of its *detriment*. When a planet is in the sign opposite to its exaltation, it is in the sign of its *fall*. Each of these positions will be listed in the study of each planet. You will also find a further explanation of the dignities and a table listing each planet's dignity, exaltation, detriment and fall on page 30.

☽ MOON

rules	Cancer ♋	anatomy	breasts, stomach,
exaltation	Taurus ♉		fluid balance of the
detriment	Capricorn ♑		body, digestion,
fall	Scorpio ♏		glandular secretions,
glyph	Moon in first		left eye of male,
	quarter		right eye of female
represents	*domestic, nurturing urge*		
keyword	*emotions*		

The Moon's influence in the chart is very important because it is the closest planet to the Earth and moves through the zodiac rapidly. It represents the female principle: mother, wife and women generally. Instincts, moods, tides, phases, receptivity, fluctuations, feelings, habit patterns, reflex actions. Its action fluctuates and changes. Governs personal interests, desires, needs, magnetism, growth and fertility, the need to touch, impressionability and consciousness. Rules liquids, commodities, sailing, brewing, nursing, trades-people and the public in general. *Where you find the Moon in the chart shows where you are subject to emotional ups and downs.*

☿ MERCURY

rules	Gemini ♊ , Virgo ♍	anatomy	nervous system,
exaltation	Aquarius ♒		brain, sight, mouth,
detriment	Sagittarius ♐ , Pisces ♓		tongue, respiratory
fall	Leo ♌		system, hands
glyph	winged cap of god		and arms, general
	Mercury		ruler of all hormones
represents	*intellectual urge, the avenue of expression*		
keyword	*reasoning ability*		

Never located more than 28° distant from the Sun. Considered neuter. Rules reason, ability to communicate, intellect, awareness, dexterity, rationalization, transmission, words, opinion and sensory perceptions. Its action is quick, uncertain, volatile. Deals with travel (especially short trips), brothers and sisters, children, clerking, speaking, writing, bookkeeping, secretaries, neighborhood activities, letters and mailings, means of transportation, trade, emotional capacity and technique. *Where you find Mercury in the chart shows where and how you communicate best.*

♀ VENUS

rules	Taurus ♉ , Libra ♎	anatomy	throat, chin, cheeks,
exaltation	Pisces ♓		sense of taste,
detriment	Scorpio ♏ , Aries ♈		kidneys, ovaries,
fall	Virgo ♍		internal reproductive
glyph	mirror of vanity of		organs, venous blood
	the goddess Venus		circulation, sensory
			organs of skin

represents *social urge, sense of value*
keyword *affection*

Never located more than 46° distant from the Sun. Venus is the planet of love; in early times it was called the *lesser benefic*. Rules art, culture, aesthetics, possessions, partners, beauty, charm, good taste, sentimentality, sweets and sugar, color, harmony, poetry, paintings, jewelry, singing, drama and music. Venus's action is gentle and harmonious. Governs emotional contacts, tenderness, moral character, marriage and unions of all kinds. Also, sociability, disposition, luxuries, pleasure and appreciation. Venus is the planet of love and sensuality, not sex. *Where you find Venus in the chart shows what you really enjoy.*

☉ SUN

rules	Leo ♌	anatomy	the heart, upper
exaltation	Aries ♈		back, spleen,
detriment	Aquarius ♒		circulatory system,
fall	Libra ♎		the sperm, right eye
glyph	shield of Helios,		of male and left eye
	or circle of infinity		of female
	(the dot represents		
	the person within)		

represents *power urge, personality, ego*
keyword *inner self*

The main expression of the individual. Shows the qualities of leadership and success. It represents the masculine principle, the father, husband and men in general. The Sun rules health, vital principles, authority and bosses, rank, title, high office, progress, dignity, energy, sense of identity and capacity for experience. Its action is fortifying and vitalizing. *Where you find the Sun in the chart is the life and heart of the horoscope; this is where you want to shine.*

♂ MARS

rules Aries ♈
co-rules Scorpio ♏
exaltation Capricorn ♑
detriment Libra ♎ , Taurus ♉
fall Cancer ♋
glyph shield and spear of Mars, the god of war

anatomy the muscular system, external reproductive organs, head and face, red blood corpuscles, motor nerves, bladder, adrenal glands

represents *action, aggressive urge, initiative*
keyword *energy*

Deals with your animal nature, desire and sexual energies. Shows ambition, force, power, construction, work, strife, competition and death. Governs surgery and operations, weapons, war, accidents, inflammation, wounds and cuts, burns, scalds, violence, tools, iron and steel. In earlier times it was known as the *lesser malefic*. Mars's action is sudden, self-assertive and disruptive. Mars can be used destructively and angrily, in a fighting way, or with courage and strength. *Where you find Mars in the horoscope is where you expend the greatest energy.*

♃ JUPITER

rules Sagittarius ♐
sub-rules Pisces ♓
exaltation Cancer ♋

anatomy arterial blood circulation, the liver, thighs, hips, feet,

detriment Gemini ♊
fall Capricorn ♑
glyph first letter of the
Greek spelling for
the god Zeus
represents ***benevolent, protective urge***
keyword ***expansion***

right ear, upper
forehead, glycogen
and fatty tissues,
pancreas

Rules wealth, leisure time, big business, the higher mind, optimism, height, growth, morality, prosperity and indulgence. Also higher education, philosophic reasoning, aspirations, sports, luck, long-distance travel, hunting and fondness for animals. Jupiter is the judge, the lawmaker and the helper. In earlier times Jupiter was known as the ***greater benefic.*** Jupiter's action is orderly and promotes health and growth. ***Where you find Jupiter in the horoscope is where you often have good fortune and like to spend your leisure time.***

♄ SATURN

rules Capricorn ♑
sub-rules Aquarius ♒
exaltation Libra ♎
detriment Cancer ♋
fall Aries ♈
glyph sickle of Chronos,
the god of time

anatomy the skin, the skeletal
system (including the
teeth), ligaments,
knees, left ear and
auditory organs,
gall bladder,
parathyroid glands,
body protein

represents ***urge for security and safety***
keyword ***the teacher***

Rules form, discipline, responsibility, organization, ambition, capacity for a career, limitations, sorrows and delays. Saturn rules theories and scientific law, older persons, depth, patience, timing, tradition, conventionality, orthodoxy and productive use of time. Saturn represents the principles of truth, of contraction, of solidification, of wisdom and of aging. Its action is slow and lasting. Saturn is the taskmaster of the horoscope. In earlier times it was known as the ***greater malefic. Where you find Saturn in the horoscope is where you feel least secure and tend to overcompensate.***

♅ URANUS

rules **Aquarius** ♒   anatomy **the higher nervous**

exaltation **Scorpio** ♏   **system, body**

detriment **Leo** ♌   **electricity, the ankles**

fall **Taurus** ♉

glyph **derivation of letter "H" for its discover- er, Herschel, in 1781**

represents *freedom urge ("divine discontent")*

keyword *the awakener*

Rules inventions, originality, science, electricity, magic, the occult, light, astrology, psychology, x-rays, airplanes and insight into nature's laws. It is futuristic, humanitarian, intellectual, eccentric, bohemian, egotistical and utopian. It also governs creative will, sudden change, revolution and dictators, individualism, ingenuity, rebellions and autonomy. Its action is sudden, unexpected and often violent. Uranus is a breaker of traditions. It is neutral and sexless and considered by many to be the upper octave of Mercury and the first of the transcendental planets. Recent research also associates Uranus with natural disasters, particularly earthquakes. *Where you find Uranus in the horoscope is where you tend to do the unusual.*

♆ NEPTUNE

rules **Pisces** ♓   anatomy **the spinal column,**

exaltation **not yet established**   **nerve fibers, feet,**

detriment **Virgo** ♍   **pineal gland,**

fall **not yet established**   **telepathic functions,**

glyph **trident of Poseidon, the sea god**   **white corpuscles of the blood, kinesthetic functions**

represents *spiritual or escapist urge*

keyword *intuition*

Rules maritime matters, liquids, music, movies, stage and television, glamour, dreams, illusion, delusion, spirituality, ideals, mystique, hunches and the things we take deeply for granted in life without questioning. Rules fog, petroleum, mystery, anesthetics, flattery, intangibles, fragrances, second sight, love of poetry, color and dancing. Neptune governs drugs and drug addiction, alcoholism, hypochondria, sleepwalking, trances, hypnosis, immateriality and abnormality. Neptune's action is subtle, gradual and sometimes insidious. It is the higher octave of Venus and the second of the transcendental planets. *Where you find Neptune in the chart is where you tend to deceive yourself and/or others; it is also where you seek the ideal.*

♇ ♀ PLUTO

rules	Scorpio	anatomy	the eliminative and reproductive systems, pituitary gland, abnormal growths (warts, tumors, birthmarks, moles, etc.)
exaltation	not yet established		
detriment	Taurus		
fall	not yet established		
glyph	one is derived from the letters "PL" for its discoverer, Percival Lowell, in 1930; the other represents the cross of matter topped by the crescent moon and above hovers circle of infinity		

represents *destroying or reforming urge, fusion*

keyword *transformation*

Pluto traditionally rules the underworld and that which is hidden from view (including the unknown worlds within you, your submerged or subconscious self). Also represents all replication processes like conception and printing. Pluto governs the masses, waste, subversion, atomic power and crime. It rules phobias and obsessions, slow growth, group factors, transmutation, beginnings and endings, birth and death, isolation, coercion, disappearance, kidnapping, anonymity, bacteria and viruses. Represents generation, regeneration and degeneration. It exposes that which has been developed secretly or undercover. It governs vacancy, plumbing, dictatorships, unpopular causes and the exclusive. Pluto's action is slow, ponderous and inevitable. It is the last of the transcendental planets and is considered a higher octave of Mars. *Where you find Pluto in the chart you'll find complexity; it is where you'll have to solve problems alone and unaided.*

⊕ EARTH

rules Taurus ♉ , (tentative)

detriment Scorpio ♏ , (tentative)

keyword *reality*

Earth is always the exact opposite of the Sun by sign, degree and house placement. It shows how and where you meet the world. It relates to the physical plane and mundane matters. It represents your mission in life.

The Nodes of the Moon

The nodes are not celestial bodies; they are points in celestial longitude where the Moon crosses over the ecliptic (or path of the Sun). The Moon's North Node is listed by position in the ephemeris and the South Node is always its direct opposite, having the same number of degrees and minutes but of the opposite sign. Example: If the North Node is at 10° Aries 50' then, the South Node is at 10° Libra 50'.

☊ NORTH NODE   (or dragon's head)

A point of gain, of increase and added confidence. It is where you take in or are given to. *Where it occurs in your chart is where you should strive for fulfillment.*

☋ SOUTH NODE   (or dragon's tail)

A point of release or letting go. It is where you must give or are taken from. *Where it occurs in your chart is where you might take the easy way out.*

Figure 3: Table of Dignities.

Planet	Dignity	Detriment	Exaltation	Fall
☽ Moon	♋	♑	♉	♏
☿ Mercury	♊ ♍	♐ ♓	♒	♌
♀ Venus	♉ ♎	♏ ♈	♓	♍
☉ Sun	♌	♒	♈	♎
♂ Mars	♈ (♏)	♎ (♉)	♑	♋
♃ Jupiter	♐ (♓)	♊ (♍)	♋	♑
♄ Saturn	♑ (♒)	♋ (♌)	♎	♈
♅ Uranus	♒	♌	♏	♉
♆ Neptune	♓	♍		
♇ Pluto	♏	♉		

Dignities

Dignity: When a planet is in the sign it rules, it is *dignified.* This strengthens our response to it. *If a planet is dignified, you control your circumstances.*

Detriment: When a planet is in the sign opposite the one it rules, it is in *detriment.* It does not operate at full power and takes on more of the sign's than the planet's coloration. *If a planet is in detriment, you are visiting where you must conform to rules and regulations.*

Exaltation: Every planet has one particular sign, apart from the one it rules, where it expresses itself harmoniously. This is the sign of its *exaltation.* The complementary forces are increased and the virtues magnified. *If a planet is exalted, you feel comfortable in a friend's home.*

Fall: If a planet is in the sign opposite to its exaltation, it is in its *fall,* because here it has difficulty expressing its real nature. *If a planet is in its fall, you must stay in someone else's home and you do not really feel comfortable there.*

Quiz

This test is a review of how well you've learned the material in this lesson. See if you can pass this quiz. You'll find the answers in the Appendix on page 284.

1 . Using their glyphs (symbols), list the planets in order of their speed through the zodiac.

2. Give the proper sign for:
    a. the Moon's exaltation
    b. Jupiter's exaltation
    c. Saturn's detriment
3. Give the planet which fits each description:
    a. represents the intellectual urge
    b. represents the power urge
    c. in its fall in Capricorn
    d. in its detriment in Capricorn
    e. rules the thighs and hips
    f. rules the motor nerves
    g. in its detriment in Cancer
    h. governs drugs
    i. is known as "the awakener"
    j. rules the skin
    k. rules morality
    l. is in its fall in Scorpio
    m. is exalted in Aries
    n. shows where you must solve your problems unaided
       and by yourself
    o. represents the social urge
    p. rules the public
    q. rules the masses
    r. planet's action is subtle
    s. planet's action is unexpected
    t. this planet rules Leo
    u. this planet rules Sagittarius
    v. not discovered until 1930
    w. rules the heart
    x. rules the nervous system
    y. the planet of "divine discontent"
4. List the three transcendental planets.

Lesson 4: The Houses

Learning to Interpret House Meanings

We know that the signs are fixed divisions of the heavens. The houses, on the other hand, are relative divisions of the heavens, depending on the birthplace and the birthtime of the individual. The rotation of the Earth causes the signs and the planets to pass through all twelve houses each day. The sign that is on the eastern horizon at the exact time of birth is called the *Ascendant* or *rising sign*.

Each house represents a basic field of activity. The meanings of the houses are modified when they are occupied with planets. It is important to realize from the beginning that having no planet in a house does not mean that there is no activity in that area. No house is ever empty; each house has a planet that rules the sign on its cusp. Since there are twelve houses and only ten planets, you cannot possibly have a planet in every house.

The houses relate to conditions, while the signs tell us about character traits. If you were to compare astrology to acting, you would say: The planets are the actors, the signs are the roles they play, and the houses are the settings or situations in which the cast portrays its roles. Mercury is always Mercury, but in Gemini it portrays a different role than in Libra; when Mercury is in the third house the setting is different from the sixth house.

The houses never change position. The Ascendant (or first house cusp) is always the eastern point of the horizon, where the Sun appears to rise each morning. Correspondingly, the *Descendant* (or seventh house cusp) is always on the western point of the horizon, where the Sun sets each evening. The *Midheaven*, commonly referred to as the *MC* (the tenth house cusp) is always at the very top or southern point of the horoscope. Its opposite point, the *IC* (the fourth house cusp) is always at the lowest point of the wheel or the northern point. The reference to the tenth house cusp as the MC stems from its name in Latin, *medium coeli*, which means middle of the heavens. The reference to the fourth house cusp as the IC stems from the Latin, *imum coeli*, meaning the lowest heavens.

As you learned in lesson 1, when you filled in the flat wheel, each house is influenced by a sign of the zodiac; each house has a planetary ruler, and each house is classified as angular, succedent or cadent.

Keeping in mind that each house represents a certain field of activity in our lives, let us now turn our attention to a detailed explanation of the houses.

FIRST HOUSE   angular
natural sign Aries ♈   natural ruler Mars ♂
keyword *identity*   a house of *life*

The cusp of the first house is the Ascendant or rising sign. It is one of the most important points in the natal chart, and it shows the exact degree and sign that was on the eastern horizon at the moment of birth. The Earth's rotation causes one degree of the zodiac to rise above the eastern horizon approximately every four minutes; for this reason, you can see how important it is to have an accurate birthtime.

The first house, and in particular the Ascendant, shows your personality, your natural disposition and tendencies, your individuality and the way you express yourself. It shows how people see you and the way you want others to see you. It is the way you "package" and "market" yourself. It represents your physical body, your health and your early childhood years. It shows your approach to life, your worldly outlook, your appearance and bearing and the beginnings of all enterprises.

SECOND HOUSE

succedent

natural sign **Taurus ♉**   natural ruler **Venus ♀**

keyword *values*   a house of *substance*

The second house shows financial affairs, possessions (except real estate), investments, earning power, and any gain or loss through your own efforts. It indicates your inner talents and resources, your need for fulfillment, your emotional feelings, your sense of self-worth and your sense of values. Since many people believe that liberty is largely a matter of money, this is the house of personal liberty. It is also the house of material debt.

THIRD HOUSE

cadent

natural sign **Gemini ♊**   natural ruler **Mercury ☿**

keyword *awareness*   a house of *side-by-side relationships*

The third house shows the local environment you live in, your brothers and sisters, and all forms of communication, such as speaking and writing. It also indicates means of transportation including short trips. It shows the adaptability of your mind to learning and to new ideas, your ability to relate to your environment, and your taken-for-granted skills. It indicates the conscious and objective portion of your mind and your primary schooling.

FOURTH HOUSE

natural sign Cancer ♋   angular

natural ruler the Moon ☽

keyword *security*   a house of *endings*

The fourth house shows your home and your parents, the family you came from (your roots) and the home you will establish. This includes your heritage, heredity and ancestry, your psychological roots and your private life. This house shows property, such as houses or real estate, and all that is secluded. It is a house of endings: the closing years of life, the ending of all matters, fame after death and the place of burial. It shows the parent who has the greater influence on you as a child, your subjective self and the foundation upon which you build your character.

FIFTH HOUSE

natural sign Leo ♌   succedent

natural ruler the Sun ☉

keyword *creativity*   a house of *life*

The fifth house shows children, love affairs, romance, pleasures, amusement, holidays, vacations, games, speculations, hobbies and avocation. It indicates your emotional attitude and the love you give. It shows your enterprise, as well as sports, originality and creative outlets. It also indicates dramatic, literary or artistic ability. The fifth house shows publication, politics, the fine arts, social affairs, pregnancy and the education of children.

SIXTH HOUSE

natural sign Virgo ♍   cadent

natural ruler Mercury ☿

keyword *duty*   a house of *substance*

The sixth house shows your work, your health and your habits. It indicates employment, employees, tenants, servants, pets and dependents. It shows service given to others, routine matters, your clothes and how you wear them, hygiene, interest in food and diet, sickness and all conditions affecting your health. This house indicates aunts and uncles, self-adjustment and your unconscious mind. Here work and health are linked together.

SEVENTH HOUSE

angular

natural sign Libra ♎   natural ruler Venus ♀

keyword ***cooperation***   a house of ***face-to-face relationships***

The seventh house shows both business and marital partnerships, marriage, divorce, contracts, lawsuits, bargains, agreements, any dealings with the public and the public's response. It shows your open enemies, your cooperation with others or your lack of cooperation. It indicates what you most lack in yourself, since it is the opposite of the first house which shows your strongest personality traits. This house shows your attitudes toward marriage: your mate, the kind and quality of the marriage, and how many marriages you may have. It also shows your grandparents and any people who act as your agent or in your behalf.

EIGHTH HOUSE

succedent

natural sign Scorpio ♏   natural ruler Pluto ♀

keyword ***regeneration***   a house of ***endings***

The eighth house shows the support you receive from other people, including financial, moral, spiritual and physical. It indicates legacies, trusts, wills, taxes, insurance matters, as well as secrets, sex, spiritual and physical regeneration, psychological rebirth and degeneration and death. The eighth house shows occult matters, sleep, deep research, investigation and hidden assets. It also includes the assets of partners and alimony. It is the house of surgery, and along with the sixth house, it shows types of illness.

NINTH HOUSE

cadent

natural sign Sagittarius ♐   natural ruler Jupiter ♃

keyword ***aspiration***   a house of ***life***

The ninth house shows your higher mind, the superconscious. It indicates religion, law, science, ideals, higher learning, philosophy, psychology, profound mental study, your dreams and your visions. It shows distant travel, foreigners, foreign dealings, commerce, big business, imports and exports. The ninth house shows the church as a spiritual factor, the clergy, in-laws, grandchildren, intuition, ethics and public opinion in general. It indicates the lessons we learn through living.

TENTH HOUSE

angular

natural sign Capricorn ♑   natural ruler Saturn ♄

keyword *honor*   a house of *substance*

The tenth house shows your profession, your reputation and your standing in the community. It indicates your ego, status, fame, promotion, ambition, business and social activities, your employer, the government or any other authority over you. It shows your achievements, how the world sees and evaluates you, and the influence you exert in your own circle. Here we see the church as an organization and the opposite parent from the one represented by your fourth house.

ELEVENTH HOUSE

succedent

natural sign Aquarius ♒   natural ruler Uranus ♅

keyword *social consciousness*   a house of *group relationships*

The eleventh house shows your capacity for friendship, your attitude toward your friends and acquaintances and all non-emotional relationships. It indicates what you most desire in life, your goals, the love you receive as well as money obtained from a profession. This house shows step-children, foster children and adopted children, as well as circumstances over which you have little control. Here we see your humanitarian interests, the way you use others, large and small organizations, and the clubs and social groups to which you belong.

TWELFTH HOUSE   cadent

natural sign Pisces ♓   natural ruler Neptune ♆
keyword *subconscious*   a house of *endings*

The twelfth house shows your unknown or hidden strengths and weaknesses. It shows sorrow, suffering, limitations, handicaps, secrets, seclusion, frustration and behind-the-scenes action. It indicates places of confinement, jails, hospitals, mental institutions, etc., and restraint, inhibitions, exile, secret enemies, hidden dangers, self-undoing and clandestine affairs. It shows the things we hide from others. Research, background, subjective sustainment, inner consciousness, the subconscious mind, spiritual debts to be paid (karma), but also charity, sympathy and public welfare. It is often called the closet or dustbin of the horoscope because it is here we sweep away or hide problems which are too painful to face or difficulties that we refuse to acknowledge.

Houses Within Houses

Just as the fifth house shows your children, the ninth house (the fifth from the fifth house) shows your children's children; i.e., your grandchildren. When counting houses in this manner, be sure to start with the house in question. For example, the fifth becomes house 1 as you begin your count, the sixth is house 2, the seventh is house 3, the eighth is house 4, and the ninth becomes house 5. The ninth house is five houses from the fifth house.

The fourth house, as a house of endings, shows the conditions at the end of your life. Thus, the eighth house shows the end of life conditions for your children because it is four houses from the fifth house, the house of your children. Count: fifth, sixth, seventh, eighth.

The second house shows your money; it is second from the first house (you). Thus, the eighth house shows your partner's money for it is second from the seventh house (your partner).

These are just a few examples of the basic principles involved in turning the wheel to glean additional information from each house.

Figure 4: Wheel of Houses This chart gives the basic meanings of each house.

House Division by Element

As you know from lesson 1 each sign is part of a grouping by element. Because each sign has a natural house position, we can group the houses in the same way, according to the ruling element of each.

Fire: The *houses of life* or *personal houses*. People with many planets in these houses are inspirational and dynamic. They have great energy and enthusiasm, motivating power and religious convictions.

> First house: body.
> Fifth house: soul.
> Ninth house: spirit, mind.

Earth: The *houses of substance* or *possessive houses*. People with many planets in these houses are stable and usually are the backbone of their communities and families. Their outlooks and vocational aptitudes are concrete and practical.

> Second house: possessions, finances.
> Sixth house: occupation.
> Tenth house: recognition, environment.

Air: The *houses of relationships* or *relative houses*. People with many planets in these houses are the "people who need people." These house placements all describe the individual in relation to other members of the community.

> Third house: relatives and neighbors, those we do not select, consanguine.
> Seventh house: close relationships and partners, those we select for one to one relationships, conjugal.
> Eleventh house: social and mental relationships, those we select for shared interests, congenial.

Water: The *houses of endings* or *terminal houses*. People with many planets in these houses are sensitive and feeling; they are the psychoanalysts and religious figures. These houses describe the innermost soul, and the probable way that we will leave this earth. Not *when*, just *how*.

Fourth house: the end of the physical body.

Eighth house: liberation of the soul, death.

Twelfth house: philosophic death, the results of the course of life we choose to take.

The Division of the Houses by Quality

As you learned in lesson 1, there is another system of house division that is also important to keep in mind. The twelve houses can be divided into three groups of four houses each, which correspond to the cardinal, fixed and mutable qualities. They are called *angular, succedent,* and *cadent.*

Angular houses (corresponding to the cardinal signs): The angular houses are the first, fourth, seventh and tenth. These angles correspond to east (the Ascendant), west (the Descendant), north (the Imum Coeli or IC) and south (the Midheaven or MC). These are the angles, or axes, of the horoscope. Planets in angular houses have great potential for dynamic action and their influences are intensified. In other words, the angular houses have cardinal qualities. Some books refer to planets in angular houses as *accidentally dignified.*

Succedent houses (corresponding to the fixed signs): The succedent houses are the second, fifth, eighth and eleventh. They are called succedent because they follow or succeed the angular houses. They are not as powerful, but, just like the fixed signs, they give stability and purpose. They are also the financial houses.

Cadent houses (corresponding to the mutable signs): The cadent houses are the third, sixth, ninth and twelfth. These houses do not have as much opportunity for action as the angular houses, nor do they confer great stability like the fixed houses, but they are adaptable and get along well with others. They are usually referred to as the mental houses. In figure 4, page 39, you will see the basic meanings of each house presented in wheel form.

The Meridians

Now that you have learned the basic meaning of each house, we will introduce you to the *meridians*. The meridians are another part of the flat wheel, and they are an important factor in reading a horoscope.

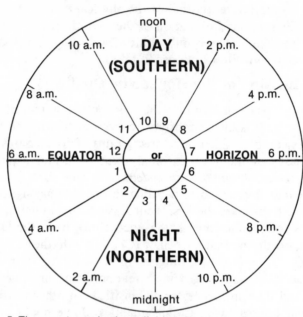

Figure 5: The equator or horizon divides the horoscope into southern (day) and northern (night) hemispheres.

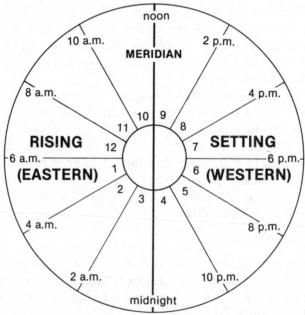

Figure 6: The meridian divides the horoscope into eastern (rising) and western (setting) hemispheres.

The horizontal axis of the horoscope is called the equator or horizon, and the vertical axis of the horoscope is called the meridian. By using each of these divisions (figures 5 and 6) we divide the horoscope into halves. The horizontal axis refers to consciousness; the vertical axis refers to power.

In figure 5 the equator divides the chart into day and night sections, because the horizon divides the chart along the sunrise-sunset axis. The *day planets* are all those that appear in a chart above the horizon, and the *night planets* are those that appear below the horizon.

Generally speaking the day or light half of a horoscope represents outgoingness and objectivity while the night section or dark half represents subjectivity and instinct. If you have many planets above the horizon, you will be quite objective and you will want to rise above your position at birth. The public and your career will be important to you. If you have many planets below the horizon, especially if these include the Sun and the Moon, you will be somewhat subjective and content to work behind the scenes.

In figure 6 the meridian axis divides the chart into an eastern half and a western half. These two sections are formed when we divide the chart along the noon to midnight axis. This meridian divides the planets into *rising planets* and *setting planets* (see figure 6). The rising planets are those in the eastern half of the horoscope, covering the time from midnight to noon. The setting planets are those in the western half of the chart, covering the time from noon to midnight. If there are many rising planets in your horoscope, you have a strong free will and are in charge of your own life. This is a sowing incarnation. If there are many setting planets in your chart, you are more flexible and involved with the destinies of others. This is a reaping incarnation.

You will also note in figures 5 and 6 that we have shown the time of day that each house represents. This becomes important when you want to erect your own charts; you will be able to check the accuracy of your calculations. For example, if you know that someone was born at 2 a.m. you know that the Sun will have to fall somewhere in the second or third house.

Quiz

Please answer each of the questions below. The correct answers will be found in the Appendix on page 284.

1. Using symbols, list the three fire signs.
2. Using symbols, list the three earth signs.
3. Using symbols, list the three air signs.
4. Using symbols, list the three water signs.
5. List the angular houses.
6. List the succedent houses.
7. List the cadent houses.
8. Using symbols, list the cardinal signs.
9. Using symbols, list the fixed signs.
10. Using symbols, list the mutable signs.
11. Which sign is the opposite of Taurus?
12. Which is the creative house?
13. Which sign is ruled by Saturn?
14. Which is the fixed water sign?
15. Which sign has a co-ruler? What planet is it?
16. Which two signs have sub-rulers? What are they?
17. Which sign opposes Sagittarius?
18. Which is the cardinal air sign?
19. Which is the house of seclusion?
20. Which are the houses of life?
21. Which are the houses of substance?
22. Which house cusp represents the north?
23. Which house cusp is the Ascendant?
24. Which two signs does Mercury rule?
25. Which other planet rules two signs? Which signs?

A Brief Comment Before We Proceed

At the end of lesson 4, students invariably want to learn the mathematics of erecting a horoscope.

We can't blame them for this eagerness; this is a fascinating subject, and of course, everyone wants to see the horoscopes of their friends and relatives. But the knowledge you have learned so far is only the rudimentary beginning of astrology. It is interesting and enlightening, but like all half-knowledge, it can be dangerous. Until you have learned more astrology, you are bound to misunderstand and misjudge charts, and you could do yourself and others an injustice. For these reasons, we do not teach you how to do the calculations in this book. We want to turn out astrologers who know how to read a horoscope before they learn to erect one.

Lesson 5: Delineating a Chart

Introduction

In lessons 1 to 4, you have learned the most basic principles of astrology: the signs of the zodiac, the planets, the houses, and how all are grouped together by similarities. If you understand these principles, and the keywords have become a part of your subconscious, you will have little trouble learning the other techniques and additional refinements that are a part of *delineating* (interpreting) a horoscope. Logic, common sense and a knowledge of human nature will aid you in interpreting a horoscope if you have grasped the significance of these basic principles.

The meanings of the signs, planets and houses are astrological words, and we are now going to learn to put them together to make simple astrological sentences. In learning any language there are certain rules for constructing sentences, and you must learn the rules for constructing astrological sentences as well.

Using the Keywords in Delineation

As explained in lesson 1, the flat wheel in astrology starts with Aries on the cusp of the first house, Taurus on the cusp of the second house, etc. Thus, the Sun in the first house will always reflect some qualities and traits of Aries, regardless of the sign in which the Sun is actually located. It is important that you keep this rule in mind.

To illustrate, let us take an example: the Sun in Cancer in the first house. A keyword for the Sun is *the inner self*. Some keywords for Cancer include *devoted, maternal, domestic* and *sensitive*. Keywords for the first house include *identity, personality* and *self-expression*. And, finally, keywords for Aries, the natural first house sign, include *dynamic* and *active*. These keywords can be put together to make an astrological sentence:

> *The devoted, maternal, inner self will be expressed in an*
> Cancer   Sun   first house
> *active and dynamic way.*
> Aries

Here's another example: The Moon in Gemini in the fifth house. Important keywords for the Moon are *emotions* and *instincts;* some keywords for Gemini include *versatile* and *literary;* keywords for the fifth house include *creativity* and *love you give*; while keywords for Leo, natural sign of the fifth house, include *creative* and *generous*. Interpreted astrologically you can say:

> *Emotionally versatile, you give love generously.*
> Moon   Gemini   fifth house
> Or: *You are instinctive and creative in literary pursuits.*
> Moon   fifth house   Gemini

Now let's broaden the concept: Venus in Capricorn in the ninth house (whose natural sign is Sagittarius). Capricorn is *responsible* and *cautious*; Sagittarius is *broad-minded* and *optimistic*; Venus represents the *affections* and the *moral character*; and the ninth house represents *philosophy* and *aspirations*. Thus, we might deduce that this individual's

aspirations and philosophical approach would be in a responsible manner, but the natural optimism of Sagittarius would
broaden the usual cautious nature of Capricorn.

Once you understand why the house position of a planet
modifies the nature of the sign in which the planet is placed,
you will also understand why a planet operates differently
depending on the type of house it is in. For example, a person
with the Sun in Taurus (a fixed sign), placed in a cadent house
will be more adaptable and less obstinate than a person whose
Sun in Taurus falls in a succedent house. The cadent houses
correspond to mutable signs and the succedent houses correspond to fixed signs. If that same Sun in Taurus were in an
angular house (corresponding to cardinal signs), the individual
might still be stubborn but would lose some of the patient and
stable qualities and become more of an initiator.

You will remember from lesson 4 that we drew an analogy
between the planets and the cast for a play. The cast does not
change; the Sun, for example, is always the inner personality,
the heart of the horoscope and the life-giver. The signs are the
roles that this cast plays, and they do not change either;
Taurus is always Taurus and retains the basic character of this
sign. However, the houses are the various settings in which the
cast portray their roles, and they can and do change a lot.
They range from the outgoing *I* of the first house to the
possessive *mine* of the second house to the people-oriented *we*
of the seventh house, and so on through the wheel.

With all this in mind, let us now turn our attention to the
delineation of a horoscope using the keywords we have
learned so far.

Delineating a Sample Horoscope

Figure 7 is the natal horoscope for Franklin Delano Roosevelt.
He was born on January 30, 1882 at 8:41 p.m. eastern standard time in Hyde Park, New York.

First, let us look at the general makeup of his chart. It is important to see the chart as a whole before we begin to take it
apart. Note that Roosevelt has seven planets above and three
planets below the horizon. (See the numbers in the circles in
the center of the chart.) Thus, we may conclude that this man
has many extroverted and objective qualities. He also has
three planets east and seven planets west of the meridian.

Figure 7: The Natal Horoscope of Franklin Delano Roosevelt Born January 30, 1882 at 8:45 p.m. local time (8:41 Eastern Standard Time) in Hyde Park, New York. Longitude 73° W 56′, latitude 41° N 48′.

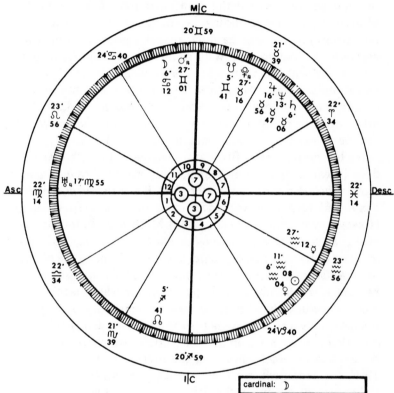

The Aspectarian: This provides an overview of the horoscope. We list the planets, the Ascendant (A) and Midheaven (M) by quality, element and so forth. For example, next to the word "mutable" we list Mars, Uranus, the Midheaven and the Ascendant because these are all are found in mutable signs in this chart.   At the bottom of the list the planets are categorized by house: the houses of life (L), the houses of substance (S), the houses of relationships (R) and the houses of endings (E). For further explanation, see page 50.

cardinal:	☽
fixed:	♄ ♆ ♃ ♇ ♀ ☉ ☿
mutable:	♂ ♅ M A
fire:	*none*
earth:	♄ ♆ ♃ ♇ ♅ A
air:	♂ ♀ ☉ ☿ M
water:	☽
angular:	♂ ☽
succedent:	♀ ☉ ♄ ♆ ♃
cadent:	☿ ♇ ♅
dignity:	☽
exaltation:	☿
detriment:	☉ ♇
fall:	

L: 3	S: 3	R: 0	E: 4

Thus, we may conclude that his life is bound up closely with the destiny of others.

If you look at the box below the wheel in figure 7, you will see that we have sorted the planets, the Ascendant and the Midheaven into the groupings we have learned. You will see that Roosevelt has one cardinal planet, seven fixed planets, and two mutable planets. With so many planets in fixed signs we can say that this man is very *determined, set in his ways, stable* and *resolute*. He has a *penetrating mind* and an *excellent memory*. Since we find both his Ascendant and Midheaven in mutable signs, we can add some *adaptability* and *flexibility* to his basic character (lesson 1).

He has no planets in fire signs, five planets plus his Ascendant in earth signs, four planets plus his Midheaven in air signs and one planet in a water sign. He is *practical, dependable* and *earthy* since planets in earth signs predominate. However, with four planets plus his Midheaven in the air element, we must add great *intellectuality, the ability to comprehend abstract thinking, logic, broadmindedness, the ability to communicate well* and *the ability to detach himself when necessary*. With only a single planet in the water element we might conclude that he has a lack of sensitivity or responsiveness; however, that planet is the Moon, which is not only dignified in Cancer but in the tenth house, which astrologically is called *elevated* since it is the highest point in a chart. Thus, the Moon will work with much strength.

The lack of planets in the fire element might worry us for a moment until we observe that Roosevelt has three planets in the personal houses (or houses of life), which correspond to the fire element (see lesson 4). He has three planets in the houses of substance, no planets in the houses of relationships, and four planets in the houses of endings. The houses of endings correspond to water, which gives him more sensitivity than is obvious when first glancing at his chart.

He has two planets in angular houses, five planets in succedent houses and three planets in cadent houses, again showing us his basic *fixity of purpose* and also *financial ability* (lesson 4).

As we mentioned above, the Moon is at home or dignified in Cancer. It is in Cancer that the Moon works at its best. We also see that Mercury is exalted in Aquarius. Here Mercury can express itself harmoniously, magnifying its virtues. The Sun is in its detriment in Aquarius. This weakens the qualities of the Sun but by no means causes it to act negatively, especially since the Sun is at home in the fifth house, the natural house of Leo, ruled by the Sun.

With this quick overview of the chart, we already have a good understanding of some of Roosevelt's major character traits. Now, let us look more deeply. The first planet to look for is the Sun, since this is the main expression of the individual, *the inner self* and *the inner personality*. It is *the heart of the chart*. We find his Sun in Aquarius in the fifth house. We would describe him as *independent, progressive, individualistic, intellectual, humane* but rather cold and impersonal (no fire in the chart), rather *fixed in his opinions, logical* and *communicative.* If you look at the keywords for Aquarius in lesson 1, you will notice that we picked keywords selectively. Why didn't we use the keyword *shy?* With seven planets above the horizon (which often denotes an extrovert), we would automatically eliminate this word. You must apply this same reasoning and judgment in selecting all keywords for use in your delineation. Also, we did not pick the keywords *eccentric* or *rebellious.* With five of his planets in earth he would be much too practical to be eccentric or rebellious; he would probably use those energies in being progressive and humane.

Aquarius is ruled by Uranus. Therefore we say that the Sun in Aquarius is ruled by Uranus, and in Roosevelt's case Uranus is in Virgo in his twelfth house (lesson 3). This rulership will add *practicality* (earth) to mental Aquarius (air). Coming from the twelfth house, it will add *hidden strength* and will often work on a subconscious and intuitive level (lesson 4).

Let us select some fitting words for the Sun's fifth house position. Because Leo is the natural sign of the fifth house, we will have to add some Leo overtones to this placement. We would add feelings of *pride, dignity, self-assurance* and a *flair for the dramatic* (lesson 2). Those with the Sun in the fifth house like *fun, pleasures, romance, love affairs* and *children.* In our keywords for the fifth house (lesson 4) we note that one of the words given is *politics;* that most certainly applies to FDR. But why not the keywords *dramatic ability* or

theater? We would not use these words because there is not
enough Leo, or drama, in the chart. For Leo, there is just the
fifth house position of the Sun; we see that there is practicality
instead of fire. This same reasoning would apply to the
keyword *fine arts.*

While you are taking the chart apart and examining it in
detail, never lose sight of the overall picture, and try to keep
everything in perspective as you exercise your judgment.

The next planet to consider is the Moon. We know that it
represents *emotions, instincts, moods, urges and desires*
(lesson 3). We've already pointed out that FDR's Moon is
strong because it is dignified in Cancer. Some keywords that
we can use are *sympathetic, tenacious, patriotic, a good
memory, rather selfish* and *somewhat touchy.* With his Sun in
progressive Aquarius he would not be *too cautious*; with his
ability for detachment, he would not be *overly sensitive*, and
with his urges and emotions placed high in his tenth house, he
would not be *maternal* or *domestic.* (See lesson 2.)

When the Moon is in Cancer it is its own ruler, so we don't
need to add other words at this time. However, because his
Moon is in the tenth house, we must add nuances of Capricorn
(the natural sign of the tenth house). We might use the
keyword *responsibilities* since there is so much earth in his
horoscope. It also makes him *status seeking,* and we could
even say that *the mind rules the heart* (lesson 2).

Because the Moon represents desires and urges, fitting
words for the Moon's tenth house position (lesson 4) would be
desire for honor, reputation and *fame.* The ego is very
developed. This position is excellent for government service.
The tenth house also indicates how the world sees you; FDR
would represent a fatherly or paternal image. The tenth house
also represents one of the parents. With the Moon signifying
the mother or wife in a man's chart, we can assume that the
tenth house represented his mother and that he saw her as very
mothering, protective and *loving* towards him, in other words
the Cancer feeling.

Now, we turn our attention to the next most revealing factor, the Ascendant. The Ascendant describes *the outer personality*; how people see you and your physical appearance.
FDR's Ascendant is Virgo. Therefore, people would see him
as *industrious, studious, methodical, factual* and *a bit critical*

(lesson 2). Virgo's ruler, Mercury, is in Aquarius, thus we realize that this Virgo Ascendant will be more *humane* and less *petty,* more *scientific* and less *skeptical* than the average person who has a Virgo Ascendant. People would trust a person who projects these qualities; they would feel that he is reliable. With Mercury positioned in the sixth house (the house of *work* and *service*), we could say that he has *a natural ability and desire to work and serve others*.

Mercury is a very important element for understanding human nature. Mercury represents *the reasoning ability, the avenue of expression, the intellect* and *basic awareness* (lesson 3). FDR's Mercury is exalted in the sign of Aquarius. It is in the sixth house, and the ruler of Aquarius, the planet Uranus, is in Virgo in the twelfth house. Thus his reasoning ability shows *independence, progressiveness, logic, intellectuality* and so on (lesson 2).

With Mercury's ruler Uranus in Virgo, we blend in the *logical* and *practical* approach. Since the sixth house is the natural house of Virgo (ruled by Mercury), Mercury is positioned well here (accidental dignity), and it takes on considerable Virgo coloring. The sixth house is the house of *work, duty, health, habits* and *service* (lesson 4). Thus we can see why much of FDR's *thinking* and *avenue of expression* went into work and serving his people. It also shows why his health became an important factor in his life. Mercury represents the *nervous system*, and he was afflicted by polio, which is basically a nervous disorder.

Quiz

By now you should have gotten the idea of what delineating a horoscope is all about. To test this, try to delineate the planets Venus, Mars, Jupiter and Saturn, using the same techniques we have just used above. When you have completed your delineation turn to the Appendix (page 285) to see how well you did.

Lesson 6: The Aspects

Introduction

There is only one more basic subject to learn in order to understand and read a horoscope. That subject is *aspects.*

When planets are placed at a specific number of degrees away from one another, they are said to be *in aspect* to each other. Aspects are of great value when interpreting character and also when reading events. The different aspects are listed on page 55.

If we use our previous analogy in which the planets are the actors, the signs are the roles they play, and the houses are the settings where the roles are played, then the aspects would show us *how* the actors play their roles.

Some aspects are said to be flowing or harmonious and other aspects are said to be challenging and inharmonious. Flowing or harmonious aspects are *pacifying, mollifying* or

Table of Aspects

Major Aspects

Aspect		Angle	Orb	Keyword
♂	Conjunction	0°	7°	Emphasis
⚹	Sextile	60° 2 signs	5°	Opportunity
☐	Square	90° 3 signs	7°	Challenge
△	Trine	120° 4 signs	7°	Flow
☍	Opposition	180° 6 signs	7°	Awareness
⚻	Inconjunct (quincunx)	150° 5 signs	5°	Adjustment

Minor Aspects

ℙ	Parallel	Same declination	1°	(Similar to conjunction)
⊻	Semi-sextile	30° 1 sign	1°	Reactive
N	Nonagon	40°	1°	Testing
∠	Semi-square	45° 1½ signs	1°	Irritating
S	Septile	51 3/7°	1°	Repercus- sions
Q	Quintile	72°	1°	Talent
⚼	Sesqui- square	135° 4½ signs	1°	Abrasive
BQ	Biquintile	144°	1°	Harmonious on mental plane

easy. The challenging or inharmonious aspects are considered *tension-producing, stimulating* or even *irritating.* But keep one thing in mind: no aspect is either good or bad. Too many flowing trines and sextiles can make you a dull and uninteresting person; everything seems easy and life flows in an uneventful and probably boring pattern. A few challenging squares, oppositions or conjunctions can stimulate you and give you depth of character; a little tension makes life more interesting. On the other hand, too many squares and oppositions with no trines or sextiles to create flow may make you bitter, stubborn, resentful and irritating to yourself and to those around you. Astrology is no exception to the rule that we need some of everything to create a whole human being.

If you look at the Table of Aspects on page 55 you will see that we have listed both *major aspects* and *minor aspects.* The major aspects are the most important aspects and the only ones you need to learn at this time. We've included the less important aspects here for your information only, to present you with the entire picture. Don't try to learn them now; just keep them for future reference. The column labeled Orb gives you the number of degrees of difference from the exact angle that is allowable for each aspect. However, the influence is strongest when the aspect is closer or even exact (also called *partile*) and the influence is weaker as the orb widens (also called *platic*).

Also, note in the Table of Aspects that the glyph for each aspect is given. It is important that you memorize these glyphs, for you will use them frequently from this point on.

Basic character is formed by the most exact aspects in the chart. Please be aware that different astrologers use different orbs. Some will never go past 6°, while others will allow as much as 14°. The orbs here are the ones we have found to work most consistently.

To get a quick look at the basic character you may wish to indicate the exact aspects (within 1°) in darker ink when you complete an aspectarian. (See page 73.)

When you think of squares or oppositions, remember the division by qualities which you learned in lesson 1. These divisions form the basic pattern for squares and oppositions. For example: the cardinal signs are Aries, Cancer, Libra and Capricorn. The sign of Aries always squares Cancer and

Capricorn; Cancer always squares Aries and Libra; Libra always squares Cancer and Capricorn, and Capricorn always squares Aries and Libra. By the same token, Aries and Libra always oppose each other, and Cancer and Capricorn always oppose each other. This same principle applies to the fixed and mutable signs. Of course, planets in these signs must fall within the allowable orb in order to form aspects. (See the diagram on page 68). For example: the Moon at 10° Aries squares Mars at 15° Capricorn.

$$☽ 10° ♈ □ ♂ 15° ♑$$

This illustration has an orb of 5°, from 10° to 15°. If the Moon were at 10° Aries and Mars at 23° Capricorn, the orb would be 13° and too wide to form an aspect.

This same principle applies to trines, but trines are based upon the division by element. (See lesson 1.) Each fire sign trines the other fire signs, each earth sign trines the other earth signs; each air sign trines the other air signs; and each water sign trines the other water signs. (See the diagram on page 68.)

For example: Jupiter at 14° Leo trines Saturn at 18° Sagittarius.

$$♃ 14° ♌ △ ♄ 18° ♐$$

Here we have an orb of 4°. However, with Jupiter at 14° Leo and Saturn at 25° Sagittarius, the orb would be 11°, too wide to form an aspect.

This gives you a general idea of what aspects are. Now, let's discuss the six major aspects in more detail.

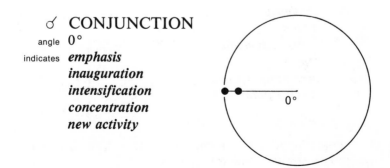

♂ **CONJUNCTION**

angle **0°**

indicates *emphasis*
inauguration
intensification
concentration
new activity

A conjunction is two or three planets located within an orb of 7°. Usually the planets are all within the same sign, but occasionally they are found in adjacent signs. For example: Venus at 28° Aries conjunct Mars at 3° Taurus. In this case the orb is 5°.

♀ 28°♈ ☌ ♂ 3°♉

The principle characteristic of a conjunction is that it gives more emphasis to a sign, since two or more planets are involved. The action of a conjunction is direct, and it affects you on an outer and obvious level.

Conjunctions are considered favorable or unfavorable depending on the specific planets involved. When you realize that these planets are merely a focus of activity, then there is nothing necessarily good or bad about them. For example, Jupiter shows expansive growth, and Saturn's function is orderly, limiting and crystallizing. Whether the conjunction of these planets is favorable or not depends on what is doing the growing and what is being limited or restricted. The expanding of a tumor is unfavorable; the same tumor being restricted is beneficial. The growth or expansion of a career is beneficial, but of course the limitation or restriction of a career is unfavorable.

A group of three or more planets in conjunction is called a *stellium*. A stellium creates its own action, and greatly emphasizes the sign and house in which it occurs.

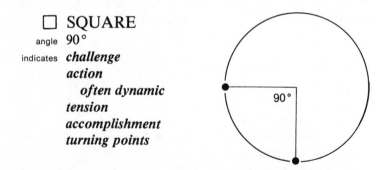

□ **SQUARE**

angle **90°**

indicates *challenge*
action
    often dynamic
tension
accomplishment
turning points

90°

The square involves two planets that are 90°, or three signs, apart. The orb we allow for squares is 7°.

The potential of any chart lies in its squares. If you do not understand them they can be stumbling blocks, but if you handle them wisely they can be stepping stones or building blocks. Action and decision are the essence of any square. It is important to note whether the square is cardinal, fixed or mutable. In cardinal squares the action is quick; in fixed squares the action is slow and deliberate, and in mutable squares the action is variable, depending to a great extent on the influences of others. This follows from the attributes which we learned in lesson 1.

A *T-square* or *T-cross* involves three planets, where two of the planets are in opposition.

Before we proceed, we would like to insert a brief note about how to read a string of aspects, like the T-square given in the following example. When reading a string of aspects always read each aspect as an aspect to the first planet listed, in this case the Sun. Thus we would read this aspect:

$$\odot 15° \approx \square \quad 4 19° \, m \quad \mathcal{S} \, \Psi 16° \, \Omega$$

The Sun at 15° Aquarius squares Jupiter at 19° Scorpio, and (the Sun) is in opposition to Neptune at 16° Leo, forming a T-square. In the diagram below, you can see where the name comes from, because the configuration resembles a T.

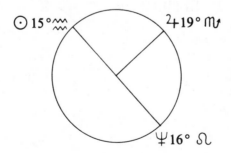

A *grand cross* or *grand square* involves four planets, with two pairs in opposition. Again, this name becomes obvious when you look at the configuration below. Note that all four of the signs involved in a given quality are represented. For example: Mars at 20° Taurus squares Neptune at 21° Leo, squares the Sun at 20° Aquarius and is in opposition to Jupiter at 18° Scorpio.

$$♂ 20° ♉ □ ♆ 21° ♌ □ ☉20° ♒ ♂ ♃ 18° ♏$$

Here the Sun opposes Neptune, and both square Jupiter and Mars, with Jupiter and Mars also opposing each other. This is a ***grand cross*** in fixed signs. The configuration in the horoscope would look like this:

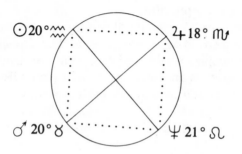

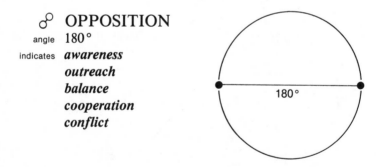

♂ OPPOSITION

angle 180°

indicates ***awareness***
outreach
balance
cooperation
conflict

The opposition involves two planets that are 180° or six signs apart. The allowable orb is 7°.

This is the widest possible aspect. Its potential value is to develop perspective and awareness. Oppositions show opposing factors at work, which complement each other when reconciled. They present challenges just as squares do, but they are a different type of challenge. An opposition involves recognizing a lack within yourself and using the polarity of the two signs to meet that lack. Imbalance then becomes balance. Reconciliation of the opposing forces is usually achieved through awareness and understanding.

For example: Mercury at 16° Gemini opposing Mars at 11° Sagittarius:

$$\text{☿}\,16°\,\text{♊}\,\text{☍}\,\text{♂}11°\,\text{♐}$$

In this example we see that the mind (Mercury) is *quick, clever, literary, expressive* and *curious* (Gemini) but lacks *idealism, broadmindedness,* and a *philosophical approach* (Sagittarius). By the same token, the energies (Mars) are directed in fields that involve *philosophy* or *higher education* and things are done with *enthusiasm* and *optimism* (Sagittarius). However, the *intellectuality* and *ability to express* in *clever, witty* or *literary* ways is lacking (Gemini). Thus, when this person learns to use the Gemini/Sagittarius polarity, creating a balance of the opposite poles through increased awareness, this aspect will become constructive and useful.

△ TRINE

angle **120°**

indicates *flow and ease*
idealism
inspiration
harmony
indolence

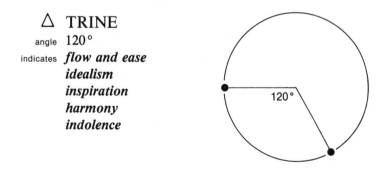

The trine involves two planets that are 120° or four signs apart. The allowable orb is 7°.

The trines are generally favorable. A trine permits easy interaction between two planets, but there is also no compulsion to use the planets advantageously, because there is no stress or tension here. Trines are not always a positive aspect; they may contribute to a tendency to choose the line of least resistance, or they may cause indolence. Trines go with the natural flow of things; they indicate natural creativity, talent, the ability to express things easily and pleasures. A trine might be compared to the fun of skiing downhill while the square might be compared to the struggle to climb the hill. Look at the sense of accomplishment when you reach the top of the hill and look back upon what you have conquered. On the other hand, the trine shows the joy of life and the love of living. Both of these aspects are parts of life.

A *grand trine* involves three planets about 120° apart (using a 7°orb) with all three planets in the same element. For example the Moon at 12° Sagittarius trines Mercury at 10° Aries and Neptune at 16° Leo. Mercury and Neptune are also trine each other; thus these three planets form a grand trine.

☽ 12° ♐ △ ☿ 10° ♈ △ ♆ 16° ♌

As you can see, all three fire signs are present, and we refer to this grand trine as a *grand fire trine*.

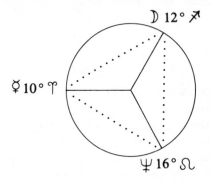

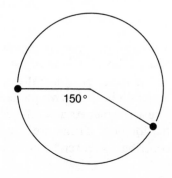

⊼ INCONJUNCT
(quincunx)

angle 150°

indicates *adjustment*
reorganization
lack of perspective
strain

The inconjunct involves two planets that are 150° or five signs apart. The allowable orb is 5°. In this aspect the signs involved are totally unrelated to each other. They share neither the same quality nor the same element, nor are they both active or passive. With nothing in common it is much harder to integrate these forces, and this aspect calls for many adjustments. The inconjunct demands a change of attitude, a change of habit pattern and a need to adjust to conditions indicated by the planets and houses in question. Often health and/or finances are involved in some way.

* SEXTILE

angle **60°**

indicates *opportunity*
attraction
self-expression
affability

The sextile involves two planets that are 60° or two signs apart. The allowable orb is 5°. Active or positive signs sextile each other; passive or negative signs sextile each other. Fire and air signs sextile each other; so do earth and water signs. With this compatibility, sextiles create an ease in understanding, in the gathering of information and in expression. The planets cooperate with each other.

As always, keep in mind which planets are involved, as well as which signs and which houses. For example: Moon sextile Mars. Here we are combining *the emotions* (the Moon) with *physical energy and drive* (Mars). If the fifth and seventh houses are included, *love affairs* and *partnerships* are involved. If the sextile is in Aquarius and Aries, then we are dealing with *intellect* and *independence* (Aquarius) plus *individualism* and *impulsiveness* (Aries). Let's assume that the Moon is in the fifth house and Mars in the seventh house:

$$☽14°\text{♒} \; \text{⚹} \; ♂17°\text{♈}$$

This would indicate that what you seek in love affairs or romance (fifth house) is similar to what you seek in a partner (seventh house). The sextile helps to blend and integrate these two planetary forces.

General Rules and Guidelines for Aspecting

Keep these general rules in mind when you analyze a horoscope for aspects.

1. Each sign has thirty degrees in it, from 0° to 29°.

2. Aspects are always figured by counting signs, not houses; otherwise you might overlook a sign that is *intercepted* in a house. Just because a sign is not on a cusp does not mean that it is not there. It is, and it has thirty degrees just like any other sign. If the first house cusp is in Cancer and the second house cusp is in Virgo, the sign Leo is intercepted in the first house. Each house does not necessarily contain thirty degrees.

3. When a planet is exalted or dignified (see lesson 3) it can integrate well and can handle all aspects in a more positive manner.

4. Check for *out of sign* aspects; these occur when a planet is at the very beginning or end of a sign. For example: Jupiter at 4° Leo square Saturn at 28° Aries.

$$♃\,4°\text{♌} \; \square \; ♄28°\text{♈}$$

This is an out of sign square, but it is within the allowable orb, so it is still a square.

5. An *applying* aspect is stronger than a *waning* aspect. For example:

Applying: the Moon at 10° Taurus trine Mercury at 16° Virgo.

$$☽10°\text{♉} \; \triangle \; ☿16°\text{♍}$$

Waning: the Moon at 16° Taurus trine Mars at 10° Virgo.

$$☽16°\text{♉} \; \triangle \; ♂10°\text{♍}$$

In the applying aspect the Moon is moving toward Mercury and is thus said to be applying; in the waning aspect the Moon has moved past Mercury and is thus said to be waning. The faster planet is always listed first, whether applying or waning. The applying aspect shows something you are *working towards;* the waning aspect shows something that has been *recently learned.* The relative speed of the planets is shown in lesson 3. The aspecting (faster) planet is the *doer*, and the aspected (slower) planet is the *receiver* of the action.

6. Aspects to the Sun are the root, seed and plant of the character. Basic character is formed by the most exact aspects in the horoscope. Aspects show tendencies, abilities and disabilities, rather than attainment. In other words, the natal chart shows your potential, but your free will dictates how much or how little you do with it.

7. Since Mercury is never more than 28° away from the Sun, the only aspect it can form with the Sun is the conjunction. Since Venus is never more than 46° away from the Sun, the only aspects it can form to the Sun are the conjunction, the semi-sextile and the semi-square. Because we are only studying the major aspects now you needn't look for more than conjunctions between Venus and the Sun.

Understanding the Basic Meanings of Aspects

In the example of the Moon sextile Mars which we gave on page 63, we illustrated once more the logic of astrology. The basic meaning of each sign, each planet and each house never changes; the keywords stay the same. As time goes on and your knowledge increases, you will add your own words based on your understanding of the nature of each sign, planet and house.

This same logic and basic understanding continues when you are learning to aspect. You already know that in astrology we always keep the flat chart or natural wheel in mind. (See lesson 1.) When we delineated Roosevelt's horoscope (lesson 5), we added a Capricorn overtone to his Cancer Moon located in the tenth house because in the flat chart Capricorn is the natural sign of the tenth house.

The conjunction is a 0° aspect. Keeping the flat wheel in mind, we always start with the first house; the first house is the natural house of Aries and its planetary ruler is Mars. Thus all conjunctions have a first house/Aries/Mars feeling, a feeling of *drive, activity* and *intensity,* no matter where a conjunction actually occurs in a chart. This adds to the feeling of *emphasis* which naturally occurs when two or more planets are placed together in a chart. (See lessons 2, 3 and 4.)

The square is a 90° aspect. In your mind picture a 90° angle. This angle again starts with Aries, and 90° to one side takes us to Cancer/Moon and the fourth house. In the other direction 90° takes us to Capricorn/Saturn and the tenth house. We are talking of an angular and cardinal feeling. Cardinal always implies *dynamic action* and *intensity* (lesson 4); thus the square always signifies *action, challenge, stimulation* and *stress.*

The opposition is a 180° aspect, and it does just what the word says: one planet opposes the other. Opposite to Aries/Mars and the first house we find Libra/Venus and the seventh house. It is an angular and cardinal position, and its challenges and dynamics are similar to the square, but here the *I-oriented* Aries is now reaching out to the cooperative *we-oriented* Libra. Aries needs to learn cooperation and balance. When Aries changes self-awareness into awareness of others, the conflict of this opposition becomes a cooperation. All oppositions reflect this Aries/Libra conflict, regardless of the actual position of the aspect.

The trine is a 120° aspect. It involves Aries/Mars and the first house and either Leo/Sun and the fifth house or Sagittarius/Jupiter and the ninth house. Because Aries, Leo and Sagittarius are the three fire signs, this is a harmonious aspect, *creative* (Leo/Sun) and even at times *indulgent* (Sagittarius/ Jupiter). All trines reflect this basic pattern which we see in the flat wheel, no matter which element they occur in.

The inconjunct is a 150° aspect. It involves Aries/Mars and the first house and either Virgo/Mercury and the sixth house or Scorpio/Pluto and the eighth house. *Quick, impulsive* Aries has to cope with the *exact, studious* and *down-to-earth* Virgo in matters related to *duty, work, health* or *habits* (the sixth house). Some sort of adjustment is needed to draw these diverse attitudes into alignment. On the other side of the wheel, Aries/Mars/first house needs to cope with the *penetrating, determined* and *over-sensitive* Scorpio in matters relating to *other people's resources* or in areas of *research* and *regeneration.* Both of these instances show two natures that are very divergent. A clear perspective and some kind of reorganization are needed before these signs can function well together. You can see that the inconjunct is a difficult aspect; it can produce stress and strain because it is always an aspect between divergent energies.

The sextile is a 60° aspect. It involves Aries/Mars and the first house and either Gemini/Mercury and the third house or Aquarius/Uranus and the eleventh house. In either case we are dealing with the combination of fire with air, which are compatible elements. Here outgoing Aries joins hands with *communicative* and *intellectual* Gemini and the third house or with *humane, intellectual, progressive* and *friendship-oriented* Aquarius and the eleventh house. All sextiles are between compatible elements (either fire and air or earth and water) and are always combinations that work in an affable way, expressing themselves easily.

TRINES (120°)

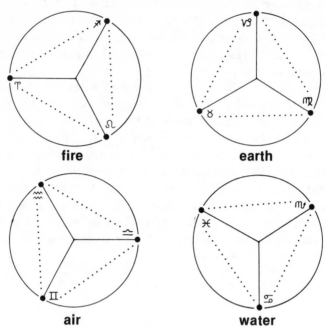

fire   earth

air   water

SQUARES (90°) and OPPOSITIONS (180°)

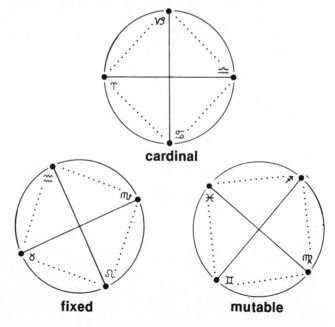

cardinal

fixed   mutable

SEXTILES (60°)

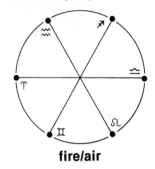

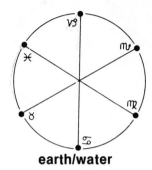

fire/air   **earth/water**

INCONJUNCTS (150°)

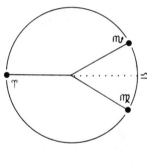

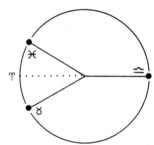

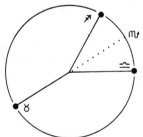

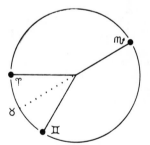

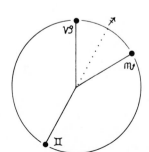

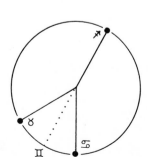

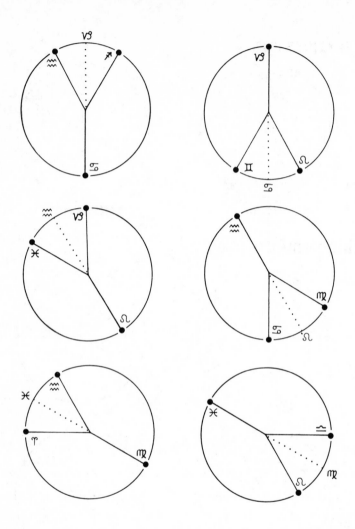

Lesson 7: Aspecting

Aspecting the Horoscope

Now that we have explained what aspects are and their relative position to each other, we will teach you how to find these aspects using the horoscope of Franklin D. Roosevelt. (See the chart with the aspectarian on page 73.)

In the aspectarian beneath the horoscope, list the longitude for each planet. Write these longitudes in the aspectarian in the column headed longitude for each of the planets.

Moon The longitude for the Moon is 06° ♋ 12 ′. Write this next to the symbol for the Moon (☽). The orb we allow for the Moon is 7° for the conjunction, square, opposition and trine. If we add 7° to this Moon position we reach 13° ♋ 12 ′; if we subtract 7° we reach 29° ♊ 12 ′. This allows a 7° orb on either side of the Moon and we know that any planet whose longitude falls between these figures will be in aspect to the

Moon. (If you have any problem in seeing this, look at the completed horoscope in the Appendix on page 286.)

•Mercury is located at 27° ♒ 12′ longitude; it is out of range by 2°.

•Venus is at 06° ♒ 04′, and we can see that it makes an exact aspect to the Moon. Now we must determine what kind of aspect it forms. Venus in Aquarius is fixed, air, active; Moon in Cancer is cardinal, water, passive. They are not in the same quality, thus not in conjunction, square or opposition. They are not in the same element, thus not in trine aspect either. Nor are they sextile. (See page 68.) However, you will note that they are of dissimilar signs and 150° apart, so they are inconjunct (quincunx). The symbol for the inconjunct is (⚻). Place this symbol in the box where the Moon and Venus intersect in the aspectarian, thus:

•The Sun is at 11° ♒ 08′; it makes the same aspect as Venus.

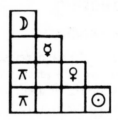

•Mars is located at 27° ♊ 01′. Our orb of 7° puts Mars 2° out of orb for a conjunction with the Moon.

•Jupiter is located at 16° ♉ 56′. This location is 3° beyond the allowable orb.

•Saturn is located at 6° ♉ 06′, which we can see makes an exact aspect to the Moon. It is neither square nor in opposition because Taurus and Cancer are not of the same quality. They are not trine, because Taurus and Cancer are not of the same element. However, both are in passive signs and 60° apart;

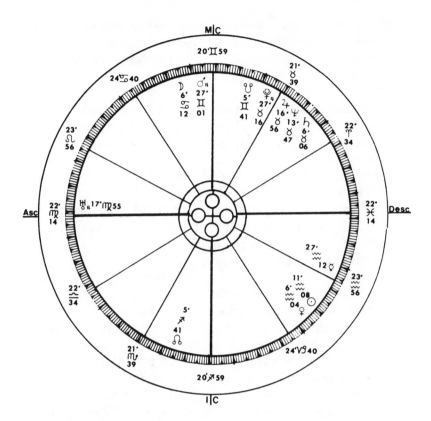

Figure 10: The Natal Horoscope of Franklin Delano Roosevelt Please complete the aspectarians. The completed aspectarians can be found on page 286 in the Appendix.

longitude										
	☽									
		☿								
			♀							
				☉						
					♂					
						♃				
							♄			
								♅		
									♆	
										♇

cardinal:	
fixed:	
mutable:	
fire:	
earth:	
air:	
water:	
angular:	
succedent:	
cadent:	
dignity:	
exaltation:	
detriment:	
fall:	

L:	S:	R:	E:

thus, the Moon and Saturn are sextile to each other. Write the symbol for a sextile (✶) in the aspectarian.

•Uranus is located at 17° ♍ 55 '. It does not fall within the orb we allow. Neither does Neptune at 13° ♉ 47 ' or Pluto at 27° ♉ 16 '.

Mercury We now go on to aspect the planet Mercury. Mercury is located at 27° ♒ 12 '. Adding 7° to this position we arrive at 4° ♓ 12 '; subtracting 7° from this position we get 20° ♒ 12 '.

•Venus at 6° ♒ 04 ' is out of allowable orb.

•The Sun at 11° ♒ 08 ' is also out of allowable orb.

•Mars at 27° ♊ 01 ' makes an exact aspect to Mercury, since Aquarius and Gemini are both air signs, we see that Mercury and Mars trine (△) each other.

•The planets Jupiter, Saturn, Uranus and Neptune are all out of orb. But Pluto at 27° ♉ 16 ' makes an exact square (☐) because Taurus and Aquarius are both signs of the same quality; they are both fixed and 90° apart.

Be sure that you put the proper symbols into the correct boxes in the aspectarian.

Venus We continue by aspecting the planet Venus, located at longitude 6° ♒ 04 '. Adding and subtracting 7° to this position gives us 13° ♒ 04 ' and 29° ♓ 04 ' respectively.

•The Sun at 11° ♒ 08 ' is within orb and both Venus and the Sun are in the same sign; thus the two planets are conjunct (☌).

•Mars is too far away for the orb we allow, and Jupiter is also out of orb. However, Saturn at 6° ♉ 06 ' makes an exact aspect, a square (☐); Taurus squares Aquarius. They are both fixed signs.

•Uranus makes no aspect, nor does Pluto; however, Neptune at 13° ♉ 47 ' is within orb and it squares (☐) Venus.

Sun The Sun is located at 11 ♒ 08 '; the allowable orb is from 4° ♒ 08 ' to 18° ♒ 08 '. Jupiter (16° ♉ 56 '), Saturn (6° ♉ 06 ') and Neptune 13° ♉ 47 ') are all within the allowable orb and are all in the sign Taurus; therefore they all form square aspects to the Sun. There are no aspects from the Sun to Mars, Uranus, or Pluto.

Mars Mars, located at 27° ♊ 01 ', makes no other aspects except those you have already found.

Jupiter Jupiter at 16° ♉ 56 ′ is trine (△) Uranus (17 °♍ 55 ′) and conjunct (♂) Neptune (13 ° ♉ 47 ′).

Saturn Saturn at 6° ♉ 06 ′ is conjunct (♂) Neptune at 13 ° ♉ 47 ′.

Outer Planets Uranus at 17 ° ♍ 55 ′ is trine (△) Neptune at 13 ° ♉ 47 ′. Neptune makes no aspect with Pluto.

This is a simple method for finding aspects. If necessary, refer to pages 55 and 68 to familiarize yourself with the various aspects. If you have learned the material in lessons 1, 2 and 3, aspecting should be quite easy.

Now that we have shown you how to aspect, turn to page 76. Here is another chart for you to aspect: the horoscope of actress Judy Garland. After you have filled in the complete aspectarian, check your answers against ours on page 288.

Summary of Lessons 6 and 7

In these two lessons we have shown you the planetary angles within a horoscope and their importance to a full delineation. In lesson 6 we explained the different aspects and their meanings; in lesson 7 we taught you how to actually find these aspects in a chart.

It takes a beginner a lot of time to completely aspect a horoscope; however, with practice this procedure becomes easier and faster. We suggest that you practice aspecting other charts that you have until you are thoroughly familiar with the procedure.

After planets, houses and signs, aspects are the last basic astrological element you must learn. You will discover as we proceed that everything else is based upon these four building blocks. If you have built your foundation well, mastery of the remaining lessons should be relatively easy.

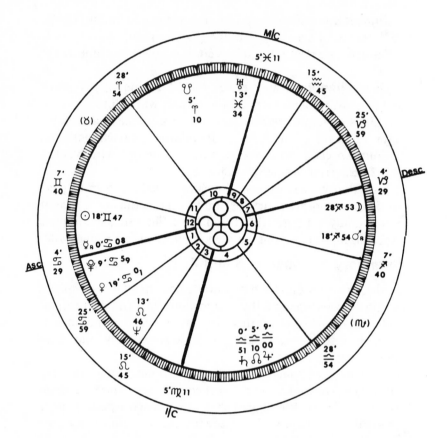

**Figure 11: The Natal Horoscope of Judy
Garland** Born June 10, 1922 at 5:30 a.m.
Central Standard Time in Grand Rapids,
Minnesota. Longitude 93° W 32′,
latitude 47° N 14′.

longitude										
	☽									
		☿								
			♀							
				☉						
					♂					
						♃				
							♄			
								♅		
									♆	
										♇

cardinal:	
fixed:	
mutable:	
fire:	
earth:	
air:	
water:	
angular:	
succedent:	
cadent:	
dignity:	
exaltation:	
detriment:	
fall:	

L:	S:	R:	E:

Part II
Introduction

Up to this point, you have learned the basics of astrology. These basics form the foundation on which we shall now build. If you are familiar with the signs, planets, houses and aspects, it will be easy for you to add to this knowledge. In Part II of this book, we expand on these basic premises.

As you realized in our rudimentary delineation of Roosevelt's chart, a few keywords can help us to see and understand a lot. But that was only a beginning. We want to teach you to go more deeply into a chart, to be able to delve into the traits, characteristics and potentials of any horoscope. The keywords you learned in Part I are your first point of reference. You now have developed a certain feeling and understanding of astrology. The next step is to learn to use your own logic, thinking and intuition. Experience has shown us that you'll need more than just keywords to understand the many possible variations of a horoscope. You will need detailed explanations, more actual examples and your own thinking to describe the possibilities present in a horoscope. This will be your second point of reference.

What you do with this second point of reference will make the difference between your becoming an excellent astrologer or just a cookbook astrologer. If you use our phrases and examples as you would a recipe (i.e., take one spoonful of the Moon in Aries, add three pinches of Saturn in the third house), then you have not really understood the principles of astrology. What we shall try to teach you is to 1) look at a horoscope without losing sight of the entire picture presented by the horoscope and 2) always think and always discriminate in your choice of words and phrases.

Let's take a typical example. One of the sentences describing the Moon in Gemini is, *You are generally incapable of long-sustained feelings or undivided loyalties.* On one occasion, one of our students had this combination and she got angry when she read this. She explained to the rest of the class that she was very loyal! This is the kind of example that teachers love, because it gave us a chance to explain how astrology works. The student in question had the Moon in Gemini, but her Moon was ruled by Mercury in Cancer. She also had the Sun, Venus and Pluto in Cancer. All four planets were conjunct, a four-planet stellium. Her Moon in Gemini had some Gemini qualities, but with all of this Cancer emphasis, her Moon naturally had many Cancer characteristics and sensitivities, which include her loyalty.

In astrology nothing stands by itself; we can't say anything without considering the entire chart. A sense of the whole chart is always more indicative than each placement considered individually. The different factors in a horoscope do not cancel or negate each other, but they change the overtone. Thus a Moon in Gemini influenced by Cancer will work differently than a Moon in Gemini influenced by Leo or Capricorn.

This may sound complicated now, but as you proceed with Part II, you will become more familiar with the complexities of astrology. You will actually delineate a chart and check your interpretation against ours, and these things will fall into place. Practice is the key. Eventually you will have your own experience to rely on, you will develop your own vocabulary, and you won't need our sentences anymore. For this, Part II will give you a firm starting point.

To make everything even clearer, we have included the names of some prominent people who have the same planetary positions as those being discussed. We find that these examples always help our students, and we hope they will help you too.

Lesson 8: The Sun
Some General Comments on this Lesson

In lesson 7 your review work was to aspect the horoscope of Judy Garland. In the next ten lessons, as we give you more details on each planet, we ask you to delineate each planet in Judy Garland's horoscope. As always, you can find our answers and our interpretations in the Appendix. It is very important that you actually do these delineations, because this is what astrology is all about: delineating, interpreting and judging what you see. You can only learn this by doing it. As you delineate each planet and decide which of the given keywords or phrases to use and then check in the Appendix to see if we chose the same phrases and why, you are exercising the practice that eventually makes the master. This experience will be your basic learning of astrology; everything that comes afterwards will be just further refinements of the same technique and knowledge.

A Basic Overview of Judy Garland's Horoscope

Before we begin to delineate Judy Garland's horoscope, we must first look at the whole picture to get a basic overview of her personality.

She has five planets plus her Ascendant in cardinal signs, only one fixed planet, and four planets plus her Midheaven in mutable signs. Therefore Judy is *active, ambitious, enthusiastic* and *quick*. With many mutable planets added to this cardinal feeling, and considering that she has four planets in cadent houses (which relate to mutable), she is *versatile, changeable, sympathetic* and *intuitive* (see lesson 1).

Six planets in water signs give her great *sensitivity*, make her *emotional* and *easily influenced*. The fact that she has no planets in earth shows that she lacks a certain practicality and that she does not always have both feet on the ground (see lesson 4). This lack of the earth element is somewhat compensated for by four planets in the houses of substance which are based on the elements and relate to earth. We also see that she has four planets in the houses of endings, which relate to water and re-emphasize her *sensitivity* and *depth of feeling*.

Garland has six planets east and four planets west of the north-south meridian, which is not a significant division. Three planets above and seven planets below the horizon, one of the seven being the Moon, shows that her basic inclination is *subjective* (lesson 1).

The planet Saturn is exalted in Libra, and therefore Saturn can express its nature harmoniously (lesson 3).

This gives you a good basic sense of Judy Garland's horoscope. The next step is to delineate the *heart of the chart*, the *life-giver*, the Sun. This lesson covers the Sun in greater detail. At the end of this lesson, we will ask you to choose the right keywords for the Sun, the sign of Gemini, and the twelfth house and then the phrases and words given in this lesson which you feel fit Judy Garland's horoscope. And don't forget to delineate all the aspects that the Sun makes in this chart.

Our interpretation can be found in the Appendix, on page 289.

You will notice that next to the Sun in the first house and the Moon in the second house it says *accidental exaltation*.

Next to the Sun in the fifth house and the Moon in the fourth house it says *accidental dignity*. This indicates that the Sun in the first house equates to the Sun in Aries where it is exalted, and the Sun in the fifth house equates to the Sun in Leo, where it is dignified. Therefore the Sun, as if by accident, works very positively in these houses. The same reasoning, of course, applies to the Moon in the second house, which is the house of Taurus where the Moon is exalted, and the fourth house, equating with Cancer where the Moon is dignified, and so on with all the planets in houses equating to the signs where they are either exalted or dignified.

The Sun in the Signs

The Sun represents your *inner self,* your *personality* and your *ego,* so you will have to consider the following descriptions within that context.

☉ ♈ SUN IN ARIES
keyword *enterprising*　　　　　　　　　　exaltation

Militant, headstrong and ambitious, you are quick, dynamic and enthusiastic. You are a leader, not a follower, and you do well in positions of authority and management. You are an excellent artisan. You like to do your own thing in your own good time, and you are opinionated and at times even arrogant. You can be insensitive to the needs of others, yet you rarely hold a grudge. Your overt self-confidence can hide a deep feeling of inadequacy. Your aim is energetic leadership. *President Thomas Jefferson, dancer Arthur Murray, sportscaster Howard Cosell, singer Diana Ross, actor Warren Beatty.*

☉ ♉ SUN IN TAURUS
keyword *practical*

Persistent, determined and cautious, you are a plodder who needs time to adjust to new ideas. Because you are fond of art and music, you can excel in these fields. Retentive and steadfast, you rarely scatter your forces. You prefer to assume responsibilities seriously and practically. You like gracious living and have an inner drive to build a firm foundation, often based on financial security. Headstrong, you are slow to anger, but when you do get angry you get furious. Sympathetic and understanding, you are a faithful friend but an implacable enemy.

Singer Barbara Streisand, baseball player Willie Mays, newspaper publisher William Randolph Hearst, singer Ella Fitzgerald, conductor Zubin Mehta.

☉ ♊ SUN IN GEMINI
keyword *adroit*

Sensitive, talkative, vacillating and sympathetic, you must cultivate perseverance, or your restlessness will inhibit true accomplishment. Variety is the spice of your life. You love to socialize, and you try to avoid deep emotionalism. You are eloquent, love to read and have many hobbies. You can be vague and irresponsible and need a constant change of scene. You should channel your ability and talent for communication so it does not become idle chatter.

Writer Ralph Waldo Emerson, actress Marilyn Monroe, pianist Erroll Garner, President John F. Kennedy, actor Errol Flynn, attorney F. Lee Bailey, actor Tony Curtis.

☉ ♋ SUN IN CANCER
keyword *feeling*

You are innately attached to your home and family and are patriotic, maternal and imaginative. Although quiet, conscientious and receptive, you are deeply concerned with what others think of you. You need to feel needed, and through genuine concern for humanity you can overcome your natural shyness. You like to cook and entertain, and you are an avid collector. When necessary you can be manipulative to achieve your aim, which is emotional security. You need a quiet place for retreat, since you respond so strongly to influences in your environment.

Writer Henry David Thoreau, actor Bill Cosby, lyricist Oscar Hammerstein, writer Pearl Buck, artist Rembrandt van Rijn, actor Bob Crane.

⊙ ♌ SUN IN LEO
keyword *self-expressive*   dignity

You are a natural leader with many friends. You are active, generous, youthful and optimistic. In spite of your self-assurance and dignity, you have a great fear of being laughed at or disgraced. Affectionate, you love to display your feelings. Though you may not have many children of your own, you are fond of children and they respond warmly to you. Patience is not your strong suit, and you must learn to discipline your fiery enthusiasm and overly dramatic approach to life. You cannot be pushed, but flattery goes a long way with you. Creative and emotionally exuberant, you make a good actor or teacher, and you enjoy the good life.

Actress Lucille Ball, Emperor Napoleon Bonaparte, actress Mae West, ex-First Lady Jacqueline Kennedy Onassis, artist Andy Warhol, actor Robert deNiro.

⊙ ♍ SUN IN VIRGO
keyword *conscientious*

Modest, discriminating and thoughtful, everything you do you do well. You give great attention to detail, but you can carry this to extremes, becoming fussy, overly critical and even interfering. You worry a lot, but you are not easily discouraged. Once you overcome a sense of modesty, you are very articulate and express your ideas well. You enjoy routine, are service-oriented and very responsible. You are thoughtful and fond of learning, and you rarely look your age.

Actress Greta Garbo, actor Gene Kelly, Governor George Wallace, artist Grandma Moses, writer H.G. Wells, White House chief of staff Hamilton Jordan, actress Sophia Loren.

☉ ♎ SUN IN LIBRA
keyword *moderate*   fall

You believe in compromise, which makes you a good diplomat. You love beauty and refinement. You do not like to get your hands dirty and usually avoid any field that may require this. Charming and companionable, you operate best in a partnership. You generally marry young and sometimes often. You are social, gracious, gregarious, and you love to entertain and have a good time. Peace and harmony are important to you, and you can go to great lengths to achieve them.

First Lady Eleanor Roosevelt, etiquette writer Emily Post, baseball player Mickey Mantle, TV show host Ed Sullivan, actor George C. Scott, President Dwight D. Eisenhower.

☉ ♏ SUN IN SCORPIO
keyword *probing*

Determined, aggressive and shrewd, you are rarely passive or neutral about anything. Deep, often quite secretive and reserved, you are at times jealous, resentful and even vengeful. Your recuperative powers are remarkable. You are a truth-seeker; you have keen judgment and penetrating insight, and these qualities enable you to exercise a great deal of authority over others. Science, medicine or any field of intrigue are right up your alley. Willpower and persistence are your strong points, and although you are somewhat reticent, when prodded you can become outspoken and direct.

Artist Pablo Picasso, strongman Charles Atlas, baseball player Roy Campanella, Queen Marie Antoinette, singer Mahalia Jackson, murder cult leader Charles Manson.

☉ ♐ SUN IN SAGITTARIUS
keyword *forthright*

You are gregarious and enthusiastic, and you espouse high principles such as universal love and world peace. Happy-go-lucky, honest, cheerful and optimistic, at times you are restless, careless and extravagant. Your tolerance allows you to work well with all people, and you accept them for what they are. You are extroverted, and your bluntness and impatience can unknowingly hurt others who are more sensitive. You are fond of sports, the outdoors and travel. "Don't fence me in" could be your motto.

Industrialist Andrew Carnegie, conductor Arthur Fiedler, writer Mark Twain, statesman Winston Churchill, writer Louisa May Alcott, actress Liv Ullman.

⊙ ♑ SUN IN CAPRICORN
keyword *cautious*

Ambitious, serious and dedicated to duty, life may seem difficult for you, but you ultimately triumph. Although you are self-disciplined, responsible and practical, at times you can wallow in self-pity. Your reasoning ability is excellent, and you have a strong sense of purpose and direction. You may appear somber and reserved in your dealings with others, but once you give your trust you are a loyal and steadfast friend. Socially-oriented, you are willing to work hard for anything you want, and your self-esteem is extremely important to you.

Statesman Daniel Webster, medical missionary Albert Schweitzer, FBI director J. Edgar Hoover, General Robert E. Lee, pianist Oscar Levant, President Richard Nixon, actress Faye Dunaway.

⊙ ♒ SUN IN AQUARIUS
keyword *unconventional*   detriment

Original, independent, individualistic and freedom-loving, you can be rebellious and perverse if you do not handle these qualities well. Your strong likes and dislikes can make you seem stubborn and unyielding. Anything different has great appeal to you, and you are often attracted to the occult, astrology or causes of any kind. It is easier for you to love many people than just one, which can make you seem cool and detached. Unpredictable, curious and intellectual, your aim is to express useful knowledge.

Naturalist Charles Darwin, feminist Betty Freidan, aviator Charles Lindbergh, actor Hal Holbrook, singer Marian Anderson, actor John Travolta.

☉ ♓ SUN IN PISCES
keyword *imaginative*

The dreamer of the zodiac, you are compassionate, tolerant, kind and loving. You are easily influenced by others because you don't want to hurt anyone. It is hard for you to make decisions and you need to overcome your desire to escape from anything that is difficult. Creative, spiritual and often mystical, at times you can be indolent and impractical. You may seem to lack self-confidence, but in your own quiet way you accomplish a great deal. Charming and likeable, you are good to those in distress and are fond of animals. Pisces, more than any other sign, will draw its strength or weakness from the rest of the horoscope.

Poet Edna St. Vincent Millay, poet Elizabeth Browning, dancer Rudolf Nureyev, dancer Cyd Charisse, actor Sidney Poitier, consumer advocate Ralph Nader.

The preceding notes also apply to the sign on the Ascendant. When delineating the Sun, you must not only consider the sign but also the house it is placed in. For example, the Sun in Gemini in the eighth house will express itself with Scorpio overtones, while the Sun in Gemini in the tenth house will have a Capricorn approach, in addition to Gemini characteristics. However, with the sign Gemini on the Ascendant (the cusp of the first house) the true Gemini personality will be evident.

The Sun in the Houses

SUN IN THE FIRST HOUSE
keyword *vital*   accidental
                                             exaltation

Strong-willed, confident, optimistic and happy, this place-ment intensifies the Sun sign. You usually have a happy childhood, a strong constitution and good health. You have leadership ability and like to dominate. You are extroverted, courageous and enthusiastic, but with too many challenging aspects you can be dictatorial, egotistic and pompous. The Sun in the first house takes on many Aries characteristics.

Governor Huey Long, President Lyndon Johnson, actress Lucille Ball, FBI Director J. Edgar Hoover, actor Warren Beatty.

SUN IN THE SECOND HOUSE
keyword *financial*

You are constantly searching for values. This placement in-dicates an ability to attract money, but you can't always hang on to it. You love splendor; your possessions can be status symbols. Influential friends usually come to you. You come from a well-to-do home or have a successful parent. Ex-travagance and financial success are characteristic here, but it is also important for you to learn to share. The Sun in the second house acts much like the Sun in Taurus.

Comedian Jack Benny, political philosopher Karl Marx, Senator Edward M. Kennedy, actress Ellen Burstyn, actor Robert deNiro, dancer Joel Gray, singer Beverly Sills.

SUN IN THE THIRD HOUSE
keyword *communicative*

Observant, optimistic, scientific and flexible, you have the ability to make the right decisions at the right time. A good speaker and writer, you enjoy getting involved in neighborhood affairs and traveling. Brothers and sisters are important to you, and your early environment was probably happy. You can be either impartial and self-reliant or arrogant and domineering. The Sun in the third house acts much like the Sun in Gemini.

Poet Alfred Tennyson, Chief Justice Earl Warren, conductor

Arturo Toscanini, poet Carl Sandburg, astronaut Neil Armstrong, Governor John Connally, singer John Davidson.

SUN IN THE FOURTH HOUSE
keyword *domestic*

You have strong parental ties and a happy home life, unless you have too many challenging aspects; then there is a desire to leave home early. You experience good health in old age. This house placement is excellent for all phases of real estate. You have a strong urge for self-protection that may surface as an ultimate need for security. This house shows the roots of a person's being, the depths not apparent on the surface. The Sun in the fourth house reflects many tendencies of the Sun in Cancer.

Medical missionary Albert Schweitzer, pianist Liberace, actress Greta Garbo, inventor Thomas Edison, columnist Jack Anderson, singer Lena Horne.

SUN IN THE FIFTH HOUSE
keyword *magnetic*   accidental dignity

Strong, popular, creative and self-indulgent, you find great joy in love and children. You are successful with the opposite sex and may have many love affairs. You handle children well but rarely have a large family. You are likely to express yourself through acting, teaching, art, sports or speculation. With difficult aspects, you may exploit others or be an exhibitionist. The Sun in the fifth house works much like the Sun in Leo.

Writer George Sand, actor James Dean, The Duke of Windsor, dancer Fred Astaire, singer Alice Cooper, musician John Lennon, publisher Larry Flint.

SUN IN THE SIXTH HOUSE
keyword *capable*

You are a good worker and organizer, and you take pride in your achievements. Determined and faithful, you have a high regard for beauty, diet, health and hygiene. A regular routine is necessary for your emotional well-being. A positive attitude can help you overcome physical weakness or poor health. You would do well either in service fields or in sports. The Sun in the sixth house is similar to having the Sun in Virgo.

Baseball player Jackie Robinson, film director Alfred Hitchcock, boxer Muhammad Ali, singer Glen Campbell, singer Eartha Kitt, basketball player Kareem Abdul Jabbar.

SUN IN THE SEVENTH HOUSE
keyword *companionable*

Partnership is your keynote and you function best when working with someone else. However, you must learn that your partner's wishes are as important as your own. Because you are easy to get along with, you are popular and well-liked. Marriage is important to you, and you will profit through any partnership or union. If there are difficult aspects, this placement can bring notoriety. Usually you are lucky in any dealings with the law or courts. The Sun in the seventh house and the Sun in Libra work in very much the same way.

Actress Jean Harlow, murder cult leader Charles Manson, actress Carole Lombard, singer Mick Jagger, actor Clint Eastwood, Lieutenant William Calley.

SUN IN THE EIGHTH HOUSE
keyword *regenerative*

This is a very political placement; you are able to attract the support of other people. You may have an inheritance, a legacy, or perhaps you manage other people's money. You are very creative, and sex is important to you. Intent on self-improvement, you can be interested in occult fields and in issues of life after death. You might have difficulties in your early life, linked somehow to your father. With challenging aspects, you could have financial trouble either through mismanagement or an extravagant partner. The Sun in the eighth house takes on many overtones of the Sun in Scorpio. *President Harry S. Truman, President John F. Kennedy, poet Lord Byron, financier John D. Rockefeller Sr., heiress Barbara Hutton, financial writer Sylvia Porter.*

SUN IN THE NINTH HOUSE
keyword *adventurous*

The Sun in the ninth house is an excellent placement for success in law, travel or orthodox religion. You have a flair for foreign languages, and you get along with almost anyone. You could marry a foreigner whom you meet on a long journey, or perhaps you have a foreign-born parent. You are a serious student with philosophical leanings, and you would make a good and devoted teacher. At times you can be impractical and if you use this placement negatively, you can be a daydreamer on the one hand or a fanatic on the other. The Sun in the ninth house acts much like the Sun in Sagittarius.
Dictator Benito Mussolini, explorer Robert Peary, presidential adviser Bernard Baruch, explorer Roald Amundsen, ecologist Jacques Cousteau, film director Roman Polanski.

SUN IN THE TENTH HOUSE
keyword *responsible*

You feel the need to prove your importance, so you are usually successful and sometimes famous. If you are not in the public eye, you are nonetheless a leader in your own circle. This is an ideal placement for politics, as you are ambitious and intrigued with power. Sometimes you are rebellious and arrogant, but people always notice you. The Sun in the tenth house and the Sun in Capricorn often work in the same way. *Civil rights leader Martin Luther King, artist Vincent Van Gogh, poet Anne Morrow Lindbergh, composer Igor Stravinsky, actor Burt Reynolds.*

SUN IN THE ELEVENTH HOUSE
keyword *individualistic*

You do your own thing, and generally you achieve what you want. You are either very social with many friends, or you are the loner who goes your own way. Good at meeting challenges, you are usually an excellent organizer who can inspire others to help you in all your undertakings. You are often a leader in some new field or involved with service on a large scale. The Sun in the eleventh house and the Sun in Aquarius operate similarly.

Writer Ernest Hemingway, General Douglas McArthur, actress Ethel Waters, artist Salvador Dali, anthropologist Margaret Mead, singer Cher, actor Robert Reed.

SUN IN THE TWELFTH HOUSE
keyword *secretive*

Although you may lack self-confidence and need a lot of solitude, you are able to integrate the subconscious part of your nature. Your life before thirty may be somewhat restricted. Some kind of work in institutions, charities, labor or research appeals to you, although you usually prefer to work behind the scenes. This is often the placement for actors, since actors can hide their real feelings by playing a role. If there are difficult aspects, you may be your own worst enemy; you must learn to serve and should not let yourself wallow in self-pity. The Sun in the twelfth house operates like the Sun in Pisces; this placement depends more on the total horoscope than any of the other Sun placements.

Writer Zelda Fitzgerald, Secretary of State Henry Kissinger, newspaper publisher William Randolph Hearst, labor leader James Hoffa, TV personality Paul Lynde, comedian Jim Backus.

The Sun in Aspect

Any aspect to the Sun stresses the *inner self*, the *personality* and the *ego*.

The conjunction emphasizes the *self.*

The opposition gives *self-awareness* or *awareness of some-one else.*

The square *challenges the ego* and creates *tension on the personality level.*

The trine *gives the personality an opportunity to flow harmoniously.*

The sextile makes it *easy for the ego to express itself.*

The inconjunct tells you that *an adjustment must be made* before the inner self can express itself positively.

Conjunctions

☉ ☌ ☽ SUN CONJUNCT MOON

This aspect can be limiting and can show extremes of temperament according to the sign. You tend to one-sidedness by narrowing your outlook. You can be self-willed and driving, but you keep personal contacts at a distance. The Sun conjunct the Moon indicates a new Moon at your birth.
Political philosopher Karl Marx, writer Leo Tolstoi.

☉ ☌ ☿ SUN CONJUNCT MERCURY

You are a forceful thinker, and you are impulsive, ambitious and creative. At times you can be reflective and introspective, but you can also be egocentric, inflexible and stubborn, showing a lack of impartiality.
French President Charles de Gaulle, actress Liv Ullman.

☉ ☌ ♀ SUN CONJUNCT VENUS

You have a charming disposition, a great love of life, and you are affectionate and social. You may delay marriage, and once married you may limit your family, but you have a fondness for children. You have a strong sense of love and eroticism. You are persuasive and eager to be liked, and you lead a

charmed life. A very close conjunction can lead to egotism, pompous attitudes and overly high expectations.
Actress Carol Burnett, playwright George Bernard Shaw.

☉ ♂ ♂ SUN CONJUNCT MARS

Hard-working and self-assertive, you have willpower and drive. This is a beneficial aspect because the power of the Sun is expressed through the energy and action of Mars in both the house these planets are in and the houses they rule. You are quick tempered but just as quick to forget. You are enterprising, dramatic and competitive, with strong leadership ability. You do not shy away from danger.
Industrialist Andrew Carnegie, astronaut John Glenn, singer Bobby Darin.

☉ ♂ ♃ SUN CONJUNCT JUPITER

This is a very beneficial aspect. It suggests success, generosity, luck and zest for life, which can lead to great accomplishments. It brings enthusiasm and optimism, but a lack of moderation can lead to physical problems. You are not overly ambitious but do like recognition for your efforts. You need to find a field that stimulates your imagination.
Singer Maria Callas, TV writer Rod Serling.

☉ ♂ ♄ SUN CONJUNCT SATURN

You are sober and industrious, and you achieve well earned material success, often with a one-track mind. You mature early and learn from your experiences. Emotional problems and personal sorrow may be caused by the lack of a father or by a strong father and your wish to live up to his expectations. Because you are hardworking, you need a demanding profession.
Governor George Wallace, writer Somerset Maugham.

☉ ☌ ♅ SUN CONJUNCT URANUS

Talented but unpredictable, you are a leader with a flair for the unusual. Self-aware and imaginative, you can be arrogant and stubborn, and at times you may be accused of erratic behavior. You could be attracted to a modern career, especially in the political arena. With this aspect, divorce is common, since personal freedom is so necessary for you.
Writer Arthur Conan Doyle, President Herbert Hoover, actress Vivian Leigh.

☉ ☌ ♆ SUN CONJUNCT NEPTUNE

Because you are uncertain of your capabilities, it is difficult for you to express yourself with self-confidence. You are artistic, musical and interested in the occult. Since you have an enthusiastic devotion to duty, you would do well in a service-oriented career. At times you adopt a fantasy viewpoint and escape into a world of your own instead of facing yourself and your life.
Writer Horatio Alger, songwriter Cole Porter.

☉ ☌ ♀ SUN CONJUNCT PLUTO

This is a point of great force in a chart. You have strong desires on all levels: physical, mental and spiritual, and you can be an extremist driven by an obsession for power. You are incapable of understanding weakness or lack of drive in others, so you must deal with your intolerance and egotism. You will fight anything that you consider an injustice.
Writer Emile Zola, newspaper publisher William Randolph Hearst.

Squares and Oppositions

☉ □ ☽ SUN SQUARE MOON
☉ ☍ ☽ SUN OPPOSITION MOON

The Sun is the self-assertive principle and the Moon is the sensitive, feeling urge, so there is conflict between the ego and the emotions. This conflict can express itself through personality, health, parents and partners. There can be acute discord within the self in trying to reconcile the "male" and "female" principles. There may be contention between professional and domestic factors or between the parents. Perhaps there is trouble with the partner which could lead to divorce and financial hazards. Yet this inner tension gives great drive and the ability to achieve. The square or opposition can indicate that the parents were not getting along at the time of conception of the child.

Bishop James Pike (□), TV personality Merv Griffin (☍).

⊙ □ ☿ SUN SQUARE MERCURY
⊙ ☍ ☿ SUN OPPOSITION MERCURY
⊙ □ ♀ SUN SQUARE VENUS
⊙ ☍ ♀ SUN OPPOSITION VENUS

Since Mercury is never more than 28° and Venus is never more than 46° away from the Sun, they can make no other major aspects than the conjunction.

⊙ □ ♂ SUN SQUARE MARS
⊙ ☍ ♂ SUN OPPOSITION MARS

You are aggressive, outspoken, enthusiastic and combative. You love to take chances and can be somewhat accident-prone. You may have a chip on your shoulder and come on too forcefully, making others angry. You are strongly physical and need a partner who can match you stride for stride. "Think before you speak" should be your motto.

Boxer Muhammad Ali (□), composer Ludwig van Beethoven (☍).

☉ □ ♃ SUN SQUARE JUPITER
☉ ☍ ♃ SUN OPPOSITION JUPITER

You can be haughty and egotistical and feel as though you can act as you please, but once you learn your priorities you can reach any goal. You may show blind optimism, a love of hazard and a tendency to overindulge in food, sex and drink. This aspect often produces a wheeler-dealer or a con artist. The fields of sports and law could appeal to you. A good Saturn aspect can be helpful.
Writer Gore Vidal (□), tennis player Billie Jean King (☍).

☉ □ ♄ SUN SQUARE SATURN
☉ ☍ ♄ SUN OPPOSITION SATURN

With this aspect your self-expression is limited, especially in your youth, and you learn everything the hard way. Your judgment is good, particularly in career situations. Once you taste success, you can become self-assured. This aspect often prohibits a close rapport with the father, or it can bring his early loss. Severe dental problems or arthritis can be the physical manifestation of Saturn's limiting action on the natural ebullience of the Sun. This aspect often brings marriage to a widow or widower or someone of diverse age.
Basketball player Kareem Abdul Jabbar (□), writer Upton Sinclair (☍).

☉ □ ♅ SUN SQUARE URANUS
☉ ☍ ♅ SUN OPPOSITION URANUS

You are impulsive, rash, eccentric and sometimes unprincipled. You go your own way and do your own thing without much regard for what others think or feel. You are original but impractical, and this aspect often gives you tremendous personal magnetism. Nervous and accident-prone, you seem to attract upsetting conditions and events.
Jockey Steven Cauthen (□), band leader Guy Lombardo (☍).

⊙ □ ♆ SUN SQUARE NEPTUNE
⊙ ☌ ♆ SUN OPPOSITION NEPTUNE

Because you underestimate your ability to succeed, you are often unable to follow through on your intentions although your motives are noble. You are sensitive to suffering, fond of animals and excessively emotional, which you try to hide. You tend to become involved in situations where others lean on you. If Neptune is angular you must guard against deception, as you may let yourself become the victim of fraud or scandal.
Senator Howard Baker (□), General George Patton (☌).

⊙ □ ♇ SUN SQUARE PLUTO
⊙ ☌ ♇ SUN OPPOSITION PLUTO

You are willful, sometimes boastful, arrogant and rebellious, and you have trouble harnessing your energy into constructive channels. Other people think they know you, but they never really do. You must learn to control your temper and to develop moderation in all your relationships. Management is your forte, but first you must learn to compromise. A career in drama would be a good way for you to blow off steam.
Tenor Luciano Pavarotti (□), actor Henry Winkler (☌).

Trines and Sextiles

⊙ △ ☽ SUN TRINE MOON
⊙ ⚹ ☽ SUN SEXTILE MOON

Popular, tranquil and happy, you are not very ambitious, but you can be successful without much struggle. You have a harmonious balance between your ego and your emotions. You can expect an easy life, a comfortable home and assistance from others. Your greatest problem is a tendency to be apathetic when you should assert yourself.
Comedian Will Rogers (△), baseball player Willie Mays (⚹).

⊙ △ ☿ SUN TRINE MERCURY
⊙ ⚹ ☿ SUN SEXTILE MERCURY
⊙ △ ♀ SUN TRINE VENUS
⊙ ⚹ ♀ SUN SEXTILE VENUS

Since Mercury is never more than 28° and Venus is never more than 46° away from the Sun, they can make no other major aspects than the conjunction.

○ ⊙ △ ♂ SUN TRINE MARS
⊙ ⚹ ♂ SUN SEXTILE MARS

You are daring and adventurous, with a strong body and great energy. You can accomplish anything you set out to do. You have a strong sense of honor and integrity, and you can make quick and incisive decisions. The fields of law, management, sports and politics attract you.
Racecar driver Al Unser (△), baseball great Stan Musial (⚹).

⊙ △ ♃ SUN TRINE JUPITER
○ ⊙ ⚹ ♃ SUN SEXTILE JUPITER

Happiness and contentment are usually your lot and people like you, but you have a tendency to be lazy and apathetic unless Jupiter or the Sun aspects Saturn. You are a bit self-indulgent and rarely in want, and if you apply yourself you can attain wealth. You are intellectual, judicious and nearly always take the broad viewpoint.
TV journalist Bill Moyers (△), actor Burt Reynolds (⚹).

⊙ △ ♄ SUN TRINE SATURN
⊙ ⚹ ♄ SUN SEXTILE SATURN

Your success in life comes through your own efforts, through your ability to concentrate and organize. You are responsible

and you lead a moral, well-ordered existence. This aspect usually promises a long life and general good health. In a woman's chart this aspect indicates a successful father or husband or both.
Prince Rainier of Monaco (△), golfer Gary Player (✶).

⊙ △ ♅ SUN TRINE URANUS
⊙ ✶ ♅ SUN SEXTILE URANUS

Your leadership, popularity and talent attract others to you. Although you are not always tactful, your enthusiasm, optimism and laughter are infectious. You may join a cause or a movement and if you do it is with total dedication. Your intuition, hunches and imagination are strong. In a woman's chart this aspect often indicates a happy marriage to an authority figure.
Astronaut Neil Armstrong (△), blind writer Helen Keller (✶).

⊙ △ ♆ SUN TRINE NEPTUNE
⊙ ✶ ♆ SUN SEXTILE NEPTUNE

You are visionary, imaginative and creative. This is an aspect often found in the horoscopes of writers and artists. You also have insight into business and stock market investments, and you could be interested in some scientific field. You are romantic and tender and are usually devoted to your home, mate and family.
Artist Norman Rockwell (△), columnist Walter Winchell (✶).

⊙ △ ♀ SUN TRINE PLUTO
⊙ ✶ ♀ SUN SEXTILE PLUTO

You are a born leader. With sound motivation, intense application and opportunities to advance, you make positive use of your creative energies. You have strong recuperative abili-

ty, concentration and willpower. You can gain from another's loss, or you may receive an inheritance or legacy.
Musician Al Hirt (△), football player Joe Namath (✶).

Inconjuncts (Quincunxes)

☉ ⚻ ☽ SUN INCONJUNCT MOON

You must make an adjustment in the way you handle your emotional needs and your conscious will. You can abuse your health if you give in to overwhelming demands on your time and energy. Romantic rejection is possible until you stop looking at your loved one through rose-colored glasses.
Actor Humphrey Bogart, actress Helen Hayes.

☉ ⚻ ☿ SUN INCONJUNCT MERCURY
☉ ⚻ ♀ SUN INCONJUNCT VENUS

Since Mercury is never more than 28° and Venus is never more than 46° away from the Sun, they can make no other major aspects than the conjunction.

☉ ⚻ ♂ SUN INCONJUNCT MARS

There is a conflict between will and desire, and this creates strain in everything you undertake. Unsure of your capability, you often overcompensate by acting haughty and arrogant. You must learn to handle your anger and resentment; when you show your dependability others will soon see you in a different light.
Actress Lauren Bacall, ex-First Lady Betty Ford.

☉ ⚻ ♃ SUN INCONJUNCT JUPITER

Because you lack a feeling of independence, you tend to overextend yourself. Either you take on too many respon-

sibilities and occupations, or you pursue too many pleasures and hobbies. Because education is important to you, you should encourage it. If you practice moderation in everything you do, you can avoid health and personality problems which could manifest themselves as tumors, obesity or pomposity.
Record executive Neil Bogart, Senator Hubert Humphrey.

⊙ ⊼ ♄ SUN INCONJUNCT SATURN

Your health may suffer because you can become too involved with your work, with doing your own thing or with letting others take advantage of you. You find it difficult to deal with authority, and your downfall can be a self-righteous attitude. Learn to relax and to become more receptive to others.
Actress Lana Turner, swimmer Mark Spitz.

⊙ ⊼ ♅ SUN INCONJUNCT URANUS

Because you feel that you have to prove yourself to others through partnership, friendship and your profession, you always seem to be on the defensive. Because of this need, you tend to project a know-it-all attitude that is hard for others to deal with. You must learn to stress your resourcefulness, creativity and originality, rather than your need to top everyone else.
Comedian Fred Allen, columnist Art Buchwald.

⊙ ⊼ ♆ SUN INCONJUNCT NEPTUNE

You have a tendency to self-sacrifice, and you seem to attract those who need you in some capacity, and later you resent what you see as their exploitation of you. There can be debilitating health problems which you should attend to promptly. You must learn to say no, because by always helping others you deplete your own energies.
Comedian Jerry Lewis, singer Sonny Bono.

⊙ ⊼ ♀ SUN INCONJUNCT PLUTO

Your work may involve great danger or matters of life and death. You push yourself tirelessly, and you must learn to take care of yourself, or your health can suffer because of your relentless drive. This strong drive may be based on an inner dislike of yourself, which you must try to overcome, perhaps through professional help.

Writer Norman Mailer, Chairman Mao Tse Tung.

Lesson 9: The Moon

Some General Comments on this Lesson

Before you start lesson 9, we hope that you have delineated
the Sun in Judy Garland's chart and checked it with our
delineations in the Appendix.

In this beginner's manual we do not give you any detailed
notes on the Ascendant. However, the Ascendant describes
the way people see you. We want to show you that even
without notes you can get a good idea of how the Ascendant
works.

Judy Garland's Ascendant is Cancer (the cusp of the first
house is at 4° 29 ' Cancer), ruled by her Moon in Sagittarius
in the sixth house. Thus people would see her as *sympathetic,
helpful, emotional, patriotic, having a good memory, touchy,
rather easily hurt, a bit sorry for herself.* Because of her
Gemini Sun, we eliminated certain words: *tenacious, maternal*

and *domestic*. Since neither Gemini nor the Moon in Sagittarius evince *brooding*, we also eliminated that word. Now add some of the Sagittarius flavoring like *freedom loving, optimistic, enthusiastic, talkative, exaggerative,* etc. and you get a pretty good feeling of how she comes across. Again, be discriminating in your choice of words, keeping the entire chart in mind. Where you find the Ascendant ruler by house position is where the native really wants to be. Since the Moon, ruling the Ascendant, is in the sixth house of work, you make a mental note that work and all other sixth house matters are very important to her and then you go into more depth when you delineate the Moon.

Now start with lesson 9, the Moon. When you have familiarized yourself with it, delineate Judy Garland's Moon the same way you did her Sun and check it against our interpretation in the Appendix on page 290.

The Moon in the Signs

The Moon represents the *emotions,* the *instincts* and the *feminine principle.* The following descriptions should be considered within this context.

☽ ♈ MOON IN ARIES
keyword *emotionally aggressive*

You respond to life as if it were an adventure, and you are open to new ideas. You relate to experience as a means for self-realization. You have much natural and sincere enthusiasm, but you must consciously work to develop patience. Your temper is uneven; you flare up quickly but soon forget the cause of your outburst.

You often assert your 'me first' tendencies. Your quick but changeable mind is brilliant and acute, but you also have a susceptibility to a hot temper, nervousness and even headaches.

You seem to be emotionally detached from the people around you. Your feelings are acute and sharp and you often use them as a conscious instrument for your own benefit. You hide a sense of insecurity behind an aggressive exterior; you should develop the ability to ask for help when you need it.

Your independent nature can make you courageous to the point of foolhardiness.

When you are interested, you are very warm; when you are not inwardly stirred, you are impersonal. You feel with your ego.

Your mental impressions and reactions are very quick. You trust your sense perceptions, and you are apt to act immediately without reflection; you jump into action from your quick feelings rather than from reason. You are not methodical; you resent authority, and you don't like advice.

You excel in positions where quick decisions are vital. You are changeable in your enthusiasms (even more than a person with the Sun in Aries). You have great originality, inventiveness and restlessness, but you do not have much persistence. You take the initiative in many activities, and you show excessive confidence as well as insufficient forethought. You try to dominate others emotionally and usually gain authority because you make a better leader than a follower.

Ambitious and pioneering, you live and gain by fits and starts. You dislike detail. You do not listen to advice, and you find discipline hard to accept. You need to cultivate perseverance. Your senses are well developed, especially your sight.

Others are impressed by your dynamic, self-reliant attitude.

This position of the Moon in a woman's chart may indicate jealousy and a need to dominate the partner. In a male chart it often attracts a dominant partner.

Since the Moon in the chart represents the mother, your mother, in your eyes, embodies many of the Aries traits: resolute, independent, active, outspoken and a strong influence upon you.

Conductor Leonard Bernstein, gangster Al Capone, President Charles de Gaulle, actor Marlon Brando, fighter pilot Eddie Rickenbacker.

☽ ♉ MOON IN TAURUS
keyword *emotionally stable*　　　　　　exaltation

Centered in the material plane, your emotions are attracted to material comforts and possessions. With a Taurus Moon you want the best of everything, and you rarely settle for less. The Moon is exalted in Taurus; this brings out the reflective and steady side of the Moon and de-emphasizes the Moon's changeable side.

You will stick to your ideals through thick and thin. You are blindly faithful, sentimental, affectionate and basically timid. You may lack originality, so try not to be too fixed in your ways.

Your reactions to sense impressions are slow but strong. You have an accurate memory. You will ponder over an action for a long time, using premises, ethics and ideals, and you assimilate and act upon information in a slow and steady manner. It is difficult for you to change your mind, and you resent any interference once you have reached a decision. You are a determined person, with well developed intuition and sound judgment. You want to excel in whatever you do. You are acquisitive, not only in land, art and other possessions, but also in friendship.

Your sense of touch and taste is highly developed, and you probably have a pleasant speaking and singing voice. Fond of music, art, dancing and all things that make life more pleasureable, you need to gratify your physical appetites.

You only welcome those ideas which are compatible with your stable temperament. You may be narrow-minded, and you are conservative and conventional. Pride, laziness, jealousy and too much stubbornness must be guarded against. Once set on a course, you forge ahead slowly but unswervingly.

You seldom succeed in leaving the family tradition or training and ideals that were impressed upon you by your mother with whom you are closely, though not necessarily happily, linked. You have loyal and lasting relationships in friendship, love and marriage.

This position of the Moon may indicate gardening ability. In a man's chart it attracts a loyal partner who encourages his ambitions.

Singer Glen Campbell, evangelist Billy Graham, singer Mary Martin, actor Gregory Peck, writer Oscar Wilde.

☽ ♊ MOON IN GEMINI
keyword *emotionally versatile*

You are interested in the intimate contact of the moment. Your emotional personality requires variety and novelty rather than duration and depth of feeling. You are generally incapable of long-sustained feelings or of undivided loyalties. Though at times you can be insensitive, your perceptions are quick and accurate. You sustain impressions through thought rather than feeling.

Your senses serve the intellect rather than the emotions. This results in an ability for dispassionate observation and reasoning. Your mind is changeable and at times chaotic, but you can assimilate an indefinite amount of detail. Being versatile and adaptable, you may have two or more vocations, often at the same time

You have a fondness for action and movement, either physical or mental. Your hands are able, facile and skillful and you have a well-developed sense of smell. You are not intuitive, but rather you are observant, quick to form impressions, and you are usually able to verbalize them.

You are drawn to artistic and literary professions or any area involving communications. A preference, even a need, to do several things at once is important for your psychological well-being. The intellectual ability of this placement often makes you an avid reader or a talented artisan.

You are reserved in personal matters, and at times others find you cold; you are more interested in the here and now than in the past. Torn apart by changing feelings, you can spread yourself too thin and scatter your forces; this can manifest in nervous tension. You know how to play up to others, and at times you may be too shrewd for your own good. Your restless nature is always in search of something new.

This position of the Moon may indicate superficiality and a lack of domesticity in a woman's chart. A man with this placement is attracted to an intellectual partner who can fit herself into any social role.

You see your mother as emotionally detached, social and

versatile, yet supportive of your education and early attempts at conversation.

Actress Brigitte Bardot, dancer Fred Astaire, sculptor Auguste Rodin, artist Andy Warhol, architect Frank Lloyd Wright.

☽ ♋ MOON IN CANCER
keyword *emotionally tenacious*   dignity

Maternal, sympathetic, but sometimes patronizing, you naively trust your feelings, but you are apprehensive in matters outside of your own control.

Your sense impressions are very accurate, but you do not often act upon them. Your mind is meditative and your reactions are slow and uncertain. Sensitive to outside influences, you pick up negative vibrations from others; this can make you moody and unhappy if these feelings spill over into your personal relationships. You hide your true feelings and strong emotions under a hard shell.

You have a great deal of placid affection and passivity that results in a special love for home and family; this is your primary attachment. You are inclined to gentle, peaceful, romantic love rather than grand passion. This position of the Moon promises a very deep and strong bond with the mother. If the umbilical cord is not severed in time, relationships may be problematic.

You are very intuitive and overly sensitive to outside influences; you sense conditions, both consciously and unconsciously, and are often psychic. You are easily imposed upon, and when this happens you feel a deep resentment.

You love your home, and you always need a home base to retreat to, yet you often travel and make changes in your life. Your domestic, nurturing nature likes to take care of others, and you are very understanding of their feelings.

The Moon in Cancer is thrifty, economical and careful with property and money. You don't like to see these misused or wasted. Artistic, creative and dramatic, you have a natural flair for music, poetry and acting. Your love of home and family can also express itself in true patriotism.

In a man's chart, this placement of the Moon can be a bit too emotionally sensitive. In looking for a partner, he is attracted to a woman who is more mother than mate. A woman with the Moon in Cancer is easily hurt and tends to dominate the home situation.

Singer Janice Joplin, singer Liza Minelli, actor William Holden, comedian Will Rogers, baseball player Babe Ruth.

☽ ♌ MOON IN LEO
keyword *emotionally dramatic*

Self-sufficient and self-reliant, you will leave things alone unless you are personally concerned. Once you have decided to act, you are resentful of interference and criticism. You are emotionally attached to anything that belongs to you or reflects on your ego personally.

Your sense impressions are well-developed, and you are able to make quick, accurate evaluations of other people and their motives. You have a fiery temperament, and you can quickly cut other people down to size.

Self-centered and somewhat pompous, you may lack objectivity and have a blind spot in your emotional perspective. To truly enjoy any relationship, your heart must be involved.

You usually lack curiosity, but when you are motivated, you learn quickly and accurately, although all your learning is colored by your feelings. Leo lends a nobility to the emotions, but this placement also makes it difficult to back down or to compromise. You are hard to convince, but when you open your mind and heart, you learn the quickest of all.

You have a need to be admired and applauded. Despite your basic loyalty, if you feel unappreciated you will seek appreciation and satisfaction elsewhere.

People with the Moon in Leo are sexually magnetic and charming but may also be overbearing and arrogant. In a man's chart it makes him romantic, fun and sexy, or he may tend to conceit, arrogance and an overbearing ego. Both men and women with this placement are attractive and attracted to the opposite sex. The man will seek a woman with flair, enthusiasm and good taste.

The Moon in Leo brings positions of authority and leadership, which you accept seriously and easily. You are ambitious and status-conscious; you want prominence and acclaim.

Your straightforward honesty is apparent, and your organizing ability is prominent, but take care that it doesn't become bossiness.

You love music, the arts, luxury and children, and you usually have a sunny and self-confident disposition. Your emotions are powerful, your affection is given generously, and you usually favor sophisticated pleasures.

You see your mother as a strong personality who dominated you in your youth. She tried to give you good moral and religious values.

Writer Pearl Buck, Defense Minister Moshe Dayan, Indian Leader Mohandas Gandhi, motorcycle stunt rider Evel Kneivel, singer Barbra Streisand, singer Graham Nash.

☽ ♍ MOON IN VIRGO
keyword *emotionally discriminating*

You respond to encouragement and appreciation, and you have a deep hunger for sharing experiences and self-realization with others. However, this makes you emotionally overeager; you may be prone to dictating the course of all your relationships. You are insistent and you can even be petulant. You are generous with your time and service; you want to serve people, but you have trouble understanding their feelings. You want what you want and just the way you want it.

This placement of the Moon emphasizes your mental qualities, but here the restless mental qualities of Gemini are replaced by steadiness and practicality. You don't value knowledge for its own sake, but you seek it in order to use and apply it. Your memory is excellent. You analyze and criticize all sense impressions with care. This is not the most sexual position for the Moon.

You have a fondness for science and/or the occult. You can be clairvoyant or psychometric, and you have great intuitive abilities if you choose to develop them.

You can be temperamental at times. You prefer to earn everything by your mental ability and your fertile imagination. Despite the Virgo tendency to be picky and argumentative, you appear quiet, shy and unpretentious. Although you are basically proper and conservative, your religious inclinations surface in a broad-minded way. With this mutable Moon, you have many acquaintances, frequent changes in your life and numerous short trips.

You are an excellent teacher. You do not ask personal questions unless necessary, and your curiousity only surfaces in relation to work and practical affairs. Interested in diet, health and hygiene, you have a tendency to worry and to develop a nervous disposition; your digestion may suffer as a result. This is often known as the "medicine chest Moon."

You are shrewd, with good business sense and meticulous attention to detail. You could do very well in psychoanalysis or diagnosis of any kind. You should try to counteract fussiness or a lack of self-confidence.

This position of the Moon in a woman's chart often indicates emotional insecurity which expresses itself as a lack of warmth and at times inhibition. In a man's chart it attracts a detached, nonclinging mate, because he does not want emotional demands made upon him.

Your mother may seem critical and cool to you.

Princess Anne, writer Gertrude Stein, writer William Faulkner, botanist Luther Burbank, actor Dustin Hoffman.

☽ ♎ MOON IN LIBRA
keyword *emotionally refined*

You see life as a means of self-discovery through trial and error. You seek shared experiences at every opportunity, and you have an easy, charming, gracious and impersonal feeling for humanity. You have a deep need for everyone to like you and have a natural courtesy, charm and diplomatic manner; your emotional well-being depends upon approval of others, and so you are eager to please.

You tend to live for the moment and you run the scale of highs and lows with every shift of events. You are friendly, easy-going and popular, but if you use this lunar position negatively you can be capricious, fickle and critical. Because you easily succumb to flattery, you must consciously develop self-reliance and learn how to say no. You must curb your tendencies to indolence and flirtation.

Your sense impressions are strong aesthetically; you feel a

need to serve beauty. Like Virgo, you experience the senses through the mind, and you evaluate the facts, but you do not criticize or analyze them. The airiness of Libra lacks the practical application that we saw in the earth sign Virgo. The Libra mind is more contemplative; you build great ideas, but you are not always ready to act on them. For you judgment is more important than execution.

Decisiveness is not usually a strong quality with this placement, but your illusive sweetness hides a great strength. You have a fondness for music, poetry and the arts. Although you have some ability in these fields, you usually prefer to appreciate rather than perform.

Affectionate and good-natured, you are often in demand in social circles. The people around you affect you, and your love life depends on how much you are appreciated. Partners are important to you since you work best in conjunction with others, and because you are dependent on their reactions.

The man with the Moon in Libra is looking for a refined, sociable and fun-loving partner who is attractive, well-groomed and intelligent. The woman with this position of the Moon is social, a good hostess, and she likes beautiful surroundings, decor and clothing.

As you see your mother, she put great emphasis on your manners and general behavior and tried to motivate you to recognize beauty, either artistic or natural.

Heiress/revolutionary Patricia Hearst, Duchess of Windsor, artist Toulouse Lautrec, Chief Justice Oliver Wendell Holmes, tennis player Arthur Ashe, actor Burt Reynolds, actor James Arness, dancer Rudolf Nureyev.

☽ ♏ MOON IN SCORPIO
keyword *emotionally possessive*   fall

Your emotions are intense and are often based on willful desire. You are impatient, moody and even given to brooding. Easily hurt, you can become jealous, hold grudges and take revenge. You often judge others too quickly and feel a need to dominate through subtle means.

You will not tolerate opposition to or interference with your goals, but often you will sacrifice a great deal for kindness.

You have executive ability and are resourceful and enterprising. Although abrupt and impulsive, you have self-confidence and the ability to attain success. You usually get what you go after; however, you might find that you have achieved a hollow victory.

Since you are so jealous, proud and possessive, this position of the Moon doesn't promise a harmonious marriage. The wish to dominate is often reflected in your relationship with your children; it can be the result of a parent's domination or of your over-idealization of a parent, usually the mother. With this lunar placement, a mother can be overly possessive, and she may have trouble freeing a child, especially if male.

You become emotionally intent on completing and enjoying any project you have adopted, and you can seem lacking in sympathy when so absorbed. Your personality is deep, and you have shrewd insight into other people; often you like to probe into deep and unknown fields.

You regard the senses as instruments of pleasure rather than knowledge, responding intensely and passionately to life and sex. Your ability to observe is unlimited. Your willpower is often latent, but when you use it, it is for the betterment of humanity.

A negative use of the Scorpio Moon can lead to sexual excess, inhibition, perversion or alcoholism. Your greatest need is to learn to forgive and forget. You must learn to handle your strong, deep feelings. Since your senses are so important, you should pay attention to them.

In a woman's chart the Moon in Scorpio may indicate sexual promiscuity, self-indulgence and family problems. A man with this placement seeks a sensual partner, but one gentle enough so he can possess and consume her. Being secretive and closemouthed, he needs an intuitive mate who can sense his moods.

Actor Charlie Chaplin, educator Maria Montessori, psychic Uri Geller, writer Truman Capote, actor Jim Backus.

☽ ♐ MOON IN SAGITTARIUS
keyword *emotionally idealistic*

You are socially naive and blissfully unaware of real human

differences. You react to others as if they were part of yourself; you tend to merge and melt into them.

You need and want to do everything with everybody, and you are open and friendly as a puppy. You have a keen prophetic and inspirational sense; you are always searching, restless and often lack continuity.

Your sense impressions are clear and more accurate than in nearly any other sign; thus your judgment is acute. But you should learn to think before you speak.

Your mind resents confusion and it will reject anything irrelevant to the issue at hand. When you do focus, it is on *one* thing only, to the point of seeming to have a one-track mind. Unsettled in both mind and body, you need activity and physical exercise. You have a need to roam and are fond of sports, both as a participant and an observer.

You have strong psychic and occult tendencies, and you are more sensitive than your free and breezy attitude reveals. You are a natural teacher or preacher, with a talent for religion, philosophy, poetry and music. You like to help others.

You have a high degree of independence, a need for freedom and a tendency to be somewhat offhand. You must counteract carelessness and recklessness with tact and thoughtfulness.

A man's Moon in Sagittarius may indicate a late marriage, bachelorhood or philandering. It may also mean early baldness. It can make a woman too independent and even footloose.

Your mother, or so it seems to you, lived her own life and left you pretty much to your own devices, but she generously supplied what she felt you needed.

Opera singer Joan Sutherland, President Gerald Ford, ice skater Dick Button, physicist Albert Einstein, singer Bing Crosby.

☽ ♑ MOON IN CAPRICORN
keyword *emotionally reserved*   detriment

You want to be recognized as an important and powerful person. Emotionally, you are supersensitive, and at the same time you are critical of others; however, you are untiring and considerate when you are interested or involved.

The Moon is in its detriment in Capricorn, in opposition to warm, nurturing Cancer. This lunar position emphasizes reserve and coldness. You are shy and insecure about your own worth; you have many subconscious fears, and you can be oversensitive to real or fancied slights. You seek to justify yourself by acting with personal dignity and by your great ambition to succeed. Thus you are neither truly sympathetic nor very emotional.

Your mind reacts quickly to sense impressions, but often with anger or antagonism. This position has produced people with fanatic or obsessive ideas or causes (Napoleon, Hitler, Joseph Smith).

The combination of Saturn, the ruler of Capricorn, and the Moon can show a morbid and melancholy tendency to brooding, but you can also achieve popularity or even notoriety.

This position of the Moon, more than any other, will react to the rest of the chart. The down-to-earth feeling of the Moon in Capricorn will pick up the best of a chart with easy aspects or the worst if there are too many challenges. When well-aspected, it gives leadership and administrative ability. Difficult aspects often result in a lack of creative energy, although your ambition is strong. If you do not learn to handle this position, you may incline to alcoholism, a surrender to the appetites or a calculated need to achieve power at any cost without concern for anyone else. You make enemies easily, whether they are earned or not, and this can cause trouble with your reputation.

The Moon in Capricorn indicates a strong parental influence. Your mother was quite traditional and conservative in raising you. She was practical and efficient, though social, and encouraged you to succeed in all your endeavors.

You are cautious in money matters, and you have common sense and practical ability. These traits can become extreme, leaning toward over-caution, gloominess and austerity. You need to cultivate warmth and tenderness, and you must learn that giving freely, without expecting anything in return, can be more fulfilling than self-seeking demands made on others. At work you show application; you can take responsibility and earn a high position through your persistent effort.

Women with the Moon in Capricorn tend to get the blues

and feel "No one in the world likes me." The man with this lunar position seeks a mate who can help further his social ambitions, run a comfortable home and balance the family checkbook.

Prime Minister Indira Gandhi, TV personality Johnny Carson, actress Lucille Ball, President Abraham Lincoln, Senator Robert Kennedy, singer Beverly Sills.

☽ ♒ MOON IN AQUARIUS
keyword *emotionally detached*

You consider experience a proving ground for yourself. You react to everything on a utilitarian and, at the same time, idealistic level. Release is very necessary for you, as you tend to overload yourself emotionally. You need a cause or project to release tension, or you become frustrated. This can lead to restless wandering and search or to spiritual enlightenment.

Your sense impressions are quick, and your mind and emotions react together; thus you have mental clarity and involvement. Your blending of religious, humanitarian, sexual and scientific instincts is good.

You have a universal quality and are ahead of your time. You are a charming friend and companion and an interesting conversationalist. Women with the Moon in Aquarius can become too eccentric and experimental, and both sexes must avoid being too impersonal or detached. A man with the Moon in Aquarius seeks a rather liberated mate, especially in sexual matters.

You may be inclined toward politics or education or unusual subjects such as astrology and the occult. You are likely to show originality, ingenuity, inventiveness and scientific ability. Your imagination is fertile, and you have a lot of creative energy; if you are not careful your abundance of emotional energy can cause your nervous system to suffer. You are a born mixer and joiner, especially for a cause.

You prefer the unconventional, and you value your personal independence. You are idealistic and broad-minded, but behind your friendly outgoing manner you hide a good bit of selfishness. You must consciously control erratic behavior, aloofness and unpredictability. Your early training in ethics and moral standards will bring good results.

This placement of the Moon overemphasizes friendliness, humanitarianism and kindliness. Your need for emotional independence can lead to loneliness and difficulty with emotional relationships; you may brush these off with seeming indifference. Your feeling nature can be cold because you do not understand the emotional needs of someone else. You act warm and friendly but not especially intimate, suggestive or penetrating.

You see your mother as a friend and companion. She raised you to stand on your own feet; she is a humanitarian and is not a run-of-the-mill mother in her general behavior.

Writer Taylor Caldwell, actress Linda Lovelace, composer George Gershwin, counter culture leader Timothy Leary, writer Charlotte Brontë.

☽ ♓ MOON IN PISCES
keyword *emotionally instinctive*

You are very responsive to the depths of human experience, and you have understanding and affection for all people. You are emotionally naive and continually overlook other people's shortcomings and deficiencies. However, you can be easily hurt, and you tend to cry or feel sorry for yourself at the drop of a hat.

You don't like to face facts coldly and objectively, and your relationships will suffer because your feelings are so sensitive. At times you may lack humor and common sense, and you can be like the proverbial Russian who loves to be sad.

Your senses can deceive you because of your over-developed romanticism and optimism; you wear the original rose-colored glasses. Because you want to believe the best about everything, truth and reality upset you. You usually have musical, poetic and artistic talent.

Depending on the aspects, this can be the worst or best position for the Moon. If this placement is favorable, it gives true vision; if the placement is unfavorable, it can cause total illusion or disillusion. You are quiet, retiring, amiable and sympathetic to the underdog. You are gentle, at times easygoing, unworldly and dreamy. You change your mind often; thus you can be undependable, easily discouraged and depressed.

This is the most psychic position of the Moon, yet there might be sorrow and many obstacles in reaching your goals. You need to feel sheltered and loved, and you like beauty, harmony and comfort around you because you suffer in adverse environments.

In a woman's chart, emotional excess may bring health problems. A woman with this lunar placement may marry late. This position often adds a silent magnetism that attracts men.

A man with the Moon in Pisces wants a devoted, affectionate and sympathetic mate, who is likely to be a strong influence and indispensable in his private life, but not necessarily in his career.

In your eyes, your mother is sympathetic, but she may be very involved in her own life. You don't always see her clearly, at times over-idealizing and at times underestimating her.

Scientist Marie Curie, designer Coco Chanel, writer Edgar Allan Poe, composer Maurice Ravel, artist Paul Cezanne, baseball player Joe DiMaggio.

The Moon in the Houses

MOON IN THE FIRST HOUSE
keyword *environmental*

You are emotional, sensitive and changeable, and everything depends on how you feel; thus you tend to be moody. You can be successful with the public once you overcome your basic timidity. Your need for recognition makes you eager to please, and resentful if you feel that your efforts are not appreciated. You have close maternal ties, and if the Moon is conjunct the Ascendant, it may give a mother complex. Your imagination is strong, and you are very sensitive to your surroundings. You are physically active, and if your Moon is in a cardinal or mutable sign, it can cause restlessness.

Columnist William F. Buckley, comedian Will Rogers, baseball player Babe Ruth, writer Marcel Proust.

MOON IN THE SECOND HOUSE
keyword *acquisitive*   accidental
                                         exaltation

You have shrewd business sense, are possessive and are
capable of changing other people's values. There will be many
changes in your financial standing. Sometimes you experience
gain through your mother or your spouse; this position is good
for public and business contacts with women. Money and
material possessions are important to your emotional security.
You can be very stingy or extremely generous, and you must
try to avoid these extremes. If the Moon is in a fixed sign, you
have a tendency to hold on to people and money.
*Religious leader Mary Baker Eddy, publisher Hugh Hefner,
actress Elizabeth Taylor, ex-Vice President Spiro Agnew, actor Mickey Rooney.*

MOON IN THE THIRD HOUSE
keyword *expressive*

You are dramatic, retrospective and intellectually curious; this
gives you an intriguing personality. You are restless, like to
travel and are easily swayed by your environment. Your siblings are important to you, and they are often helpful. You
may change schools often, and you usually lack concentration
when it comes to studying. You learn most by listening to
others; you have a good memory but an avid dislike for
routine.
*Industrialist Henry Ford, poet Robert Browning, actress
Suzanne Somers, actor Jack Nicholson, singer Elvis Presley.*

MOON IN THE FOURTH HOUSE
keyword *homeloving*   accidental dignity

You are intuitive and nurturing, and you love your home,
your family and your country; however, with many challenging aspects, you may be separated from them. The Moon in
this house indicates a strong attachment to a parent. You love

to collect things and are especially fond of antiques, tradition and ancestry. You may have many changes of residence, especially if the Moon is in a mutable sign. You tend to be self-centered, with me and mine as your motivating force. You are apt to insulate yourself from reality.

Comedian Bob Hope, labor leader John L. Lewis, General Douglas MacArthur, writer Truman Capote.

MOON IN THE FIFTH HOUSE
keyword *theatrical*

Your emotions are strong, whether you are expressing love for others or a desire for children. You are romantic and inclined to have many affairs in your constant search for pleasure, unless there are many planets in fixed signs in your chart. You have a great deal of charm and poetic imagination. Your creativity will surface according to the sign the Moon is in and the aspects the Moon makes. This placement promises a fruitful marriage. You are a good parent but are apt to bind your children to you. The Moon here can indicate early success, and it suggests a career in teaching, sports or the theater. Your luck in speculation is subject to fluctuation.

Filmmaker Federico Fellini, pediatrician Benjamin Spock, evangelist Billy Graham, Juan Carlos I of Spain.

MOON IN THE SIXTH HOUSE
keyword *adaptable*

The placement of the Moon in the chart shows an area of many changes; thus the Moon in the sixth house reflects changes in your occupation. You are considerate of others, especially employees, but you are a hard worker, and you expect others to work as hard as you do. You have a strong inclination toward mothering and serving people. You are a good cook; you would do well in any industry serving the public, such as markets and restaurants. Unless the Moon is in a fixed sign, you tend to be changeable in your habits. Your nervousness can express itself through illnesses, which can often be psychosomatic.

Designer Coco Chanel, baseball player Jackie Robinson, writer William Saroyan, actor Robert Redford, boxer Muhammad Ali, Governor John Connally.

✓ MOON IN THE SEVENTH HOUSE
keyword *popular*

You are socially popular, and this placement emphasizes interpersonal relationships. You are very sensitive and often are responsive to the needs of the public. You have trouble making up your mind about getting married and usually have several opportunities. Often because of your emotional dependency, you may marry early; this doesn't always work out because of your need to develop maturity in personal relationships. You may attract a sensitive and moody partner, especially if the Moon has challenging aspects in your chart. *Child actress Shirley Temple, dictator Benito Mussolini, actress Marilyn Monroe, astronaut Neil Armstrong.*

MOON IN THE EIGHTH HOUSE
keyword *intuitive*

You have an inherent need for security. You are often psychic and interested in matters that others consider morbid, such as life after death. Affection, love and sex are very important to you; if the Moon has very difficult aspects, you may misuse your sexuality. Money could come through your partner, your mother or women in general. Often you are involved in handling other people's money.
General George Patton, labor leader Caesar Chavez, film-maker Alfred Hitchcock, playwright Noel Coward.

MOON IN THE NINTH HOUSE
keyword *philosophical*

You develop a philosophy through your feelings and devotion to your ideals; your religious outlook is usually on the orthodox side. The study of the deeper things in life is important to you, and you are receptive to the superconscious realms. You are imaginative and fond of travel. You can also be a roamer, a dreamer and too restless. You are a natural teacher in almost any field.

Prime Minister Benjamin Disraeli, scientist Galileo Galilei, pianist Van Cliburn, Secretary of State John Foster Dulles.

MOON IN THE TENTH HOUSE
keyword *social*

It is probable that you will experience several career changes. You need to work with the public in some way, with women or in fields related to women. This placement of the Moon is good for all lunar occupations: marketing, commodities, shipping, as well as anything dealing with the public. Your reputation is important to you; your feelings are often dominated by your ambition and your desire for advancement. Because you need the world for an audience, this position can bring scandal. You have little private life and you may feel as though you live in a fishbowl. You need to feel socially useful.

Indian leader Mohandas Ghandi, billionnaire J. Paul Getty, singer Bob Dylan, actress Vivian Leigh, singer Graham Nash.

MOON IN THE ELEVENTH HOUSE
keyword *friendly*

Your views are unprejudiced, detached and objective, yet you frequently change your aims. You have a tendency to be a joiner, and you do well in organizational work. You have many friends and acquaintances who are helpful to you, and with whom you have an easy rapport. However, if your Moon has difficult aspects, you must be careful of being taken advantage of by false friends.

President John F. Kennedy, filmmaker Orson Welles, actress Sarah Bernhardt, writer Zelda Fitzgerald, track and field star Guy Drut.

MOON IN THE TWELFTH HOUSE
keyword *insular*

You are restless, shy, sensitive and too retiring, and you don't like strange surroundings. You need time alone to recharge your emotional batteries. You like to work in secluded or isolated ways, and often you live in a world of imagination. You are self-sacrificing; if you don't become overly involved with your patients, you could be a good nurse. The Moon here often indicates secret love affairs. You have an active subconscious, and you can be resentful of imaginary slights.
Cuban leader Fidel Castro, Nazi leader Hermann Goering, actor Gregory Peck, race car driver Jim Clark, would-be assassin Alfred Bremer.

The Moon in Aspect

Any aspect to the Moon stresses the *emotions*.

The conjunction emphasizes the *emotions*.

An opposition gives awareness of your own or another's *emotional makeup*.

The square *challenges you* and *creates emotional tension*.

The trine gives *flow and ease to your emotional capacity*.

The sextile gives the *opportunity for positive emotional expression*.

The inconjunct suggests *an emotional adjustment to be made*.

Conjunctions

☽ ☌ ☿ MOON CONJUNCT MERCURY

When the planet of the emotions (☽) is conjunct the planet of reason and communication (☿), the emphasis is on imagination, intuition, speech, voice and intellectual awareness. You are sensitive to other people's reactions. This conjunction emphasizes domestic and health matters.
Billionaire Howard Hughes, opera singer Joan Sutherland.

☽ ☌ ♀ MOON CONJUNCT VENUS

You are charming, kind and popular; this conjunction emphasizes the importance of beauty for your emotional contentment. You are creative, sensitive, tactful and naturally friendly; you love art, music and beauty. At times, you can be self-indulgent and too involved with luxury.
Ice skater Sonja Henie, composer Peter Tschaikovsky.

☽ ☌ ♂ MOON CONJUNCT MARS

You are impatient and socially uncompromising; although you are sensitive to criticism, you can also be insensitive to the feelings of others. You are daring and take great risks. This aspect gives willpower, creative ability and the capacity for leadership.
Seismologist Charles Richter, USSR chairman Nikita Khrushchev.

☽ ☌ ♃ MOON CONJUNCT JUPITER

You are sympathetic, practical and generous; success comes easily to you, but you often have an inner need for change. Unless you handle this aspect well, you may tend toward self-importance and vanity. Religion is important to you, and unless this conjunction is in fixed signs, you will travel a good deal.
Writer Jules Verne, psychic Uri Geller.

☽ ☌ ♄ MOON CONJUNCT SATURN

This conjunction emphasizes your hard-working, secretive, apprehensive and somber qualities; you have trouble giving of yourself. You lack self-confidence and feel that one or both of your parents denied you love and tenderness. Recognition of your own self-worth and emotional fulfillment comes with maturity. Your emotional disturbances and frustrations can

manifest themselves physically as cysts, gout, arthritis, etc., if you are unable to handle this aspect.
Actress Rosalind Russell, actor James Arness.

☽ ☌ ♅ MOON CONJUNCT URANUS

Exciting and independent, you express high emotional energy and a dislike for convention and conforming. You are resourceful, determined and at times perverse. You are highly individualistic, and often better at solving other people's problems than your own. You tend to have an unusual domestic life or an unusual approach to your family.
Filmmaker Orson Welles, Nazi leader Hermann Goering.

☽ ☌ ♆ MOON CONJUNCT NEPTUNE

You are restless, moody, extremely sensitive, romantic, idealistic, sympathetic and easily influenced. This conjunction emphasizes mystical and religious tendencies; it also emphasizes musical or creative inclinations. Emotionally, it is difficult for you to discern illusion from reality.
Composer Johann Sebastian Bach, stripteaser Gypsy Rose Lee.

☽ ☌ ♀ MOON CONJUNCT PLUTO

This conjunction often emphasizes an obsession with emotional and sexual matters; perhaps you want to dominate others in these areas. Your feelings are intense to the point of brusqueness and tyranny, yet love is very important to you, and you are constantly seeking emotional fulfillment. You may find it in creative fields.
Singer Barbra Streisand, Princess Margaret.

Squares and Oppositions

☽ □ ☿ MOON SQUARE MERCURY
☽ ☍ ☿ MOON OPPOSITION MERCURY

You can be unreasonable since your feelings are always involved with your judgments. You are clever, sarcastic and overly sensitive. You are also loyal to friends and causes. High-strung, restless and excitable, you must learn to compromise and to gain control of your powerful ego.
Religious leader Mary Baker Eddy (□), musician John Lennon (☍).

☽ □ ♀ MOON SQUARE VENUS
☽ ☍ ♀ MOON OPPOSITION VENUS

These aspects often show sorrow through the affections or a carelessness with them. Your parents object to your partner, or you experience a lack of domestic harmony. You are moody, gullible and overindulgent. Often you have a strong urge to be in the spotlight, as a compensation for your sense of inferiority. In a woman's chart, there may be periodic ill health and/or divorce.
Poet Robert Browning (□), writer James Joyce (☍).

☽ □ ♂ MOON SQUARE MARS
☽ ☍ ♂ MOON OPPOSITION MARS

You must consciously cultivate self-control in order to handle your quick temper and your tendency to indiscretion. Your demands, self-indulgences, intolerance, force and biting sarcasm can drive others from you and leave you lonely and bitter. Channeled properly, your energy is boundless, and you can move mountains. You are constantly involved in emotional crises which can lead to poor health, if you do not learn to handle them properly.
Industrialist Henry Kaiser (□), White House aide John Dean (☍).

☽ □ ♃ MOON SQUARE JUPITER
☽ ☍ ♃ MOON OPPOSITION JUPITER

You are emotionally expansive, often too generous and occasionally duped. You should avoid financial speculation. Somewhat apathetic, you are inclined to let things slide. There could be misunderstandings with, or separation from, an overly indulgent parent. You must consciously try to handle your wanderlust, overindulgence and apathy which can manifest themselves physically as weight problems, liver troubles and tumors. You may also have to deal with moral conflicts.
Russian mystic Grigori Rasputin (□), writer Jean Cocteau (☍).

☽ □ ♄ MOON SQUARE SATURN
☽ ☍ ♄ MOON OPPOSITION SATURN

This aspect indicates insecurity; you work harder than most people to prove yourself. You must learn to handle your frustration, depression and discontentment, as well as your tendency to cling to the past. This usually indicates an unhappy early childhood; perhaps there were disagreements with a domineering parent. Lack of self-confidence and a sense of martyrdom must be overcome before true maturity can be reached. You are likely to marry someone older and to have few children.
Actor Laurence Olivier (□), scientist Galileo Galilei (☍).

☽ □ ♅ MOON SQUARE URANUS
☽ ☍ ♅ MOON OPPOSITION URANUS

This aspect shows great intellectual ability, but you are also stubborn, fanatic and emotionally tense. Restless, touchy and impulsive, you must learn compromise in your dealings with others. This indicates unusual emotional attachments, and it may show infidelity and trouble with the opposite sex. You will have many changes of residence, and your sudden changes of attitude will often make it difficult for others to understand you.

Labor leader John L. Lewis (□), motorcycle stunt rider Evel Knievel (♂).

☽ □ ♆ MOON SQUARE NEPTUNE
☽ ♂ ♆ MOON OPPOSITION NEPTUNE

You become involved in complicated emotional relationships, due to your tendency to confuse reality with self-deception. Often these aspects show a need to escape through drink, drugs or fantasy. You are creative and artistic, but you underestimate your skill. Health problems may arise if you do not handle the square aspect well; if it is in cardinal signs, you may develop circulatory problems; if it is in fixed signs, you may develop glandular problems, and if it is in mutable signs, you may develop problems of the brain and nervous system. These aspects may also signify a harsh parent.

Storyteller Hans Christian Andersen (□), singer Janis Joplin (♂).

☽ □ ♇ MOON SQUARE PLUTO
☽ ♂ ♇ MOON OPPOSITION PLUTO

You tend to be a loner. You are intensely emotional, but your emotional flow is blocked in some way, and you would benefit from a positive use of your creative potential. These aspects indicate jealousy, impulsiveness and sensuality. Perhaps due to your relationship with your parents, you may feel rejected at times, and you may seek drastic solutions to your problems. You must learn to handle your intolerance and fanaticism.

Murder cult leader Charles Manson (□), writer Jack London (♂).

Trines and Sextiles

☽ △ ☿ MOON TRINE MERCURY
☽ ✶ ☿ MOON SEXTILE MERCURY

You have a shrewd, careful, sound, logical and judicious mind and a pleasant way of expressing yourself. These aspects show a lot of common sense and indicate few, if any, emotional anxieties. These aspects are very good for third and fourth house affairs and domestic dealings. In a man's chart these aspects can lead to a good marriage and/or a clever wife. *Conductor Henry Mancini (△), singer Maurice Chevalier (✳).*

☽ △ ♀ MOON TRINE VENUS
☽ ✳ ♀ MOON SEXTILE VENUS

You are calm, optimistic, cheerful and artistic, and you have a steady viewpoint that gives you a good perception of values. You handle people well, and you have a magnetic charm that appeals to children and animals. You are refined, charming and social. This aspect is often found in the charts of military people.
General Robert E. Lee (△), football coach Knute Rockne (✳).

☽ △ ♂ MOON TRINE MARS
☽ ✳ ♂ MOON SEXTILE MARS

You are ambitious, firm, resolute and quick; you are a worker not an idler. Intensely emotional, you often apply your energies to creative endeavors. These aspects can offset debilitating health problems, as they give great physical strength.
Singer Harry Belafonte (△), aviator Billy Mitchell (✳).

☽ △ ♃ MOON TRINE JUPITER
☽ ✳ ♃ MOON SEXTILE JUPITER

You are good-natured, friendly, helpful, and have sound reasoning and judgment. This aspect helps ninth and twelfth house matters to proceed smoothly. You are interested in religion, sports, journalism and travel. This is a good aspect for writers and philosophers. Women are attracted to a Jupiterian type of man, and men with these aspects find that women bring benefits. Because it can indicate relaxed moral values, this is often found in the charts of violent criminals. *Political philosopher Karl Marx (△), composer Wolfgang Amadeus Mozart (✳).*

☽ △ ♄ MOON TRINE SATURN
☽ ✳ ♄ MOON SEXTILE SATURN

You are thoughtful, serious, prudent, conservative and cautious. You have great personal dignity, and you will have opportunities for public advancement. This often indicates a long though not necessarily healthy life. Perhaps you will benefit from a parent, usually your mother. You are good at management, and this aspect often assures some measure of worldly success.
Tennis player Arthur Ashe (△), singer James Taylor (✳).

☽ △ ♅ MOON TRINE URANUS
☽ ✳ ♅ MOON SEXTILE URANUS

You are mentally alert and always seeking new and different avenues of self-expression. Enterprising, scientific and intuitive, you are interested in the occult, spiritualism, astrology and metaphysics. This indicates advantageous removals and changes, and this aspect favors travel if either the third or ninth houses are involved. If the fourth house is involved you will experience many changes of residence.
Writer Edgar Allen Poe (△), writer Guy deMaupassant (✳).

☽ △ ♆ MOON TRINE NEPTUNE
☽ ✳ ♆ MOON SEXTILE NEPTUNE

Both of these planets affect the emotional nature. These

aspects enlarge the scope of your life and often indicate unusual desires, but they can also bring a tendency to over-idealize and thus fool yourself. You are warm and genuine and attracted to art, music, singing and dancing. This is very good for Neptunian enterprises: oil, liquids, shipping, films and theater.
Billionaire John D. Rockefeller, Sr. (△), singer Mary Martin (✳).

☽ △ ♀ MOON TRINE PLUTO
☽ ✳ ♀ MOON SEXTILE PLUTO

These aspects indicate that you are deeply emotional, but controlled; you enjoy personal contact with others, yet you will not waste time with casual relationships. At times you may withdraw too much, and you may alienate others. Psychic and mediumistic, these aspects often indicate an ability for emotional regeneration.
Revolutionary leader Maximilien Robespierre (△), nurse Florence Nightingale (✳).

Inconjuncts (Quincunxes)

☽ ⊼ ☿ MOON INCONJUNCT MERCURY

It may be difficult for you to solve your problems because your emotions and your intellect are out of line. It is hard for you to keep secrets, and you often blurt things out without thinking. Your anxiety and restlessness can cause problems and digestive upsets.
Violinist Jascha Heifetz, composer George Gershwin.

☽ ⊼ ♀ MOON INCONJUNCT VENUS

In trying to affirm your own ego, you kowtow too much to others' opinions of you. You seem to attract people who want you to prove your love for them. Ill health can develop from

overindulgence. You must learn to evaluate what is important and what is unnecessary.
Singer Janis Joplin, fighter pilot Eddie Rickenbacker.

☽ ⚻ ♂ MOON INCONJUNCT MARS

This aspect indicates a conflict between your emotions and your desires; you must learn to bring this conflict under control. Your nervous irritability and your emotional anxiety can cause accidents and digestive upsets. You often become involved in other people's affairs in order to avoid facing your own problems.
Broadcast journalist Lowell Thomas, singer Bing Crosby.

☽ ⚻ ♃ MOON INCONJUNCT JUPITER

You overextend yourself without thinking twice about what you are involving yourself in. You must work things out beforehand and develop patience and calmness as you go about rendering service to others.
Chancellor Konrad Adenauer, TV personality Paul Lynde.

☽ ⚻ ♄ MOON INCONJUNCT SATURN

You act guilty and uneasy until you can figure out a way to show others that you really care about them. You are a hard and dedicated worker but cautious about new ways to do things. You tend to feel sorry for yourself. You have the ability to inspire others with the seriousness of your dedication.
Evangelist Billy Sunday, poet Walt Whitman.

☽ ⚻ ♅ MOON INCONJUNCT URANUS

You tend to act without sufficient deliberation and to overreact emotionally when you feel pressured. You must develop continuity of purpose. Rest and relaxation are very necessary,

so you will be able to handle the unpredictable problems that this aspect can cause in professional and domestic fields.
Actress Bette Davis, scientist Pierre Curie.

☽ ⊼ ♆ MOON INCONJUNCT NEPTUNE

You are sympathetic and overly willing to help others, even though they may not need or want it. Your sympathy may leave you open to hostility and sometimes even treachery. You must learn to see people as they really are, and you must learn not to romanticize your alliances. You should try to overcome your tendency to drift and to be unreliable.
Billionaire Howard Hughes, columnist William F. Buckley.

☽ ⊼ ♀ MOON INCONJUNCT PLUTO

You are emotionally compulsive and uncompromising, and you must avoid involvement with those who may try to charm you into their way of thinking. Your zeal to be productive and useful causes you to be easily taken advantage of.
Artist Leonardo DaVinci, billionaire J. Paul Getty.

Lesson 10: Mercury

Some Comments

By now you should have a general feeling for delineation. Please be sure to check your interpretations against ours in the Appendix; look for the many sentences we did not use and try to figure out why we omitted them.

You have probably seen that many traits and characteristics repeat themselves again and again under different aspects or placements. This is a most important factor in delineation. A person's most basic potential and character are shown by the most repetitive factors. The more certain traits are repeated, the surer you can be that these are the true characteristics of the person. Potentials that appear just once or twice may be developed but the emphasis of repetition is missing, and the person may not even know that these potentials exist.

Let's get on with lesson 10; first we will study the planet Mercury in general, and then you can work on Judy Garland's Mercury in particular.

Our answers can be found in the Appendix on page 292.

Mercury represents your *reasoning ability*, your *mind* and *the way you communicate*. Keep this context in mind as you read the following descriptions.

Mercury in the Signs

☿ ♈ MERCURY IN ARIES
keyword *impulsive*

You are imaginative, and you have good foresight and a desire to be first in everything. You can express yourself easily, and you can improvise beautifully. At times you use your nervous energies cuttingly or even sarcastically. Impetuous and impulsive, you may tend to sudden shifts and changes of viewpoint. This placement is not well adapted for sustained mental effort; therefore you need to cultivate patience and learn to not be impatient with delays. Witty, inventive and quick on the trigger, you have original ideas. Combative, you love a good debate. Sometimes you can be too headstrong or too self-centered. If there are challenging aspects from Mercury to Jupiter in your chart, you are prone to exaggeration. You tend to look at the world as you wish it to be, not as it really is. Many fixed planets in your chart will help to stabilize this placement of Mercury.

Actor Marlon Brando, actor Charlie Chaplin, Queen Elizabeth II, conductor Arturo Toscanini, physicist Albert Einstein.

☿ ♉ MERCURY IN TAURUS
keyword *factual*

You are stubborn and have definite likes and dislikes. Acquisitive and fond of money and material goods, you are interested in both the arts and the opposite sex. Your mind does not react readily to new ideas, and once you start a project you rarely give up. You never jump to conclusions; you like to hear all the evidence first. Mentally you are conservative, cautious and constructive. You depend more on life experience than on book learning. Your memory is good, and your approach is traditional. Your mind is practical, and this is an excellent position for business and management. If this placement has difficult aspects, you can tend towards mental inertia, but trying to push yourself into action will not help; you need to work at your own rate of speed.

Industrialist Henry Kaiser, singer Barbra Streisand, violinist Yehudi Menuhin, poet Elizabeth Barrett Browning, President John F. Kennedy.

☿ ♊ MERCURY IN GEMINI
keyword *conversational*   dignity

Pure logical reasoning can be carried to its highest here, especially if Mercury is well aspected. You are versatile, unbiased, and impersonal in your ability to perceive the truth. You have an excellent vocabulary at your command; you enjoy learning and are able to communicate well and easily. A highly sensitive nervous system is the basis of your agile mind. You are witty, talkative, charming and interested in everyday affairs. Your thinking is full of dash, flash and lightning, and you often use your hands to express yourself. Fond of intellectual pursuits, you could be a writer or a public speaker. You must watch your need for change and novelty, since this can lead to superficiality or a lack of thoroughness.

Writer George Sand, writer Jean Cocteau, Secretary of State Henry Kissinger, columnist Hedda Hopper, President Harry Truman.

☿ ♋ MERCURY IN CANCER
keyword *receptive*

You are very emotional and you can be swayed too easily by your senses. Arguments arouse your stubbornness because once you make up your mind you stick to your decision. Im-

pressionable and changeable, you are sensitive to your surroundings; kindness and praise are the best ways to get
through to you. Your mind is retentive, and your thinking is
creative. You have flashes of intuition, and you like poetry.
You are a sensitive listener, full of sympathy for the suffering
of others, but you might have trouble thinking objectively,
since your emotions are always involved. This could lead to
feeling sorry for yourself. You are diplomatic and have good
business ability, although much of your orientation is around
home and family. If your Mercury has many challenging
aspects, you might be evasive rather than honest.
*Writer Pearl Buck, writer Thomas Mann, attorney F. Lee
Bailey, billionaire John D. Rockefeller, Sr., poet Anne Morrow Lindbergh.*

☿ ♌ MERCURY IN LEO
keyword *positive*   fall

You think dramatically and always with your heart; because
you are visionary and idealistic, romantic attachments take a
big share of your concentration. You have dignity, a sense of
innate refinement and you like to make a good impression
upon others. You want to be considered an authority in your
chosen field, and although you are very able to solve problems, sometimes you ignore details. You are ambitious and
have good executive ability; you are an excellent teacher and
could succeed in the theater, the fine arts, education or the
stock market. With difficult aspects to Mercury you might be
too stubborn, self-indulgent and quick tempered, or you
might have a tendency to exaggerate or be self-centered.
*Ex-First Lady Jacqueline Kennedy Onassis, Cuban leader
Fidel Castro, dictator Benito Mussolini, writer Ernest Hemingway, actress Susan St. James.*

☿ ♍ MERCURY IN VIRGO
keyword *methodical*   dignity

You are critical, analytical and practical, and your thinking is

cool, logical and impersonal. Your judgment is impartial; your mind sorts and indexes all ideas, and they are ready to be used when you need them. Because your mind is versatile, you are a convincing speaker. You are interested in literature and are good at detailed scientific work and research; you can be a scholar. You may be interested in medicine, hygiene, mathematics and all detail-encompassing work. You know how to turn knowledge into material benefits. You have strong common sense, you are honest, but you can be intolerant of those less intelligent than you, or you can be too skeptical. With challenging aspects to Mercury, you are too quick to criticize and should guard against letting details get in the way of larger plans and goals. It is also wise to fight a tendency to pigeonhole everything in the universe.
President Lyndon B. Johnson, Labor leader Walter Reuther, Princess Anne, conductor Leonard Bernstein.

☿ ♎ MERCURY IN LIBRA
keyword *diplomatic*

Although you are friendly, broad-minded and rational, you can be stern when your own principles are involved. You abhor injustice; you desire to balance and to judge all things with complete fairness. You are unable to make decisions in a hurry. You hate arguments and prefer to discuss issues or to reason together. You desire intellectual attainments, love the arts, have a delicate sense of touch and like to surround yourself with well-mannered, refined and honest people. Coarse behavior or inappropriate dress really disturb you; your desire for perfection can make you hard to live with. You are curious about the thinking and behavior of other people; thus this position of Mercury is good for all types of work involving human relations, expecially psychology; it is also excellent for diplomats and arbitrators. Without enough squares and challenges to Mercury to spur you on, you might be too social, flighty and superficial.
President Dwight D. Eisenhower, playwright Oscar Wilde, singer Maurice Chevalier, writer Fannie Hurst, skier Jean-Claude Killy.

☿ ♏ MERCURY IN SCORPIO
keyword *incisive*

You are critical, skeptical and at times even secretive or suspicious. You are set in your opinions and it is difficult to convince you to change your mind. You are shrewd, forceful and apt to be too incisive with tongue or pen. Either you can needlessly wound others, or you can turn that sarcasm into an exquisite wit. This investigative and probing position is good for any of the healing professions; it is also good for chemistry, photography, detective work, occultism, research and big business. Your mind is deep but rarely charitable; your determination is boundless and your mentality is so fixed that you can overcome all obstacles to get what you want. If your Mercury has difficult aspects, you must learn to overcome your tendency to use others' weaknesses for your own advantage; also try to avoid passing judgment on those who may be less fortunate than you.

Indian leader Mohandas Gandhi, scientist Marie Curie, statesman Winston Churchill, actress Suzanne Somers, King Hussein.

☿ ♐ MERCURY IN SAGITTARIUS
keyword *independent*   detriment

You are sincere and you have a great sense of dry humor. Impulsive, you often speak without considering the consequences. You have intuitive flashes of truth, but, due to an overabundance of interests, you are apt to scatter your mental forces. Your mind does not need sharpening, only directing. Generous, progressive and honest, you hate to deceive anyone. Because you are concerned with attitudes more than with facts, you are interested in higher education, philosophy and religion. You relish intellectual status, tend to be a nonstop talker and love travel of any kind. If there are many difficult aspects to Mercury, you can have a tendency toward moral sermonizing or toward being overly pedantic in your attitudes.

Psychic Uri Geller, evangelist Billy Graham, Prime Minister

Indira Gandhi, President Charles de Gaulle, Senator Howard Baker, anthropologist Margaret Mead.

☿ ♑ MERCURY IN CAPRICORN
keyword **serious**

Hard-working, cautious and earnest, your mind is penetrating; your memory for facts and figures is excellent, and detailed work is right up your alley. When you want to make a point you can be tactful and diplomatic, but basically you tend to intellectual snobbery. You have good common sense and the ability to turn ideas into practical use. You are self-disciplined and a good disciplinarian, but you must remember to add heart to your head. You are methodical in both thought and procedure, which gives you executive and political ability. You like to uphold traditional ideas; you are realistic rather than idealistic. You also have keen awareness and good powers of concentration. You may lack the ability to laugh at yourself, but if you have a sense of humor it will be somewhat satirical. If there are difficult aspects to your Mercury, you can be too materialistic, ambitious, dogmatic and even suspicious.

President Richard Nixon, Governor Ronald Reagan, TV personality Zsa Zsa Gabor, writer Charles Dickens, scientist Louis Pasteur, actor Paul Newman.

☿ ♒ MERCURY IN AQUARIUS
keyword **original**   exaltation

You are resourceful, observant, intuitive and usually a good judge of human nature. Your mind is keen, original, independent, humanitarian and witty. You are able to absorb abstract ideas; you tend toward the occult. You are studious, sociable and often self-taught in your field. Interested in science, character study and matters of human interest, you are also fond of reading and are often involved with groups and organizations. Writing and speaking come easily to you, but you may be too talkative. Although you are open to any view, you will not change your opinion without due reflection and logical analysis. Truthful and objective, you have little care

for traditional concerns or for social acceptance. With challenging aspects to your Mercury, you may think a lot but accomplish little, or you may be stubborn and eccentric.
Composer Wolfgang Amadeus Mozart, nutritionist Adelle Davis, civil rights leader Martin Luther King, inventor Thomas A. Edison, writer Norman Mailer.

☿ ♓ MERCURY IN PISCES
keyword *reflective*   detriment

You are psychic and intuitive, and you learn by absorption rather than by study. Your memory is retentive; your mentality is reflective, romantic and poetic. You may keep your real thoughts under cover and only express them when you are with close friends or relatives. This placement for Mercury shows a duality evincing contradictory qualities; combined with your receptivity to outside influences, it's no wonder that you are often accused of being moody and sensitive. You get hurt easily. Harmonious surroundings are very important to you because you react more from the subconscious than from reason. You like to be well-informed and often have a great love for music or some sort of artistic talent. With difficult aspects, your sense of reality might be distorted and your mind may vascillate; you may tend to wool-gathering or day-dreaming; you could be pessimistic, melancholy and confused. Too many difficult aspects can give you a morbid imagination, a persecution complex or other neuroses or phobias. You should guard against self-pity or personal resentment; concentrate on seeing and thinking clearly. Use your many talents and your innate spiritual attitude to combat your potential negativity.
Psychic Edgar Cayce, dancer Vaslav Nijinsky, mime Marcel Marceau, composer Nikolai Rimsky-Korsakov, actor Steve McQueen.

Mercury in the Houses

MERCURY IN THE FIRST HOUSE
keyword *ego-conscious*

You are curious, adaptable, restless and often nervous. With easy aspects you are probably quite eloquent; with too many challenging aspects you may stammer or have a speech impediment. You have strong intellectual energy and a quick wit. Your thinking is quite *I* oriented, and you find it difficult to really understand the feelings of others. You are intelligent, and this is a good position for writers, doctors, scientists, scholars and librarians. You have a deep need to express yourself, and sometimes you speak before you think. But usually you approach your personal affairs very rationally.

Evangelist Billy Sunday, singer Barbra Streisand, writer Zelda Fitzgerald, artist Toulouse Lautrec.

MERCURY IN THE SECOND HOUSE
keyword *value-conscious*

You value that which you think can produce practical results, are oriented toward money and business, and can be either tight or very free spending, depending on the sign and the aspects Mercury makes. You like to make quick decisions and have a good mind for rational, commercial, clerical or educational occupations. This is a good position for economists, corporate planners, salespeople, writers with mass appeal, publishers, and any profession involving communications.

Nazi leader Hermann Goering, Prime Minister Benjamin Disraeli, consumer advocate Ralph Nader, Governor Ronald Reagan.

MERCURY IN THE THIRD HOUSE
keyword *communcation-conscious*   accidental dignity

You are very intelligent, with good reasoning and conversational powers. You can make quick decisions; your thinking is accurate and exact. You have literary talent, are a good secretary, an ardent letter writer and an excellent reporter. You are attracted to research and investigation. The affairs of your siblings and relatives are important to you; in fact, you might work for a relative. You are curious about all facets of

life. It is wise for you to choose a profession that keeps you on the move, since you are restless by nature. With challenging aspects you could overdo a good thing and frazzle your nerves by overwork or over-worry; you could develop intestinal problems or you may tend to exaggeration and even deceit. With a difficult Mercury it would be better to study all documents and agreements before signing. Smoking is a no-no.
Writer Charles Dickens, playwright Eugene O'Neill, psychic Uri Geller, actor Cary Grant.

MERCURY IN THE FOURTH HOUSE
keyword *home-conscious*

You are determined, your memory is retentive, and your thinking is economical. Proud of your family and interested in your ancestry, you love antiques and might be a book, stamp or coin collector. Your parents were probably educated and cultured. This is a good position for real estate, agriculture, ecology, archeology, geology and other professions related to the earth. It is possible that you will work out of your home. You might change residence often, or there may be a lot of activity in your home. Perhaps a relative will live with you. With challenging aspects, you are easily irritated and quite highstrung.
Poet Emily Dickinson, President Gerald Ford, artist Pablo Picasso, Vice President Nelson Rockefeller, boxer Max Baer, basketball player Wilt Chamberlain.

MERCURY IN THE FIFTH HOUSE
keyword *pleasure-conscious*

Your thinking is creative and you express yourself dramatically. You have good speaking ability. You can be autocratic, and you like speculation. You are busy with lovemaking, pleasure and artistic pursuits. You are fond of children, but you may not necessarily have any of your own. You are attracted to anything that stimulates your mind, such as chess or word games. Education is important to you, and you could be an excellent teacher, actor, playwright or art critic. If Mercury is strong and fixed, you may be too opinionated or conceited. *Dancer Leslie Caron, actor Marlon Brando, poet Robert Browning, financier Diamond Jim Brady, boxer George Foreman.*

MERCURY IN THE SIXTH HOUSE
keyword ***work-conscious***   accidental dignity

You are practical, reserved, systematic, efficient, fond of mental work and very observant. Education, health, hygiene, medicine, literature and engineering interest you. You are a hard worker and should guard against overwork. Because you are an excellent planner, this position is good for commercial enterprises or secretarial work. You like a variety of jobs, and you might have too many irons in the fire. Difficult aspects may lead to unnecessary worrying; this can produce ill health. Health problems in this house often stem from wrong thinking, rather than from anything physical. A sound diet is helpful.
President Dwight D. Eisenhower, baseball player Hank Aaron, actor Charlie Chaplin, General George Patton.

MERCURY IN THE SEVENTH HOUSE
keyword ***people-conscious***

Unless there are many difficult aspects to Mercury, your relationship with your partner will be honest and refined. Your marriage could be more mental than emotional, and you may have more than one marriage. You may marry someone younger than you or get married while you are very young. You are apt to choose a mate who is quick, witty and talented. People are important to you, and you have good rapport with the public at large. This is a good position for public relations, counseling, psychology and law. Challenging aspects could give you a tendency to bicker. It would be better to settle legal problems out of court, and it is wise to study contracts and documents carefully before you sign anything.

Actor Charles Boyer, ex-First Lady Betty Ford, conductor Leonard Bernstein, singer Anita Bryant, singer Bob Dylan.

MERCURY IN THE EIGHTH HOUSE
keyword *motivation-conscious*

Your insight is penetrating, and you are attracted to the occult. Intuitive, secretive and psychic, you enjoy intrigue; at times you can be sly or sarcastic. Since you are capable of handling the affairs and possessions of others, this is a good position for banking, corporate finance, taxes and insurance. This position is particularly good for politics; politicians not only handle other people's affairs, but they need other people's help and support. You may have your first sex experience at an early age. With Mercury here, the death of a relative or close friend could affect you deeply. Difficult aspects often indicate that you hold grudges. You should avoid smoking since your lungs need plenty of oxygen.

Bishop James Pike, Senator Robert Kennedy, President John F. Kennedy, President Harry Truman, singer Frank Sinatra, White House aide John Dean.

MERCURY IN THE NINTH HOUSE
keyword *education-conscious*

You are earnest and religious though with difficult aspects you could be a doubter. You are interested in higher education, philosophy, foreign countries and foreign cultures. You love to travel, and it is easy for you to learn foreign languages. You would do well in propaganda or advertising; this position is also good for teachers, professors, historians and anthropologists. You can be very intuitive, even visionary. With challenging aspects, you might be too dogmatic, headstrong or rash, and you might change your point of view too often. You may have problems with your in-laws, and it is better to live away from them.

Ex-First Lady Jacqueline Kennedy Onassis, dictator Benito Mussolini, civil rights leader Angela Davis, singer Mary Martin, President Charles de Gaulle.

MERCURY IN THE TENTH HOUSE
keyword *achievement-conscious*

You like facts, and you are very quick but not always thorough. Usually you are cheerful, successful and outgoing. You enjoy changing jobs or may hold down more than one job at a time. Your career is important to you, and you are attracted to politics or professions that involve a public life. Often a successful public speaker, you are good at communicating your ideas to others in many different ways. Alert and active, you have organizational ability. Education interests you, but only as a means to help your career. With many challenging aspects, you may become unprincipled and scheming to achieve your personal ambitions.

Cuban leader Fidel Castro, Emperor Napoleon Bonaparte, Governor Edmund G. (Jerry) Brown, composer Igor Stravinsky.

MERCURY IN THE ELEVENTH HOUSE
keyword *group-conscious*   accidental
                                   exaltation

Your mind is active and original. You like cultured friends, love new ideas and are intuitive and often idealistic. Friends and groups are very important to you, and you like to join with them to achieve common goals. You enjoy sharing your knowledge with your friends, since your friendships are more mental than emotional. Very social and unprejudiced, you probably have many younger friends. With challenging aspects, you tend to be critical, cynical, impractical and at times eccentric. If you do not choose your friends carefully problems or scandals could arise.

Boxer Joe Louis, Princess Anne, artist Salvador Dali, evangelist Aimee Semple McPherson.

MERCURY IN THE TWELFTH HOUSE
keyword *inward-conscious*

You are good at analyzing other people's problems; you are interested in the psychic realms, and your thinking can be secretive. Your mind is subtle, and you like to work in seclusion. At times you may have trouble expressing yourself. You lack self-confidence but hide your insecurity; you need to guard against living in a dream world. You base your decisions on feelings rather than on reason. If your Mercury is close to the Ascendant it will take on a first house feeling, so you would be very communicative and less introverted. With difficult aspects you may have had reading problems as a child, or you might have had an extraordinary childhood; perhaps you were raised in a foster home, orphanage or boarding school.

Evangelist Billy Graham, counter culture leader Timothy Leary, composer Johannes Brahms, writer Ernest Hemingway.

Mercury in Aspect

Any aspects to Mercury should be thought of as *mental.*
   The conjunction gives *mental emphasis.*
   The opposition gives *mental awareness* or *unawareness.*
   The square creates *mental tension.*
   The trine and sextile give *mental flow and ease.*
   The inconjunct suggests a *mental adjustment to be made.*

Conjunctions

☿ ☌ ♀ MERCURY CONJUNCT VENUS

Here we have the planet of the mind and communications conjunct the planet of affections and love; the emphasis here is on doing and saying the right thing at the right time. You are charming, gracious and easygoing. You have many artistic talents as well as the ability to express them.

Poet Rod McKuen, singer Harry Belafonte.

☿ ☌ ♂ MERCURY CONJUNCT MARS

You have great mental energy, are restless, curious and impatient, and at times you may need to slow down. Your mind is clear and incisive, constantly reaching forward and rarely glancing backward. You love debate and argument and have good writing ability. You may be satirical, controversial and hasty to judge others.

Singer Johnny Cash, seismologist Charles Richter.

☿ ♂ ♃ MERCURY CONJUNCT JUPITER

You think big and are insatiably curious. You are enthusiastic, interested in many fields and prone to exaggerate. Your intelligence is above average. Kind and optimistic, you have great verbal ability. Although you command respect, you need to develop self-discipline. This conjunction emphasizes education, history and public relations work.

Writer Marcel Proust, actor Paul Newman.

☿ ♂ ♄ MERCURY CONJUNCT SATURN

You are careful, sober, logical, methodical, tenacious, accurate and responsible; you can be the voice of authority. You are a good listener and usually prefer to work alone. This conjunction is good for business management, mathematics and architecture. With difficult aspects, you may be pessimistic, gloomy or depressed.

Physicist Albert Einstein, kidnapper Bruno Hauptmann.

☿ ♂ ♅ MERCURY CONJUNCT URANUS

You are self-willed, dramatic, colorful, inventive, creative, articulate, individualistic, progressive and independent. You are interested in astrology, science, human behavior, psychology and electronics. You need a good education. You resent interference, and with challenging aspects to the conjunction you may be eccentric and tactless.

Psychoanalyst Sigmund Freud, scientist Louis Pasteur.

☿ ♂ ♆ MERCURY CONJUNCT NEPTUNE

This conjunction will make you abnormally sensitive; you are dreamy, musical, poetic, and fond of dancing, water sports and photography. You have a vivid imagination and are visionary, but you may overidealize. You tend to escape unpleasant experiences through fantasy and deception. You should avoid artificial stimulants, especially drugs and alchohol.
Astronaut Neil Armstrong, poet Anne Morrow Lindbergh.

☿ ♂ ♀ MERCURY CONJUNCT PLUTO

Your mind is deep, subtle, persuasive and inclined to extremes. You are resourceful, probing, persistent and fascinated by the mysterious and the unknown. This is a good aspect for research, analysis, surgery, chemistry or exploration. You can be deceitful. You may have a power complex, or you may be involved with undesirable associates.
Writer Arthur Conan Doyle, scientist Galileo Galilei.

Squares and Oppositions

☿ □ ♀ MERCURY SQUARE VENUS
☿ ☍ ♀ MERCURY OPPOSITION VENUS

Since Mercury and Venus are never more than 74° away from each other, they can make no other major aspects than the conjunction and the sextile.

☿ □ ♂ MERCURY SQUARE MARS
☿ ☍ ♂ MERCURY OPPOSITION MARS

You have a good intellect but can be overly impulsive and may sometimes leap to conclusions. You are curious, and if you are not careful your expenditure of mental energy can lead to exhaustion. You need to learn concentration and compromise. You are combative, opinionated, sharp-tongued, fault-finding

and prone to headaches. This aspect is good for law, strategy, acting, drama, sports and management.
General George Patton (□), singer James Taylor (♂).

☿ □ ♃ MERCURY SQUARE JUPITER
☿ ♂ ♃ MERCURY OPPOSITION JUPITER

You want to start at the top, expect too much of others or try to take the easy way out. You can be a good bluffer. Education is important to you, but it might be interrupted. Curious and impulsive, your intentions are often better than your actions. You have difficulty focusing your beliefs, philosophies or abilities to communicate, but you can conquer these problems. You can be proficient in law, education, literature or public relations. This is a good aspect for politicians.
Writer Ralph Waldo Emerson (□), Prime Minister Indira Gandhi (♂).

☿ □ ♄ MERCURY SQUARE SATURN
☿ ♂ ♄ MERCURY OPPOSITION SATURN

You are traditional, reserved, shy, hard-working, responsible and ambitious. You may have a difficult childhood because of problems with your father; this could produce insecurities, defensiveness, a suspicious nature or could lead to depressions. Dental trouble or hearing problems are common with this position. This is a good aspect for big business and politics.
Financier Bernard Baruch (□), President Calvin Coolidge (♂).

☿ □ ♅ MERCURY SQUARE URANUS
☿ ♂ ♅ MERCURY OPPOSITION URANUS

Your mind is alert and ingenious; your thinking, eccentric. You are intellectual; it is hard to deceive you. A "rebel with a cause," you like to defy authority and you rarely accept ad-

vice. You are arrogant, nervous, daring and discontented. Your beliefs are self-exalting. This aspect is good for science, philosophy, writing and politics.
Emperor Napoleon Bonaparte (□), writer Johann Wolfgang von Goethe (☍).

☿ □ ♆ MERCURY SQUARE NEPTUNE
☿ ☍ ♆ MERCURY OPPOSITION NEPTUNE

You are unrealistic in your approach to love, romance or marriage, and you see life through rose-colored glasses. Creative, sensitive, insightful and imaginative, you can be naive or cunning, and you are easily distracted. You tend to be absent-minded, and you fear competition. Writing, music, dancing, painting, drama or social programs attract you.
Poet Elizabeth Barrett Browning (□), actress Elizabeth Taylor (☍).

☿ □ ♀ MERCURY SQUARE PLUTO
☿ ☍ ♀ MERCURY OPPOSITION PLUTO

Your speech is incisive, you tell it like it is, but you can also exhibit fantastic tact and diplomacy. You like to convert others to your ideas. You rarely show a happy mental balance; you swing from blind zeal and devotion to pessimism, nagging and quarreling. You take unnecessary risks. You would be good at research, crime detection, medicine or psychology. This aspect is good for new modes of expression in any field.
Physician Charles Mayo (□), artist Pablo Picasso (☍).

Trines and Sextiles

☿ △ ♀ MERCURY TRINE VENUS

Since Mercury and Venus are never more than 74° away from each other, they can make no other major aspects than the conjunction and the sextile.

☿ ⚹ ♀ MERCURY SEXTILE VENUS

You have many social graces and a lot of charm. You know how to compromise. Refined and easygoing, you have an imaginative style. You judge fairly and receive cooperation from others. You will be able to make money as a public speaker, writer, actor or entertainer.
Actor Gregory Peck, pianist Liberace.

☿ △ ♂ MERCURY TRINE MARS
☿ ⚹ ♂ MERCURY SEXTILE MARS

This aspect strengthens the mind; you never stop learning. You are quick, practical, perceptive, trustworthy and courageous. You know how to detect another's weakness, and you can take advantage of it. You are a convincing debater with a dramatic delivery. You are creative, literary and good at crafts. You also could be a good reporter, politician or public relations worker. You are often childless, but you are fond of children.
President Franklin Delano Roosevelt (△), actress Leslie Caron (⚹).

☿ △ ♃ MERCURY TRINE JUPITER
☿ ⚹ ♃ MERCURY SEXTILE JUPITER

You are good-natured and mild-tempered with breezy manners. Your mind is good but not necessarily original. You have excellent command of language, good comprehension and great integrity. You are honorable, fair, optimistic, easygoing, philosophical and shy. Travel is usually rewarding for you. This aspect is good for literature, journalism, publishing, teaching, foreign enterprises, public speaking and counseling.
Columnist Hedda Hopper (△), psychoanalyst Sigmund Freud (⚹).

☿ △ ♄ MERCURY TRINE SATURN
☿ ✳ ♄ MERCURY SEXTILE SATURN

You have a good memory and are practical, logical, studious, worldly and resourceful. Because of your disciplined mind, you are able to concentrate easily. You are methodical, responsible and serious, and have steady judgment. When young, you prefer older people's company. This aspect is excellent for generals, politicians, historians, scientists, writers, researchers and those in big business.
Writer Ernest Hemingway (△), dictator Benito Mussolini (✳).

☿ △ ♅ MERCURY TRINE URANUS
☿ ✳ ♅ MERCURY SEXTILE URANUS

You are original, talented, independent and brilliant to the point of genius. You are a spellbinder, very eloquent and you have great dramatic sense. Unique, enterprising, intuitive and progressive, you are impatient with ignorance. You have an excellent memory. You are a trend breaker and a trend setter. This aspect is good for philosophy, psychology, education, literature and drama.
Writer George Sand (△), actress Marilyn Monroe (✳).

☿ △ ♆ MERCURY TRINE NEPTUNE
☿ ✳ ♆ MERCURY SEXTILE NEPTUNE

This aspect shows the super salesperson. You are thoughtful, subtle and idealistic, have a great imagination, and are receptive to new ideas and methods. You have talent for acting, music, journalism and speechwriting; you can paint pictures with words.
Actress Tallulah Bankhead (△), attorney F. Lee Bailey (✳).

☿ △ ♇ MERCURY TRINE PLUTO
☿ ✳ ♇ MERCURY SEXTILE PLUTO

You are witty, diplomatic, analytical and individualistic. You have deep comprehension and good powers of concentration; you use your willpower intelligently. You can exert influence over others, you are courageous and like competition. You may expect too much from other people. This aspect is good for analysis, teaching, medicine, research and financial management.

*Financier Bernard Baruch (△), inventor Thomas Edison (*).*

Inconjuncts (Quincunxes)

☿ ⚲ ♀ MERCURY INCONJUNCT VENUS

Since Mercury and Venus are never more than 74° away from each other, they can make no other major aspects than the conjunction and the sextile.

☿ ⚲ ♂ MERCURY INCONJUNCT MARS

You are well informed, but not always able to use your information, because you take on too many responsibilities. Your efforts often go unappreciated. Although you are a hard worker, your sense of priority needs sharpening. You are mentally impatient, very impulsive and at times rebellious and irritating. Unless you moderate your activities, your health may suffer.

Theosophist Annie Besant, Field Marshal Henri Petain.

☿ ⚲ ♃ MERCURY INCONJUNCT JUPITER

You are generous with others at the expense of your own time schedule. You tend to take on too much, and then are easily frustrated. Although your education may be interrupted, a good education is necessary for you to achieve your desired goals. You can become a typical do-gooder. You may love to escape by traveling and roaming the world.

Consumer advocate Ralph Nader, poet Lord Byron.

☿ ⊼ ♄ MERCURY INCONJUNCT SATURN

This aspect shows that you have a tendency to get in a rut or to pity yourself. You have a desperate need for approval in order to compensate for your sense of insecurity. Sometimes you are forced to take care of elderly or sick relatives. You are good at mathematics and related fields. You can be ruthless, and you may take advantage of others, expressing, "I want what I want when I want it."
Composer Johannes Brahms, actress Mia Farrow.

☿ ⊼ ♅ MERCURY INCONJUNCT URANUS

Your intellectual capacity is enormous, but it comes in spurts. You are an abstract and progressive thinker. You are self-centered but always feel guilty about it. You like to serve humanity, and if you overdo it, your health may suffer. You are an indefatigable worker, but you are nervous and need to develop self-discipline. You can have excellent physical coordination, or you can be accident-prone.
Physicist Albert Einstein, tennis player Chris Evert.

☿ ⊼ ♆ MERCURY INCONJUNCT NEPTUNE

Although you are creative and inspired, you are never satisfied with the way you express these talents. You dislike routine. You need to determine what your responsibilities are, and then you must live up to them. You have a lot of nervous energy and many grandiose ideas. You can be too trusting and unrealistic, and others may take advantage of you or use you.
Writer Ralph Waldo Emerson, actor Clark Gable.

☿ ⊼ ♇ MERCURY INCONJUNCT PLUTO

Because your sense of responsibility is overdeveloped, you take on too many duties. At times you may get involved in other people's business. You are sensitive and intuitive, and you like to get totally involved in causes. You expect too much from both yourself and others; guard against draining your energies; your health might suffer.

Civil rights leader Angela Davis, President Charles de Gaulle.

Lesson 11: Venus

A Few Suggestions

Before you start reading lesson 11, we would like to give you a few suggestions.

1. Don't try to absorb too much at one time.

2. Don't jump from planet to planet. Finish aspecting and delineating one planet before you start on the next one. Don't jump to Mercury before you have finished the Sun and then the Moon.

3. For an even better understanding of what we are trying to teach you, go back to Franklin D. Roosevelt's chart and look at his aspects and house positions as you read our more detailed text.

Now go on to lesson 11—Venus. When you have finished this lesson, try to delineate Judy Garland's Venus. Our interpretation is in the Appendix on page 293.

Venus in the Signs

Venus represents *affection,* your *sense of values* and your *social urges.* Keep this in mind when you read the following descriptions.

♀ ♈ VENUS IN ARIES
keyword ***demonstrative***   detriment

You are magnetic, an idea person and a fast thinker. Restless, ardent and instigating, you may be overwhelming, and your aggression may even drive others away. Because you are outgoing and enthusiastic, you excel in social situations. Your outlook is cheerful and positive; you package yourself well, and you can be creative and artistic. With difficult aspects, you may be fickle, may dash into an early or hasty marriage, or you may even lack manners. You must develop more understanding for other people's feelings.

Singer Liza Minelli, actress Elizabeth Taylor, transsexual Christine Jorgensen, Defense Minister Moshe Dayan, actor Neville Brand.

♀ ♉ VENUS IN TAURUS
keyword ***steadfast***   dignity

Faithful and stable, your sense of touch is highly developed. You love luxury and plush surroundings, and you have an innate sense of the value of material objects. Although you are sensual, you express your sensuality passively; you let things come to you. With your charm, good looks and probably good voice, the opposite sex is bound to seek you out. You have a close rapport with nature, flowers and gardening; you can also do well in any of the artistic fields. Conventional and sociable, your emotions are deep. When you feel insecure, you become jealous and possessive. With difficult aspects, you may be too stubborn, or you may marry late in life. Since you love good food, you could have a weight problem.

Composer Nicolai Rimsky-Korsakov, poet Walt Whitman, violinist Yehudi Menuhin, actor Warren Beatty, TV personality Tom Snyder.

♀ ♊ VENUS IN GEMINI
keyword *fickle*

You are generous, friendly and detached. You need a lot of freedom. You like your partner to be intellectual, and if possible, to have a good sense of humor. You enjoy roaming the world and are literate, even poetic. You lack permanence in most of your involvements, and you may have more than one marriage. Your values in romantic matters can be quite superficial, especially if you lack fixed planets in the rest of your chart. You have pleasing manners, good relations with siblings and neighbors, and a great sense of family. Your emotions are on a more mental than feeling level, and you thrive on change and variety. Your nature is curious and you want to taste much of what life has to offer.

Poet Alfred Lord Tennyson, broadcast journalist Lowell Thomas, writer Henry David Thoreau, singer Cher, actor Eddie Albert.

♀ ♋ VENUS IN CANCER
keyword *sensitive*

Idealistic and poetic, you enjoy the nice things in life. You may be self-indulgent, but you are rarely wasteful. Your feelings are sensitive and you are easily hurt but try to hide this by keeping busy or by pretending not to care. You enjoy your home and taking care of it. If you don't have a home to take care of, you nurture the whole world. Financial and domestic security is very important to you. You are gentle, sympathetic, ingratiating and exude a quiet charm. With Venus in this position your reactions are instinctive and emotional; in a partnership you may be more a mother than mate. You like your partner to be very demonstrative. With difficult aspects, the tendency to sentimentality becomes overemphasized; you might cling to your loved ones, or your parents may object to your chosen mate.

Pianist Liberace, singer Nelson Eddy, poet Robert Browning, Prime Minister Menachim Begin, humorist Ogden Nash.

♀ ♌ VENUS IN LEO
keyword *romantic*

You are ardent and romantic, and you can be theatrical in your behavior. You love life and love. You can be a social climber, who enjoys throwing lavish parties and adores elegant people. You have great pride, and love to be noticed and to be the center of attention. Clothes and appearance are important to you, as well as children, and you like dramatic and exciting courtships. You have a great need for applause; if you do not get it at home, you'll seek it outside. Your good sense of color gives you artistic ability. The fields of acting, writing and music appeal to you. You are warm, affectionate and loyal to those you deem worthy. With challenging aspects, you can be jealous, snobbish, indiscriminate and overconcerned with sex.

Artist Andy Warhol, violinist Isaac Stern, designer Coco Chanel, designer Pierre Cardin, writer George Sand.

♀ ♍ VENUS IN VIRGO
keyword *fastidious*   fall

You are neat, even clinical, in your personal appearance and approach. You tend to analyze everything you do, and you may take every emotion apart until you have destroyed any natural or spontaneous feelings. With Venus in Virgo you may marry late or stay single, yet you have very good relations with your friends and co-workers. It is difficult for you to give of yourself emotionally; you'd rather share work interests or intellectual pursuits with others. Soft-spoken, undemonstrative and shy, you have sympathy for the underdog. You can be a good nurse or doctor, and you are very interested in health or hygiene. With difficult aspects, this position can reverse itself. Instead of shying away from love, you may pursue sex as an obsession; instead of being neat and clean, you may be slovenly and crude; instead of being hardworking, you may be lazy and secretive.

Actress Brigitte Bardot, actress Sophia Loren, labor leader Walter Reuther, comedian Will Rogers, Russian mystic Grigori Rasputin, filmmaker Dino DeLaurentiis.

♀ ♎ VENUS IN LIBRA
keyword *compatible*   *dignity*

Harmony, marriage and all social relationships are extremely important to you. You enjoy companionship, and you like to please others. Quite fair in your judgments, you have high standards of social behavior. You love beauty, luxury and intellectual stimulation, and you entertain well. Discord and loud noises can make you nervous, since your sense of hearing is well developed. Although you are not money-oriented, you appreciate what money can buy. Your talents are many, but music, public performance, painting and sculpture are particularly suited to your temperament. You are attractive to and attracted by the opposite sex; in fact you are in love with love. You can be easily hurt, but you rarely carry a grudge. Gracious and appreciative, you are eternally young at heart. With difficult aspects, you may become too superficial or gushing, and you may be unable to stand up for what you believe.

Entertainer Maurice Chevalier, artist Pablo Picasso, musician Al Hirt, pianist Ignace Jan Paderewski, actress Elke Sommer.

♀ ♏ VENUS IN SCORPIO
keyword *intense*   detriment

Your emotions are very deep, and your sexual desires are strong and passionate. You tend to be jealous and secretive, and have difficulty sensing other people's feelings. You can also be very idealistic, religious or even mystical. Because you do everything with so much intensity, you feel desolate when your advances are rejected, and your love can easily turn to hate. Even your artistic tastes are colored by pathos and drama. Your demeanor can be mysterious, and you rarely lose your dignity. With challenging aspects, you feel very insecure, and you can become preoccupied with sex. You may be selfish or even cruel.

Psychic Uri Geller, murder cult leader Charles Manson, Indian leader Mohandas Gandhi, playwright Eugene O'Neill, singer Cass Elliott.

♀ ♐ VENUS IN SAGITTARIUS
keyword *objective*

Emotionally idealistic, you are also light, humorous, sociable and even flirty. Demonstrative, friendly, sociable, outgoing, you love freedom. You have many friends and are objective in your personal relationships. You are honest, and your tastes and morals are traditional. You prefer the classical approach to the ultra-modern. You enjoy the outdoors as well as sports, travel, pleasures, fun and gambling. You like people who are philosophical or concerned with education. You may marry a foreigner. With difficult aspects, you can be too breezy, fickle or pleasure seeking. You may be too frank in expressing your feelings, or you might try to impose your beliefs on others.
Senator Barry Goldwater, Prime Minister Winston Churchill, writer Mark Twain, White House aide John Dean, producer Jack Haley, Jr.

♀ ♑ VENUS IN CAPRICORN
keyword *dedicated*

You are basically insecure, and in order to compensate for this sense of inadequacy you may seek status and material goods. Seemingly cold and calculating in your approach to marriage or partnerships, you try to protect yourself since you fear rejection. It is very difficult for you to show the tenderness you really feel. Proud and reserved in your public behavior, you may appear snobbish yet you are successful. You often repress your emotions and sexuality, but deep inside you are very sensual, even lusty. Slow to develop romantic relationships, you may either choose an older or mature partner or a much younger one for whom you feel responsible. Once someone manages to pierce your great shield of reserve, you are loyal and dedicated. With your leadership potential you could do well in business. With challenging aspects, you may be too concerned with material achievements and emotionally too detached and cold.
General George Patton, Senator Robert Kennedy, actor Clark Gable, musician Dave Brubeck, actress Diane Keaton.

♀ ♒ VENUS IN AQUARIUS
keyword *detached*

You are cool, calm, collected, friendly, popular and unselfish. You prefer liking many to loving one. You live by your own rules and regulations, regardless of how unacceptable these may be to society. Your romantic attractions are often sudden, but they are not always lasting. Your partner must be a friend as well as a lover, from whom you seek mental stimulation and plenty of variety. Not possessive yourself, you will shy away from anyone who might want to tie you down. You are intuitive, and you function well with friends and in groups. You are interested in new art forms, legal reforms and technical endeavors. With difficult aspects you may be aloof, cold, stubborn and may crave eccentric sexual experiences.
Artist Paul Cezanne, singer Janice Joplin, nutritionist Adelle Davis, scientist Linus Pauling, astronaut John Glenn.

♀ ♓ VENUS IN PISCES
keyword *compassionate*   exaltation

You are gentle, compassionate, helpful and tenderhearted. Very understanding of others, you can be quite spiritual. You are romantic and sensitive. You need love and tenderness, and without love you feel lost. Your intuition is highly developed, and you relate well to art, poetry, nature and animals. You are creative and can inspire creativity in others. However, your extreme sensitivity can leave you wide open to hurt. Knowing this, you often suffer in silence, or you may become very reticent. Self-sacrificing, you are attracted to the underdog. With difficult aspects, you become too emotionally dependent on others, or you may force others to depend on you. You may be sentimental, hypersensitive, undiscriminating and unrealistic. Try to use your artistic talents in some positive, creative way.
Poet Elizabeth Barrett Browning, psychic Edgar Cayce, civil rights leader Martin Luther King, writer Victor Hugo, Queen Elizabeth II.

Venus in the Houses

VENUS IN THE FIRST HOUSE
keyword *charming*

Venus in the first house bestows beauty, harmony, balance, personal grace, intuition, kindness, good luck and a happy disposition. You like nice clothes, enjoy social involvements and love people to spoil you. Your early life is pleasant, and you like beautiful surroundings and cultured living. You may have a sweet tooth and enjoy music and flirting. Acting is easy for you because of your outgoing personality. With difficult aspects, you may have a me-first attitude, and you can be lazy and self-indulgent.
Actress Rita Hayworth, singer Johnny Cash, actor Robert Taylor, Ethel Kennedy (Mrs. Robert F.).

VENUS IN THE SECOND HOUSE
keyword *materialistic*   accidental dignity

You have the ability to obtain money, enjoy being content and prosperous and are quite lucky. Social status is important to you, and therefore you will undoubtedly work hard toward financial success. You like to earn money in pleasant ways, and you may find a career in the arts, beauty, clothing or flowers. You have the ability to charm others, and any career that caters to women, including a public one, is rewarding. With difficult aspects, you may spend more than you earn, since you like to show off. You may also be greedy or stingy.
Attorney F. Lee Bailey, comedian Peter Sellers, publisher Hugh Hefner, comedian Jack Benny, dancer Cyd Charisse.

VENUS IN THE THIRD HOUSE
keyword *pleasant*

You enjoy pleasant relations with your brothers and sisters and had a harmonious early life. Compromise is easy for you, and generally you can always see the other person's point of view. Your mind is refined, and you express yourself well. Fond of studying, you enjoy lots of running around and short trips. Charming and intellectual, your good nature endears you to everyone. Artistic and creative, you could be a good writer; if you don't write books at least you write interesting letters. You do not like to argue; you prefer to achieve your aims by persuasion rather than by pressure. With difficult aspects, you tend to be fickle, decadent and superficial.

Cornelia Wallace (wife of Governor George F.), Governor Ronald Reagan, playwright Noel Coward, actor Lew Ayres.

VENUS IN THE FOURTH HOUSE
keyword **warm**

You love your parents, and they are probably well-off. An organized home is very important to you. You like to entertain, are sensitive to your surroundings, enjoy nice furnishings, and are interested in decorating, gardening, flowers and the arts. You may marry late, but you will be quite happy. In fact you enjoy good relationships with everyone in your home. You are optimistic by nature, and rightly so; if you live up to your own ethics you should always be surrounded by love and warmth. With difficult aspects, you can become demanding, dictatorial and jealous.

Comedian Will Rogers, ex-First Lady Betty Ford, Senator George McGovern, Emperor Hirohito.

VENUS IN THE FIFTH HOUSE
keyword *affectionate*

Your love affairs should be happy, your speculations should be successful, and your children will bring you contentment. Artistic and creative, you have a natural flair for acting and writing and can also excel in sports. The opposite sex finds you very attractive, so you will probably have many love affairs. This is a good placement for work with children and

teenagers. Your nature is affectionate, pleasure-seeking, sociable and even passionate. With challenging aspects, all the above still applies, but these things will be harder for you to achieve; more effort on your part will be required.
Actress Shirley Temple, baseball player Hank Aaron, millionaire Diamond Jim Brady, actor Peter Lorre.

VENUS IN THE SIXTH HOUSE
keyword *helpful*

You like to give service, and you get along famously with your co-workers, servants and employees. You function best when others respect your habit patterns. You enjoy artistic work, and you often do business with or for women. You prefer jobs where you need not dirty your hands. You are always ready to lend a helping hand, so this is a good position for mediators, counselors of all kinds, arbitrators and health workers. Your health is generally good, and you are conscious of your clothes and diet. With difficult aspects, you should avoid too much sugar and starch. You may tend to be self-indulgent, and you may be unwilling to make adjustments.
Psychoanalyst Carl Jung, composer Frederick Chopin, TV actress Kay Lenz, writer Rod Serling.

VENUS IN THE SEVENTH HOUSE
keyword *harmonious*   accidental dignity

Able to create harmonious surroundings, you will be happy in your marriage. Popular with the public at large, your business partnerships run smoothly. With your legal mind you can expect success in matters dealing with the law. You have a loving nature; if you do not get married it will be by your choice, not because of lack of opportunity. You have many social graces and find it easy to get along with all kinds of people. With difficult aspects, you may tend to build up resentments. This could even lead to a persecution complex.
Chief Justice Oliver Wendell Holmes, actress Jean Harlow, poet Elizabeth Barrett Browning, writer Jack Kerouac.

VENUS IN THE EIGHTH HOUSE
keyword *sensuous*

You will have many benefits through a partner, or you may gain through insurance and inheritance. You should have a long life and a peaceful death. This is a good position for big business, banking and writing. You may have spiritual tendencies; if you pursue these, you will find happiness and peace of mind. Your sexual relationships are harmonious. With challenging aspects, you may experience inertia, lack of discipline, too much sensuality and excesses in food and drink. *Writer Hermann Hesse, billionaire John D. Rockefeller, Sr., transsexual Christine Jorgensen, White House Chief of Staff Hamilton Jordan.*

VENUS IN THE NINTH HOUSE
keyword *beneficial*

You have keen intuition and enjoy the higher cultural aspects of life. Fond of study, you are usually well educated. Venus in this position smooths the path of your life. Philosophical, kind, sympathetic and helpful, your tastes are artistic and refined. You may marry a foreigner, or perhaps you will spend much time traveling abroad. If you marry, you will probably have a good relationship with your in-laws. If the aspects are challenging, you might be lazy and indifferent, or perhaps you will have too much missionary or religious zeal. *Educator Maria Montessori, writer Thomas Mann, Vice President Nelson Rockefeller, actress Mary Tyler Moore.*

VENUS IN THE TENTH HOUSE
keyword *well-liked*

You are ambitious and should enjoy social success, finding many people along your way who are ready and willing to help you. Often one of your parents is instrumental in helping you professionally. You are popular, lucky and successful with the opposite sex, but you may end up marrying for status rather than love. You are a born diplomat. Although you go along with the trend and are not really a pioneer, you are successful with the public. With difficult aspects, you may be a social climber and may not attain many of the potential benefits of this position.

Industrialists Henry Ford, Sr. and Henry Kaiser, Governor Edmund G. (Jerry) Brown, Princess Caroline of Monaco.

VENUS IN THE ELEVENTH HOUSE
keyword *amicable*

You have a variety of friends, especially of the opposite sex, and they may all be helpful to you in your career and personal life. You have many artistic acquaintances and may marry someone in your profession. You are successful working with clubs and organizations; perhaps you may be involved in philanthropy. You tend to be too idealistic and need to be more realistic in order to achieve your desired aims. With difficult aspects, you might choose the wrong friends and may suffer many disappointments through them.

Writer Ernest Hemingway, designer Coco Chanel, actress Catherine Deneuve, football player O.J. Simpson.

VENUS IN THE TWELFTH HOUSE
keyword *sympathetic*   accidental
                                        exaltation

You are kind, compassionate, charitable, sympathetic to others and often deeply inspired. You enjoy secluded places and you need time each day to recharge your batteries. Although the undercurrents of your life are smooth, you feel a compelling need to serve. Drawn to the occult, you like to probe the deeper meanings of life and love. Basically shy and easily hurt, you may have secret love affairs. You are quite resigned when in trouble. With challenging aspects you may love a person who is not free or suffer setbacks in your love life or experience the frustrations of divorce.

Actor Gregory Peck, Prime Minister Benjamin Disraeli, singer Peggy Lee, writer James Hilton.

Venus in Aspect

Any aspect to Venus should be thought of as affecting *the love nature*.

The conjunction emphasizes the *affections* and *love nature*.

The opposition shows your *awareness or unawareness of your feelings towards others*.

The square *challenges your affections and feelings*.

The trine or the sextile lends *flow and ease in feeling love and affection*.

The inconjunct suggests that *an adjustment is needed in order to realize your feelings*.

Conjunctions

♀ ☌ ♂ VENUS CONJUNCT MARS

Both sensitive and sensuous, you blend charm and energy. Romance comes easily to you, and you demand much from your loved ones. You often feel discontented and angry because you expect too much. You need freedom of expression and hate being tied down. Yours is a free soul. Your involvements are passionate; your emotions are warm and vital, and at times you may seem pushy. You are good in relating to the public, yet you also enjoy and need occasional solitude. *White House Chief of Staff Hamilton Jordan, RAF pilot Peter Townsend.*

♀ ☌ ♃ VENUS CONJUNCT JUPITER

You are charming, generous, even extravagant and popular, especially with the opposite sex. Your relations with your parents are good. You dislike vulgarity and are moral, artistic and religious. You are a good teacher and excellent at public relations. You respond well to honesty, but are often taken advantage of. You can also be lazy and self-indulgent. *Pianist Liberace, artist Toulouse Lautrec.*

☿ ♀ ♂ ♄ VENUS CONJUNCT SATURN

Your duty and happiness become identified with each other. Your judgment is good, and so is your self-discipline. You have a great need for security which you often seek in a partner who could be older than you and perhaps married before. One of your parents may have been too strict and unloving, and so you may fear close associations. You are faithful, quite serious and good at mathematics, finances and art. You are a hard worker and are protective of the dignity of the family. *Scientist Marie Curie, actor Yul Brynner.*

♀ ♂ ♅ VENUS CONJUNCT URANUS

Self-willed and emotionally tense, you have a sparkling personality and may be a genius. You crave peace, you intellectualize life, and you refuse to be taken for granted. Where uniqueness is required, you function well. If you are artistic, you will be very original in your work. Involved in many unusual liaisons, you tend to end romances suddenly, and you rarely remain true to one person, often confusing friendship and love. You are very sociable. *Actress Elizabeth Taylor, Senator Edward M. Kennedy.*

♀ ♂ ♆ VENUS CONJUNCT NEPTUNE

You are high-strung, temperamental, appreciative of beauty, artistic, poetic, and you love music. An impractical, romantic dreamer, you seek a peaceful occupation. You do not see others very clearly and may experience many disappointments in your emotional relationships. You love animals. You can be a real flirt, at times too trusting of others, and you are usually at ease in social situations. *Playwright William Shakespeare, actor Rossano Brazzi.*

♀ ♂ ♀ VENUS CONJUNCT PLUTO

Your feelings are deep, and your emotions become magnified. You can be fanatic in love; you have such intense needs that disappointments are unavoidable. Changeable yet possessive, you love life and often fall in love at first sight. Your personality is magnetic; you will fight injustice of any kind. You can be totally committed to a partner, but you expect the same commitment in return. With difficult aspects you could be perverted and degenerate.
Psychoanalyst Sigmund Freud, writer Thomas Mann.

Squares and Oppositions

♀ □ ♂ VENUS SQUARE MARS
♀ ☍ ♂ VENUS OPPOSITION MARS

Impulsive and amorous, you have a well-developed sexual nature. You express your feelings openly, but you are deeply hurt if people don't respond to you. You are often critical of others due to your own dissatisfaction with yourself. You expect too much, often engaging in family quarrels. You tend to get along better with members of the opposite sex. In a man's chart this is considered the aspect of the great lover. You can be self-indulgent and easily dissatisfied in matters of the heart. You are always romantic and often very good-looking.
Playwright Arthur Miller (□), actor William Holden (☍).

♀ □ ♃ VENUS SQUARE JUPITER
♀ ☍ ♃ VENUS OPPOSITION JUPITER

You can be vain, idle, conceited, overly emotional and may have many love affairs. Your financial sense is not well developed. You tend to exaggerate and are often self-indulgent. You may use others and yet, when others use you be bitter. Overly optimistic, you are a great pal when the going is good but can become touchy when the going gets rough. If

you can use these challenges positively, your intuition will flourish, and you can do well in public relations work, politics, counseling and the media.
Psychoanalyst Carl Jung (□), Secretary of State Henry Kissinger (♂).

♀ □ ♄ VENUS SQUARE SATURN
♀ ♂ ♄ VENUS OPPOSITION SATURN

Chronically discontented, you often sacrifice happiness for duty. Shy, sensitive and stiff with your emotions, others may find you cold. You tend to be on the defensive, and you fear rejection and lack of acceptance. You may have problems with your parents and will do better after you leave their home. Since it is difficult for you to express your true feelings, you will probably have to make many concessions in life. You should delay marriage until after age twenty-eight because you may be unhappy if you marry too young. Your big lesson is to learn to relate to others.
Producer Sam Peckinpah (□), General George Patton (♂).

♀ □ ♅ VENUS SQUARE URANUS
♀ ♂ ♅ VENUS OPPOSITION URANUS

You tend to be spoiled and used to having your way, yet you get your point across with much charm. You are self-centered and egotistic but also magnetic. Touchy and willful, you have problems with the opposite sex and often have a hasty marriage and a quick divorce. Your desire is always very strong, and you transfer your affections for no apparent reason. You resent authority and like to be different. You enjoy a conquest and then tire of what has been conquered. You try to hide a deep inferiority complex.
Millionaire Diamond Jim Brady (□) actress Deborah Kerr (♂).

♀ □ ♆ VENUS SQUARE NEPTUNE
♀ ☍ ♆ VENUS OPPOSITION NEPTUNE

You must learn to deal with your extreme idealism, your exaggerated emotions and the struggle between your intuition and your feelings. You are easily deceived and often financially misled. You would be a good mathematician, statistician or strategist. You are an escapist, and you are very sensitive to drugs. When you feel unappreciated you tend to blame others. Artistic, you love gracious living and may be born into good circumstances. However, you must overcome your great sense of insecurity.
Movement leader Angela Davis (□), Field Marshall Erwin Rommel (☍).

♀ □ ♇ VENUS SQUARE PLUTO
♀ ☍ ♇ VENUS OPPOSITION PLUTO

Your sexuality is strong, at times lustful and even lascivious. This can lead to philandering and can create many psychological inhibitions which will frustrate your love affairs. You should try to keep high standards. Although financial problems dog you, you have a great desire for wealth. You make many demands of your partner, or your partner makes many demands of you. You are always looking for an ideal, either in a partnership or in your profession. Many of your problems will be solved when you learn to compromise.
Dancer Vaslav Nijinsky (□), race driver Lance Reventlow (☍).

Trines and Sextiles

♀ △ ♂ VENUS TRINE MARS
♀ ⚹ ♂ VENUS SEXTILE MARS

Ardent and faithful in marriage, you are fond of singing, dancing, music and drama. Your nature is affectionate, warmhearted, congenial and fun loving, and you don't like to think of the seamy side of life. You enjoy family life but need and expect independence. You may lack ambition to do much with your abilities and talents because everything comes too easily to you.

Actress Carol Burnett (△), singer Harry Belafonte (✳).

♀ △ ♃ VENUS TRINE JUPITER
♀ ✳ ♃ VENUS SEXTILE JUPITER

You have a strong sense of ethics, and are graceful, charitable, sympathetic, imaginative and good at handling people. Your outgoing, affectionate personality puts others at ease; this makes you popular. You know what you want out of life, your ideals and aspirations are high but you may be too lazy and/or self-indulgent to go after what you want. You have the capability to make big money and also the extravagance to spend it. Your partnerships are generally successful; you could have numerous love affairs.

Playwright George Bernard Shaw (△), TV emcee Ralph Edwards (✳).

♀ △ ♄ VENUS TRINE SATURN
♀ ✳ ♄ VENUS SEXTILE SATURN

You are serious, faithful, self-sacrificing and thrifty, and you can gain through partnerships, business and/or older people. You work your way up slowly and steadily and will benefit from a long-term effort. You usually are a fine parent, as well as a good judge of people. You are both dependable and dependent, and you tend to be a late bloomer. Writing, poetry and music would be good outlets to overcome your innate loneliness.

Writer Hermann Hesse (△), singer Pat Boone (✳).

♀ △ ♅ VENUS TRINE URANUS
♀ ✳ ♅ VENUS SEXTILE URANUS

You have a magnetic personality, are unconventional, and

make many unorthodox contracts. You have sudden romances and marriages, but they don't always last. You are attractive to the opposite sex. Because you need an adequate outlet for your emotions, you should explore your creative potential. You have much zest for life.
Writer Erich Maria Remarque (△), actress Mia Farrow (✳).

♀ △ ♆ VENUS TRINE NEPTUNE
♀ ✳ ♆ VENUS SEXTILE NEPTUNE

You are a good problem solver because you are both sensitive and imaginative. Fond of beauty in all forms, you are drawn to refined people. You are romantic and spiritual in your outlook, and you are kind to others even in disappointment. You don't usually like hard or routine work but would do well in a service field such as nursing or social work. Your creativity could express itself well in poetry or music; you may have a preference for stringed instruments.
Actor Burt Reynolds (△), writer Johannes Wolfgang von Goethe (✳).

♀ △ ♇ VENUS TRINE PLUTO
♀ ✳ ♇ VENUS SEXTILE PLUTO

You are creative and ingenious and have a strong sense of color. With your good financial and leadership ability you could be a great teacher, preacher or politician. You form strong opinions early in life and show great dedication, intuition and honesty. You can also be overly self-indulgent; you may have weight problems as you get older.
Civil rights leader Martin Luther King (△), Secretary of State Henry Kissinger (✳).

Inconjuncts (Quincunxes)

♀ ⚻ ♂ VENUS INCONJUNCT MARS

You find it difficult to satisfy your desires. You should learn

to pay more attention to yourself instead of worrying about what others expect of you. You must overcome a negative self-image. You tend to volunteer your services, working for free; therefore others often take advantage of you. You can be too ambitious and must learn not to sacrifice love and affection in order to succeed.
Conductor Arturo Toscanini, actor Rip Torn.

♀ ⚻ ♃ VENUS INCONJUNCT JUPITER

You tend to overreact in personal ways, although you are able to act defensive with others. You try so hard to win approval that you must be careful not to become the proverbial door-mat. You often feel exploited in your romances, since you tend to make a better best friend than lover. You must learn to maintain your self-respect; this will lead to growth.
Actor Judd Hirsch, director Vittorio de Sica.

♀ ⚻ ♄ VENUS INCONJUNCT SATURN

You are capable of earning a very good living, but your hard work drive is often an overcompensation. Your fear of rejection in love leads to a need to shine in a profession or career where less personal involvement is required. You have great potential for success since this is a workhorse aspect. Depression and self-depreciation are common, but you hide them behind your dedication to work, often at the cost of love and tenderness.
Writer Ernest Hemingway, jazz musician Miles Davis.

♀ ⚻ ♅ VENUS INCONJUNCT URANUS

You are generous and indulgent and spoil others, while deep down inside you resent them. Often you take on other people's problems instead of dealing with your own. You are very communicative; in fact you are often too talkative, putting on a happy face. Or else you may become silent, sullen and

mysterious. You would benefit from any artistic outlet, especially writing.
Writer Zelda Fitzgerald, football player Larry Czonka.

♀ ⚻ ♆ VENUS INCONJUNCT NEPTUNE

Sensitive, even inspired, also very vulnerable, you need everyone to like you. You can either become a crusader, or you may waste all your resources and accomplish nothing. You look for the perfect mate and are unwilling to settle for less. Therefore, you may end up lonely and partnerless. You must take off your blinders and learn to face life realistically.
Consumer advocate Ralph Nader, singer Peter Frampton.

♀ ⚻ ♇ VENUS INCONJUNCT PLUTO

You need to learn moderation in your relationships. You experience stress with the opposite sex, sometimes to the point where you shy away from them totally, suppressing your intense love nature. You may have religious inclinations and believe in the occult and life after death. With your sharp tongue and mind, you have excellent communication abilities in writing or speaking.
Playwright Noel Coward, baseball player Ty Cobb.

Lesson 12: Mars

Some General Comments

Before you start lesson 12 we would like to explain the little Rx symbol that looks like a doctor's prescription which appears next to the symbol for Mars in Judy Garland's chart. That same Rx is also next to the symbol for Mercury. This symbol signifies that the planet is in *retrograde motion* or apparently moving backwards as seen from Earth.

For now, it is enough that you know what the symbol means. Be assured that your not knowing its full working potential in a chart will not really affect your delineation of Judy Garland's Mercury or Mars.

You may also have noticed that Cancer is on the cusp of both the first and second houses and that Capricorn is on the seventh and eighth houses. Within the fifth and eleventh houses Scorpio and Taurus are inserted in parenthesis. This sign in parenthesis is called an *interception* since it is intercepted or contained within a house even though the sign itself is not on the cusp of any house.

The interception is arrived at mathematically. When you learn the mathematics of erecting a chart, you will understand how this happens. In your future studies you will learn its meaning in a chart. But as with retrograde motion, interception is not a basic factor in interpreting a horoscope.

Please proceed with lesson 12 with this in mind. After you have studied Mars in more detail, go on to delineate Judy Garland's Mars. Our interpretation can be found in the Appendix on page 294.

Mars in the Signs

Mars shows your *sexual drive* and *where you expend your energy*. The keyword for Mars in the different signs shows the type of energy expended.

♂♈ MARS IN ARIES
keyword *dynamic*   dignity

You are vigorous, independent, dominant, autocratic and courageous. Routine bores you; it is difficult for you to compromise. Aggressive and full of initiative, you like to be in the driver's seat. Your enthusiasm is contagious, and you are often a community leader. Success is yours if you learn to channel your energy and to develop patience and sympathetic understanding. You are strong and ardent sexually. With challenging aspects you may experience uncontrolled desires, a hot temper and irritability.
Singer Ella Fitzgerald, filmmaker Orson Welles, actor Paul Newman, golfer Jack Nicklaus, football player Joe Namath.

♂♉ MARS IN TAURUS
keyword *dogmatic*   detriment

You are obstinate, practical, determined and very assured. Once you set yourself on a course of action it is difficult to turn you away from it. You have good earning power, but you are particular about how you spend your money. Although you judge others harshly, you will fight injustice to the bitter end. Your endurance is great, but you may lack thrust and mobility. At times you can be very self-indulgent. A skilled artisan, you also are good in business. Sexually you are earthy and sensual, but you must take care not to be jealous and possessive.

Dancer Rudolf Nureyev, columnist Dorothy Kilgallen, President Andrew Jackson, labor leader John L. Lewis, singer Leontyne Price.

♂ ♊ MARS IN GEMINI
keyword *spontaneous*

Your mind is always active, and you have great dexterity and manual skills. Observant, argumentative and excitable, you are very alert, active and restless. You must develop the discipline of concentration. You often feel the need for adventure and have a tendency to go off in many directions at once. You have a great sense of liberty and justice. Your speech is eloquent, yet straightforward. Sexually you alternate from deep relationships to superficial ones. This placement often requires more than one partner for total fulfillment.

Swimmer Johnny Weismuller, musician Louis Armstrong, artist Raphael, dictator Benito Mussolini, singer Dean Martin.

♂ ♋ MARS IN CANCER
keyword *temperamental*   fall

Because of your moodiness and emotional frustration, you can be quite quarrelsome, and you may become involved in discordant domestic relationships. Acquisitive and artistic, gadgets appeal to you. You are firm and calm in an emergency. If you suppress too much anger, ulcers or stomach problems may arise. Usually unwilling to sacrifice your own views, you like to work independently. This position of Mars may lead to the early loss of the mother. You are refined yet sensitive sexually. If there are inharmonious aspects, you should avoid over-indulgence.

Playwright Tennessee Williams, poet Ogden Nash, Queen Marie Antoinette, family planning advocate Margaret Sanger, filmmaker Dino DeLaurentiis.

♂ ♌ MARS IN LEO
keyword *passionate*

Generous, fun-loving, sympathetic and dynamic, you exude great personal magnetism. Demonstrative and generous in love, warm and expressive sexually, you are strongly attracted to members of the opposite sex. You are self-willed and must learn to develop a grasp of detail and a sense of humility. You tend to see everything on a large scale; you rarely suffer from a lack of self-confidence. People with Mars in this position have great sex appeal. With difficult aspects, you must avoid being domineering and too egotistical.

Actress Sophia Loren, spy Mata Hari, pianist Vladimir Horowitz, Vice President Nelson Rockefeller, singer Frank Sinatra.

♂ ♍ MARS IN VIRGO
keyword *disciplined*

You are cool, scientific and logical. You love to work and are enthusiastic when you feel you can contribute to a good cause. Because you are thorough and painstaking, you enjoy routine and can do the most monotonous tasks well. Sexually you are idealistic though not necessarily platonic. At times you may seem to lack passion and imagination; you have very little patience with social butterflies. You tend to work too hard, and overwork may bring on illness. This is a good position for a career in the medical field, and you are often a good gardener. With difficult aspects you must avoid being overly critical, scheming or suspicious.

TV personality Art Linkletter, General George Patton, architect Frank Lloyd Wright, Emperor Napoleon Bonaparte, Julie Nixon Eisenhower (daughter of the President).

♂♎ MARS IN LIBRA
keyword *controlled*   detriment

You are charming, generous, amiable, cooperative and persuasive. You like to entertain and be sociable, and are interested in new ideas. You are quick to seek justice whenever it
is lacking. You may confuse your own desires and ambitions
with those of others. Sexually, you are affected by external
stimuli such as music, soft lights and beautiful surroundings.
You may lack self-reliance and must develop the ability to
stand alone. Inharmonious aspects can make you lazy, or you
may feel that everyone should abide by your rules.
*Secretary of State John Foster Dulles, explorer Robert Peary,
composer Gioacchino Rossini, golfer Arnold Palmer, actress
Elke Sommer.*

♂♏ MARS IN SCORPIO
keyword *explosive*   dignity

You are strong and self-disciplined. Self-reliant, efficient,
dignified and intense, you seldom act until you know what is
right for you. Idealistic, probing and set in your ways, you are
very trustworthy and you expect the same from others. You
lack adaptability and the power to relax. A planner and
strategist without equal, you have an all-or-nothing attitude
that makes compromise difficult. Sexually you are strong,
powerful and secretive; if you misdirect this drive you can
become intensely jealous.
*President George Washington, scientist Jonas Salk, aviation
pioneer Orville Wright, cellist Pablo Casals, director Martin
Scorsese.*

♂♐ MARS IN SAGITTARIUS
keyword *zealous*

Your inner strength is based on a good philosophy of life. You
operate with great bursts of energy but have little endurance.
You often embrace new ideas without thorough investigation

beforehand. Full of life and vigor, you can be a crusader and are quite patriotic. Rhythm, harmony and tempo come naturally to you. Because you are gallant, extravagant and scintillating, your cheerful presence is welcome at any social gathering. Sexually, you are expansive and exploratory. With difficult aspects, you can lack follow-through, and could experience some danger through travel.

Drummer Gene Krupa, writer Francois de Voltaire, composer John P. Sousa, composer Johann Sebastian Bach, singer Joan Baez.

♂ ♑ MARS IN CAPRICORN
keyword ***commanding***   exaltation

You are magnetic, proud, earthy and well coordinated. A good organizer and reasoner, you want success and are willing to work for it. Because you are so practical, you rarely operate on impulse; thus you can function well in business. Self-control and self-discipline are your keywords. This position often brings admiration rather than love from the opposite sex. There may be a separation from a parent, usually the father, and if Mars is afflicted, there is some danger of broken bones. Strong and persistent sexually, you must learn to develop humor, humility and warmth.

Labor leader James Hoffa, scientist Louis Pasteur, explorer Richard Byrd, filmmaker Walt Disney, golfer Gary Player.

♂ ♒ MARS IN AQUARIUS
keyword ***electric***

You have high principles and a very modern outlook. Usually skilled, you can be detached and intellectual. This position often gives more thought than action. You are a good leader who can meet challenges with serenity and poise. You seldom work well unless you are in charge, and you are contemptuous of tradition unless it is substantiated with logic. You are experimental and innovative sexually, but you may lack the personal touch. With challenging aspects, you can be quite revolutionary and feel a need to overthrow the established order.

Publisher Hugh Hefner, actor James Mason, millionaire Howard Hughes, artist Leonardo da Vinci, actress Julie Christie.

♂ ♓ MARS IN PISCES
keyword *restless*

Your emotions are unpredictable, and you can be very intense. Because you are receptive and sympathetic, others easily take advantage of you. Your excessive sensitivity can stand in the way of self-confidence or decisive action, and you must develop initiative and self-reliance. You try to avoid confrontation of any kind. Though seemingly quiet on the outside, your demeanor hides an inner restlessness. You are usually shy, musical and even lazy. Sexually, you are very romantic and sensual. Difficult aspects may show a tendency to alcoholism or drug problems.

Singer Johnnie Cash, naturalist John Audubon, artist Vincent Van Gogh, writer Carson McCullers, actor Steve McQueen.

Mars in the Houses

MARS IN THE FIRST HOUSE
keyword *energetic*   accidental dignity

Since you are positive, self-assertive, combative, active and boisterous, you may be accident-prone. Your great physical strength and dynamic energy propel you headlong into things; you need to control your impatience and learn to use your energies constructively. Because you are practical and enterprising, you have good organizing ability. If Mars has challenging aspects, you may have scars on your head or face, and there may be danger of violence in your life.

South African Leader Jan Smuts, writers Booth Tarkington and Lewis Carroll, Prince Charles, Princess Caroline of Monaco.

MARS IN THE SECOND HOUSE
keyword *resourceful*

You are acquisitive, work hard for financial gain and usually earn well, spend freely and are most generous to others. If your expectations aren't met immediately, you can become very impatient. You have a tendency to get involved in get-rich-quick schemes. This is a good placement for engineers, mechanics and any other Martian pursuit such as military or government work. With difficult aspects, you may have a loud, discordant voice, and you may be unable to hang on to your assets, thus becoming involved in frequent financial crises.

Newspaper publisher William Randolph Hearst, actor Warren Beatty, Birdman of Alcatraz Robert Stroud, TV personality Merv Griffin.

MARS IN THE THIRD HOUSE
keyword *impatient*

You are impulsive, argumentative, restless and forthright. Quick at repartee, you are a strong family defender. Proper thinking is very important to you. You are both curious and aggressive; you may come on too strong and be tactless, impatient or too critical of others. You have an abundance of good ideas but are often inattentive to details because you are so active, nervous and restless. If Mars is in aspect to Uranus, you will be inventive. With difficult aspects, you may be an only child, or perhaps you have tremendous ups and downs in early life.

Aviator Charles Lindbergh, poet John Milton, actress Jayne Mansfield, writer Jack Kerouac.

MARS IN THE FOURTH HOUSE
keyword *self-reliant*

You have an aggressive need for security and are often patriotic. Because of a dominant parent or strife in your family, you probably will do better away from your birthplace. This Mars placement often indicates a military background or many changes of residence in your childhood. You need to tone down your strong emotions, and you must learn self-discipline. If Mars has difficult aspects, be careful of fire in the home. Some people with this placement prefer not to marry.

Filmmaker Walt Disney, President Richard Nixon, writer Emile Zola, General George Patton.

MARS IN THE FIFTH HOUSE
keyword *ardent*

You are athletic, impulsive and fickle. You love to compete but are a bad loser. You work well with children and can be an excellent disciplinarian. Sociable and a born promoter, you may tend to be self-indulgent and at times foolhardy. You are very sexual, romantic and idealistic. With challenging aspects, you should not gamble and must be very cautious in any speculative dealings. Your children could cause you some unhappiness, but this is usually a good house for Mars.

Actress Hedy Lamarr, writer Pearl Buck, Chief Justice Charles Evans Hughes, actor Hal Holbrook.

MARS IN THE SIXTH HOUSE
keyword *vigorous*

Mentally and physically you are a hard worker, but if you drive yourself too much, you may experience illnesses. You expect a great deal from those you work with; others may find your pace too fast. Unless you learn to control your temper, you may find it difficult to get along with fellow workers. Your great vitality can surface as athletic ability. With difficult aspects, you are prone to headaches, accidents, fevers and burns.

Red Cross founder Clara Barton, basketball player Kareem Abdul Jabbar, baseball player Henry Aaron, actor Leonard Nemoy.

MARS IN THE SEVENTH HOUSE
keyword *active*

You are a controversial person with a strong personality and a need to prove yourself. You attract verbal attack and legal difficulties, especially if Mars has strong aspects. Often you will marry early or hastily, choosing a dominant mate; unless you have a mature outlook, this can lead to separation or divorce. You like to have your own way, and everything goes well when you get it. Public opinion and that of your partner are important to you.

Comedian Charlie Chaplin, dictator Adolf Hitler, tennis player Arthur Ashe, comedienne Lily Tomlin.

MARS IN THE EIGHTH HOUSE
keyword *fervent*   accidental dignity

You are lusty, earthy and sensual, and your sex life is very important to you. It is often necessary for you to deal with other people's money, sometimes in a public capacity. You are interested in psychic matters and life after death, and may do research in these fields. This is a good position for politicians, surgeons, investigators, psychologists and psychiatrists. You flirt with and are comfortable with the idea of death, and your demise will probably be sudden. If Mars is aspected by Neptune you should avoid involvement with psychic phenomena.

Actress Marilyn Monroe, President John F. Kennedy, composer George Gershwin, baseball player Willie Mays.

MARS IN THE NINTH HOUSE
keyword *venturesome*

Independent, enthusiastic, often self-educated, you are curious and interested in serious studies. Although you can be quite skeptical, at some time in your life you probably will develop a religious zeal, bordering on fanaticism. Your mind is very restless; if you cannot travel in person, you do a lot of armchair traveling. If you have difficult aspects to Mars, you

may run into trouble in your foreign travels, or you could have some problems with your in-laws.
Industrialist Henry Ford, writers Helen Keller and Louisa May Alcott, explorer Roald Amundsen.

MARS IN THE TENTH HOUSE
keyword *driving*   accidental
                                          exaltation

If you are in the public eye, you will probably be controversial. You are active, persistent and highly motivated, and the driving force of your personality could make you an excellent executive. You will work hard to achieve a top position. If the aspects are difficult, you must protect your reputation. You may have a problem with your father, possibly a separation from him. This is a good position for a career in military, mechanical or engineering fields.
President Dwight Eisenhower, Duchess of Windsor, actress Lucille Ball, skier Jean Claude Killy.

MARS IN THE ELEVENTH HOUSE
keyword *exploratory*

You work hard to achieve your goals, whether they are material or spiritual. A social leader and born promoter, you make friends easily, but you may lose them by being too pushy or demanding. You are energetic and enthusiastic, but with hard aspects you can be touchy, overly sensitive and easily frustrated. You need to develop caution and integrity in your dealings with others. A lot of your energy goes into creative endeavors.
Artist Salvador Dali, family planning advocate Margaret Sanger, writer Rod Serling, singer Cass Elliott.

MARS IN THE TWELFTH HOUSE
keyword *rebellious*

You work and fight for the underdog, and you would make a good administrator in either a hospital or a prison. Since you can be secretive, you could also do well as an investigator or detective. This placement indicates some association with the law. This is a difficult house for Mars because your energy feels limited. With challenging aspects, you may often suppress your strong emotional reactions. You sometimes tend to buck the organization, and this can lead to sorrow, self-undoing and accidents.

First Lady Eleanor Roosevelt, writer Arthur Conan Doyle, mass murderer Adolf Eichmann, strongman Arnold Schwarznegger.

Mars in Aspect

Any aspect to Mars stresses the *energies, action* and the *aggressive urge.*

The conjunction emphasizes *applied energy.*

The opposition gives awareness of *your own or the other person's motivation.*

The square challenges you and brings out your *aggressive urge.*

The trine gives flow and ease *to the motivating force and energy you are generating.*

The sextile provides opportunity for the *expression of positive energy.*

The inconjunct shows that some sort of adjustment must be made *before the energy finds a productive outlet.*

Conjunctions

♂ ♂ ♃ MARS CONJUNCT JUPITER

Energy and enthusiasm combine to produce ambition, wealth and luck. You are liberal, self-confident and good at making decisions. Open, frank and generous, you tend to accumulate material possessions. This aspect often indicates a love of sports and the possibility of gain through a military career. Your restlessness and fearlessness enable you to take on any and all adversaries. It is easy for you to propel yourself into the limelight. If you drive yourself too hard, your biggest problem may be physical exhaustion.

Billionaire John D. Rockefeller, Sr., decathlon champion Rafer Johnson.

♂☌♄ MARS CONJUNCT SATURN

Although you have good organizational ability, you experience a conflict between inhibition (♄) and action (♂). You find it hard to control your energy flow; it is like driving with one foot on the brake and the other on the gas. However, your sense of economy and judgment enables you to take sound action. If this conjunction is challenged by difficult aspects, you may develop a persecution complex, sex problems or some physical difficulty which relates to the sign of the conjunction.

Singer Sonny Bono, French President Valery Giscard d'Estaing.

♂☌♅ MARS CONJUNCT URANUS

Willful and somewhat intolerant, you operate by your own rules and rarely submit to any restraint. You are volatile and courageous; you thrive on hard work and do your best in times of danger. Any occupation that requires both great energy and daring, such as sports, exploration, mechanics or industry, is ideal for you, as long as you realize that you must take safety precautions. With afflictions, you can be extremely accident-prone.

Boxer Joe Frazier, skier Jean Claude Killy.

♂☌♆ MARS CONJUNCT NEPTUNE

Because you are imaginative, emotional and sensation-loving, you must learn to sublimate your feelings. Your enthusiasm,

while boundless, is not always controlled; you often feel that you are above the common law. You may have a drug or drinking problem if either Cancer or the twelfth house is involved. You are magnetic and can be psychic. If you are strongly motivated you can be a crusader. With difficult aspects you must be careful in romantic affairs; you may be subject to treachery. All Mars-Neptune aspects create steam and energy; you need an escape valve.
Poet Percy Shelley, TV producer Gene Roddenberry.

♂ ♂ ♀ MARS CONJUNCT PLUTO

Highly emotional, you must learn to control your strong desires. You are a hard worker with regenerative qualities and are able to cope with any situation because of your great endurance, but your objectives can become obsessive. If you express the energy of this conjunction positively you can be dynamic and courageous; if you express it destructively, you can be cruel, brutal and sadistic.
Comedian Mort Sahl, actor Robert Mitchum.

Squares and Oppositions

♂ □ ♃ MARS SQUARE JUPITER
♂ ♂ ♃ MARS OPPOSITION JUPITER

If you do not develop discipline you can waste your talents through impulsive and misdirected energy. You are a very hard worker but are sporadic and become impatient if you don't get immediate results. You tend to overdo everything; this aspect can manifest itself negatively as discontent or resentment. Make sure that you define your goals well.
Football player Jim Brown (□), White House aide H.R. Haldeman (♂).

♂ □ ♄ MARS SQUARE SATURN
♂ ☍ ♄ MARS OPPOSITION SATURN

You alternate between aggression and apathy. Timing is not your strong point, but once you become aware of what you need to do, you can achieve success. You can be selfish and egotistical and must learn how to sublimate your will to that of others. This aspect can indicate some possibility of physical violence or the early loss of a parent. You should take care of your health.

Lawrence of Arabia (□), White House chief of staff Hamilton Jordan (☍).

♂ □ ♅ MARS SQUARE URANUS
♂ ☍ ♅ MARS OPPOSITION URANUS

Although you are self-willed and contradictory, once you learn a little self-restraint you are a leader who can go far. You are accident-prone and liable to risks, violence and overwork. It is important that you learn to recognize your limitations. You have a tendency for reckless love affairs. Marriage or an ordered way of life is probably not for you.

Actor Lee Marvin (□), playwright Arthur Miller (☍).

♂ □ ♆ MARS SQUARE NEPTUNE
♂ ☍ ♆ MARS OPPOSITION NEPTUNE

Your strong imagination and creative ability will enable you to reach great heights. However, a casual attitude can lead you into unsavory situations. You seem to look for trouble, and you are especially vulnerable to deceit. Be careful with drugs because you are susceptible to drug allergies. You are also susceptible to food poisoning and infection. You must learn to handle alcohol or it could become a problem.

TV personality Mike Douglas (□), Ethel Kennedy (Mrs. Robert F.) (☍).

♂ □ ♀ MARS SQUARE PLUTO
○ ♂ ☌ ♀ MARS OPPOSITION PLUTO

Forceful and aggressive, you come on strong. You must control your tendency to ride roughshod over others. When you are angry you may resort to physical violence. Your tendency to be abusive when frustrated can cause havoc in your personal relationships. Your strong sex drive requires a proper emotional outlet; you should not let it dominate your life to the exclusion of your creative instincts.
Governor Huey Long (□), Canadian Prime Minister Joe Clark (☌).

Trines and Sextiles

♂ △ ♃ MARS TRINE JUPITER
○ ♂ ✶ ♃ MARS SEXTILE JUPITER

You are optimistic and enthusiastic. With your broad viewpoint you make a good leader or manager. Jupiter supplies direction and Mars provides the energy. You are liberal, loyal, proud and self-confident; you are probably interested in sports, politics and travel. Even if you never achieve significant material wealth, you will always be comfortable with a steady income. Because you are secure in your own beliefs, you are a true idealist.
Joan Kennedy (Mrs. Edward F.) (△), singer John Davidson (✶).

♂ △ ♄ MARS TRINE SATURN
♂ ✶ ♄ MARS SEXTILE SATURN

You lead an organized, disciplined life and accept hardship well, in fact you may even thrive on it. You have a powerful follow-through and know when to fight and when to run. This is a good aspect for the military or engineering fields. Home, family and the respect of others are very important to you.
Actress Lauren Bacall (△), Governor Tom Dewey (✶).

♂△♅ MARS TRINE URANUS
♂⚹♅ MARS SEXTILE URANUS

You are a diligent worker who expresses enthusiasm, creative energy and physical strength. You have a tremendous drive and a positive attitude; this enables you to get a great deal accomplished in a hurry. You would do well in any field that lets you move around and be original and inventive. Your strong sexual drive expresses itself both impulsively and romantically.
Baseball player Willie Mays (△), astronaut Neil Armstrong (⚹).

♂△♆ MARS TRINE NEPTUNE
♂⚹♆ MARS SEXTILE NEPTUNE

Sympathetic and inspirational, you always look for the best in others. You would do well in service fields or in occupations which help others. Imaginative and artistic, you could be talented in music or literature. Although you are loving and emotional, you also know self-control. You can do well in any Neptunian field such as acting, medicine, shipping or oil.
Writer Louisa May Alcott (△), singer/composer Anthony Newley (⚹).

♂△♇ MARS TRINE PLUTO
♂⚹♇ MARS SEXTILE PLUTO

You use your emotional and physical energy positively; this enables you to become deeply involved and committed to righting society's wrongs. You will probably dedicate yourself to helping others. Your courage and self-confidence mark you as a leader; you have good aptitude for many fields, including technology, medicine, sports, surgery and industry.
Governor John Connally (△), writer Ross MacDonald (⚹).

Inconjuncts (Quincunxes)

♂ ⚻ ♃ MARS INCONJUNCT JUPITER

You tend to take on more than you can handle in your work, then you find it difficult to live up to your promises. Philanthropic, sympathetic and kind, you feel a need to take care of others, whether or not they want you to. When other people reject your offers of help, you then feel hurt. You may be victimized by people who take advantage of your willingness to become involved in unrealistic goals.
Statesman Benjamin Franklin, Prime Minister Menachim Begin.

♂ ⚻ ♄ MARS INCONJUNCT SATURN

It is not easy for you to determine where your responsibilities lie, and you find it difficult to cooperate with people. You either think that others are more talented and capable than you, or you arrogantly assume that you are the only one who knows the proper way to handle things.
Writer Oscar Wilde, comedian Bill Cosby.

♂ ⚻ ♅ MARS INCONJUNCT URANUS

You feel constantly under pressure. When you are frustrated you act hastily and with antagonism. You must learn to think before you speak, or you may alienate others. Vulnerable to public criticism, you must develop patience and learn to listen to other people's ideas.
Governor George Wallace, pop star David Bowie.

♂ ⚻ ♆ MARS INCONJUNCT NEPTUNE

This aspect shows a tendency to exaggerate and to have unrealistic ambitions that may be hard to realize. You leave

yourself open to deception in personal relationships because you expect the best of everybody. Those around you may find it difficult, if not impossible, to live up to your ideals.
Showman P.T. Barnum, tennis player Arthur Ashe.

♂ ⚻ ♀ MARS INCONJUNCT PLUTO

You are compulsively aggressive and domineering in your work; this can result in opposition and a lack of cooperation from your co-workers. You must learn to relax and roll with the punches, or you may suffer from total mental and physical exhaustion. Don't let others make too many demands on your time and efforts.
Writer Edward Bulwer-Lytton, Governor Pat Brown.

Lesson 13: Jupiter

Important Comments

By now you have delineated five planets in Judy Garland's chart. If you have followed the procedure of checking our keywords and explanations, if you have been discriminating with words and phrases and if you have looked at our answers in the Appendix and thought about why we omitted certain words and phrases, then you should understand the principles involved in delineation. You are probably finding this process easier and easier as you go along.

But before you become overly sure of yourself as an astrologer, let us re-emphasize one of the most important facets of astrology, the *free will*.

There is a nice saying that has been around for years that tells it all: *The stars impel, they do not compel!* The chart shows your basic traits, characteristics and potentials, but what you do with these depends totally on your choice, your attitude and your free will.

Applying this to Judy Garland's chart, we saw that she not only had musical and acting talent, but she could also have been a writer. Obviously, since we know her life fairly well (at least her public life), she did not choose to use that particular talent, putting her effort into acting and singing instead.

We also noticed at least two or three times that her home and family were very important to her. Yet we know, according to her daughters, that although she was a loving mother, she did not have much time to be a homemaker. That doesn't mean that she did not have the inclination. She chose her career above her family; that was her free will. Of course, in hindsight you can say that she had a very ambitious mother who pushed her into a career from early childhood on and that she got used to hard work and fame before she was old enough to have a family. However, had she really wanted to, she could have renounced it all and become a homemaker. She didn't. Her Moon, ruler of her Ascendant, is in the sixth house of work; so is her Mars, the planet of action; therefore work was important to her. But with three planets and the Ascendant in the home-loving, domestic and nurturing sign Cancer, she could have gone either way. This is what we mean by free will.

We cannot predict what a person will choose in life; nobody knows which potentials someone will use. All we know is what you are born with: what is easy for you and what is difficult; what is good for you and what may hurt you. The rest is up to each individual, your choice and free will.

Now we will go on to lesson 13. After you have studied it, please delineate Judy Garland's Jupiter. Our answers are in the Appendix on page 295.

Jupiter in the Signs

Jupiter represents the principle of *expansion* in a chart; therefore the keywords indicate possible types of growth and expansion.

♃ ♈ JUPITER IN ARIES
keyword *enthusiastic*

You are heroic, militant, ardent, generous and have executive ability, a talent for leadership and a strong wish for freedom of action. Able to analyze past errors and profit by them, you are capable of innovations in the fields of philosophy and education. You can be too egocentric and should channel this me-first tendency into ways to inspire others. With difficult aspects, you can be rash, impetuous, willful and even atheistic.

Religious leader Mary Baker Eddy, actress Shirley Temple, broadcaster Lowell Thomas, writer Helen Keller, comedienne Lily Tomlin.

♃ ♉ JUPITER IN TAURUS
keyword *manifest*

At home with financial dealings, you may be a whiz when it comes to investments and finance. You would do well in your own business or working with other people's money, perhaps as a stockbroker or a banker. With good aspects, you have a deep understanding of the true value of life. You like the luxury that money can buy. Quietly stubborn, you dislike being pushed and are concerned with justice and orthodox religion. If your Jupiter is afflicted, your expensive tastes can lead to self-indulgence, dissipation and laziness.

Musician John Lennon, architect Frank Lloyd Wright, Pope John XXIII, Senator William Fullbright, Governor John Connally.

♃ ♊ JUPITER IN GEMINI
keyword *fluctuating*   detriment

You are self-educated, diplomatic and broad-minded, and your great originality and alertness can make you the idea person in some organization. Although you are basically cheerful and fun-loving, you have a temperamental streak which can show itself unexpectedly. You express your talents in many ways; you could own a boutique, write or teach philosophy or run a mail-order business. Separation from your siblings and more than one marriage are strong possibilities with Jupiter in Gemini. With challenging aspects, you must avoid being an intellectual snob and must learn to handle your restlessness.

Actress Ingrid Bergman, industrialist Henry J. Kaiser, actor Steve McQueen, composer Igor Stravinsky, boxer Muhammad Ali.

♃ ♋ JUPITER IN CANCER
keyword ***generous***   exaltation

Your grace, sympathy and poise indicate your ability for public relations. Because you enjoy contact with all sorts of people, you can also excel in sales work. Jupiter in Cancer indicates a good family background and a deep love of children; you tend to establish a secure home and share it with friends and relatives. Take care not to become too sentimental or too involved with your family; you also must watch a tendency to overeat. You handle money well, and you can profit from real estate.

Writer Marcel Proust, actor John Wayne, President Harry Truman, millionaire Jay Gould, musician Paul McCartney.

♃ ♌ JUPITER IN LEO
keyword ***exuberant***

Helpful and ambitious, you are able to cope with almost any situation and would do well in the political ring. Because you are anxious to figure out and achieve your goals, you act while others dream. You have a dramatic and colorful personality and much enthusiasm for the good life. Your many talents make you a natural entertainer or public person. With challenging aspects, you can be conceited or arrogant and you may overdo everything. Your health is generally good, but you could develop heart and/or weight problems.

Singer Johnny Cash, President Lyndon B. Johnson, writer Victor Hugo, jockey Willie Shoemaker, actor Rex Harrison.

♃ ♍ JUPITER IN VIRGO
keyword *dutiful*

You are able to gain the cooperation of others and you set high standards in whatever you do. You are a natural scholar with lofty ideals and you must watch your tendency to expect too much from others. You are analytical, practical and kind, however you may be too narrow in your affections. Virgo's concern with details can conflict with the natural expansiveness of Jupiter; so you may make mountains out of molehills. Cleanliness and order are very important to you unless Jupiter has difficult aspects; then you can be sloppy, lazy, dissatisfied and bohemian. You do well in mental health, education, nutrition or hospital work.

Senator Barry Goldwater, comic-strip artist Al Capp, poet Robert Frost, Prince Philip of Great Britain, singer Mick Jagger.

♃ ♎ JUPITER IN LIBRA
keyword *hospitable*

You are poised, sincere and domestic. You cherish your leisure time and its pleasures and tend to let the rest of the world go by. Your artistic ability, good taste and fine conversational instincts make you very popular. You are concerned with justice, and others will trust your judgment. You need a partner. Refined and idealistic, you may dislike manual work. With difficult aspects, you may tend to make moral decisions for others and desire to be all things to all people. Sometimes you operate on a double standard, and you may have legal problems.

Singer Bing Crosby, writers Gertrude Stein and George Sand, singer Cher, actress Sophia Loren.

♃ ♏ JUPITER IN SCORPIO
keyword *persevering*

Active, you have great faith in yourself and like to exercise willpower over others. You like luxurious living and will probably earn enough to assure it. Courageous and faithful, you approach life with deep insight and are interested in the mystical and the occult. You are intense and uncompromising about your beliefs and standards. Your judgment is shrewd, and you can have magnetic healing power. Archaeology, music, medicine, corporate finance, taxes and insurance are all areas which should appeal to you. With challenging aspects, you must learn to handle deviousness, bad investments and maybe a loss of inheritance.

Gangster Al Capone, writer Jack London, murder cult leader Charles Manson, evangelist Billy Sunday, singer Elvis Presley.

♃ ♐ JUPITER IN SAGITTARIUS
keyword *temperate*   dignity

You are able to sense opportunity and act upon it. Because you are sociable, you need to be among people, and you like youngsters and animals. You enjoy making life brighter for others. You are usually a director or manager, rarely a subordinate, and you are farsighted and often a deep thinker. Fond of luxury, you can spend money on a whim. Optimistic and outgoing, you are drawn to the outdoors, religion and sports. Difficult aspects can make you narrow-minded, self-righteous, reckless and indiscriminate.

Football coach Knute Rockne, golfer Ben Hogan, President Jimmy Carter, artist Toulouse Lautrec, singer Alice Cooper.

♃ ♑ JUPITER IN CAPRICORN
keyword *expedient*   fall

You are honorable, puritanical and austere. Ambitious, you need a career that provides enough financial assets for good security. You are conservative and could successfully run your own business, or you could also do well working for a large organization. Your patience and dedication enable you to attain wealth, but you can be penny-wise and pound-foolish. You abhor waste and extravagance, you have high morals which you adhere to, and you excel in land dealings. Im-

properly handled, this position of Jupiter can make you miserly, bigoted, overly orthodox and a martyr.
Explorer Christopher Columbus, political philosopher Karl Marx, ex-First Lady Pat Nixon, filmmaker Walt Disney, TV personality Johnny Carson.

♃ ♒ JUPITER IN AQUARIUS
keyword *tolerant*

Inspiration is your guide and you have a great need to help people. You do not like routine work. You are very respectful of others' views and receptive to new ideas. Just, considerate, sociable and studious, you are quite political and have an impartial and democratic approach to life. You make no racial, class or religious distinctions. You will do well in any career because of your good judgment, intellect and originality. Challenging aspects may cause you to be tactless, intolerant, unrealistic and revolutionary.
President Dwight Eisenhower, Rose Kennedy (mother of President John F.), writer John Steinbeck, actress Jane Fonda, White House aide H.R. Haldeman.

♃ ♓ JUPITER IN PISCES
keyword *imaginative*

You are kind, quiet, friendly and unassuming. You are naturally drawn to others and spend time trying to help them. Because of your sympathetic nature and the quiet assurance of your mannerisms, you are popular. You champion the underdog, and at times you can be too compassionate. You would make a good doctor, nurse or veterinarian. You are not ambitious in the worldly sense and need periodic seclusion. With afflictions, this placement can cause self-sacrifice, shirking of responsibility and over-emotionalism. It can also produce social parasites.
Artist Leonardo Da Vinci, President Abraham Lincoln, pediatrician Benjamin Spock, writer Edgar Allan Poe, writer Ross MacDonald.

Jupiter in the Houses

JUPITER IN THE FIRST HOUSE
keyword *cheerful*

Broad-minded, breezy and optimistic, you love travel and the open air. Your kind, happy disposition attracts helpful people. Logical and poised, you have a good sense of humor, tremendous vital force and an interest in sports (at which you usually excel). You are an executive type. When mishandled, Jupiter here can make you too pleasure-loving, self-indulgent, lazy, extravagant, conceited and impatient; you could also have weight problems.
Writer Guy deMaupassant, singer Ethel Waters, President Charles deGaulle, White House aide John Dean.

JUPITER IN THE SECOND HOUSE
keyword *prosperous*

You are fortunate financially because you can do much with little. This is a very good position for business, but the type of business depends on the house Jupiter rules and the sign it is in. Banking, stocks and bonds, travel, sales, import-export and insurance may all be good fields. You have an inner optimism and others find you likeable and appealing. With difficult aspects, you may have a tendency to be a showy spendthrift, and you can suffer financial losses because of your careless attitude toward money.
Actress Linda Lovelace, Field Marshall Erwin Rommel, writers Grace Metalious and Alex Haley.

JUPITER IN THE THIRD HOUSE
keyword *optimistic*

Your success comes through educational matters or through writing and communication. You are witty and happy-go-lucky. You have good relationships with your relatives, with a lot of give-and-take. You are practical; your ideals are high;

your intuition is strong, and you possess good common sense. Because you have a restless mind, you need a non-routine job. With difficult aspects, you are too talkative, imprudent and prone to exaggerate.

Singer Enrico Caruso, President Jimmy Carter, labor leader Walter Reuther, actress Linda Darnell.

JUPITER IN THE FOURTH HOUSE

keyword *loyal*   accidental exaltation

You are devoted to your home and family and often receive help from your parents. You do well in your place of birth and can expect to be comfortable in your old age. You enjoy open spaces; perhaps you would like to live in a large home on a hill. Your generous, outgoing personality needs expansive and pleasant surroundings. With challenging aspects, you can be grasping and greedy and suffer a loss of parental influence. Sometimes this placement indicates a very militant early home.

Actress Carol Channing, writer James Joyce, labor leader John L. Lewis, writer Leo Tolstoi.

JUPITER IN THE FIFTH HOUSE

keyword *buoyant*

You have a love of grandeur and do things in a big way. Sports, children, creative activities and romance are only some of your varied interests. You are lucky in speculation and gambling, particularly if Jupiter is well-aspected. This placement can indicate a large family; your children will be successful and beneficial to you. It is a good position for teaching, publishing and entertainment. When misused, you can be too daring, reckless and overly sensuous.

Nazi leader Hermann Goering, philosopher Isaac Newton, aviator Amelia Earhart, singer Edith Piaf.

JUPITER IN THE SIXTH HOUSE
keyword *philanthropic*

You are a cheerful and lucky worker, as work is always available to you and usually well paid. You have good organizational ability, are generous and get along well with your fellow workers. Your health is good and your recuperative powers are strong. If Jupiter is afflicted, you may have a tendency for tumors, liver and weight problems, or you may have an arrogant attitude that turns others away from you.
Musician Guy Lombardo, singer Liza Minelli, nurse Florence Nightingale, producer Sam Peckinpah.

JUPITER IN THE SEVENTH HOUSE
keyword *notable*

This placement usually indicates a fortunate marriage and/or business partnership. Unless the aspects are extremely difficult, Jupiter in the seventh house rarely brings divorce. There may be good luck in legal affairs and a tendency to marry someone with money. Jupiter here usually indicates someone who lavishes affection on a spouse. Be careful not to be overly optimistic in your dealings with others if Jupiter has difficult aspects.
Ice skater Dick Button, Indian leader Mohandas Gandhi, evangelist Billy Graham, ex-First Lady Jaqueline Kennedy Onassis.

JUPITER IN THE EIGHTH HOUSE
keyword *discerning*

You are resourceful and handle money well. You could handle money for others in fields such as accounting, banking and business management. This placement promises a long life and a peaceful demise. Your attitude towards life and death is good. You may obtain money through partnership or inheritance. You are emotional and have a strong sex drive.

With difficult aspects, you can be extravagant, dishonest and lacking in judgment.
Scientist Louis Pasteur, writer Oscar Wilde, baseball player Maury Wills, actor Yul Brynner.

JUPITER IN THE NINTH HOUSE
keyword *orthodox*   accidental dignity

You are faithful, tolerant, devoted, aspiring and interested in religion and philosophy. You enjoy life abroad, get along well with foreigners and definitely should travel. Higher education is a must, and you have a flair for languages, writing and publishing as well as lecturing and public speaking. Your faults are arrogance and a love of display, but Jupiter here usually works in a positive way.
Chancellor Konrad Adenauer, fighter pilot Eddie Rickenbacker, writer John Steinbeck, TV personality Steve Allen.

JUPITER IN THE TENTH HOUSE
keyword *successful*

Because of your leadership ability, self-reliance and trustworthiness, this position is excellent for success in business and/or politics. You have many opportunites to advance. Socially, you are very active. Your strong sense of justice indicates that you would do well in law. Your moral standards are high. You are proud, materialistic and ambitious; recognition comes early in life. With difficult aspects, you can be arrogant and overbearing.
Actor James Dean, boxer Muhammad Ali, composer George Gershwin, Queen Victoria.

JUPITER IN THE ELEVENTH HOUSE
keyword *benevolent*

You set goals for yourself and usually achieve them with minimum effort. Sociable and pleasure-loving, you have many friends and helpful aquaintances. You are successful in large organizations, groups, clubs or religious affiliations. Your judgment is good; your intuition is strong, and you can benefit through travel. You probably have a large family to whom you are devoted. When used negatively, you can take advantage of your friends, and you may be a leech.

Singer Nelson Eddy, actor Ryan O'Neal, pianist Ignace Paderewski, labor leader James Hoffa.

JUPITER IN THE TWELFTH HOUSE
keyword ***charitable***

This placement of Jupiter gives great protection; it is like having an angel on your shoulder. You are kind, hospitable and like to give secretly. Very resourceful when you are in trouble, you are always ready to help someone else; you need to be needed. You are very dependent on other people's reactions to you. Success usually comes in your middle years. This placement is good for work in medicine, research, poetry, dancing, acting or social work. When misused, you may be self-indulgent, doubting, and you may act in haste with poor timing.

Scientist Galileo Galilei, colonizer Cecil Rhodes, baseball player Babe Ruth, Secretary of State George Marshall.

Jupiter in Aspect

Any aspects to Jupiter stress *expansion, philosophic reasoning* and *protection*.

The conjunction emphasizes *expansion*.

The square and opposition challenge you to *the proper expression of your expansive urge*.

The trine and sextile make it *easy for you to operate positively*.

The inconjunct requires a *reorganization of the protective principle*.

Conjunctions

✓ ♃ ☌ ♄ JUPITER CONJUNCT SATURN

Although life seems hard and there is constant struggle, you have a specific mission to fulfill and go about this with great singleness of purpose. This conjunction shows an integration of fundamental motives: poise (♃) and hard work (♄). You are usually fortunate within the establishment and have big-business ability as well as intellectual and political power. If you are religious, it is in an orthodox way. When there are challenging aspects to this conjunction, you may lack discrimination and inner guidance.
Physicist Enrico Fermi, writer Alex Haley.

✓ ♃ ☌ ♅ JUPITER CONJUNCT URANUS

You are restless and dislike restriction. This conjunction shows a deep respect for knowledge; you may be a genius and feel that you must learn everything there is to know. You are interested in anything new and progressive, and you may have a strong belief in the occult. Generous and encouraging to your friends, you will often have opportunity for unexpected travel.
Vice President Walter Mondale, war correspondent Ernie Pyle.

♃ ☌ ♆ JUPITER CONJUNCT NEPTUNE

You have a fertile imagination that you can express in numerous creative fields. Musical, artistic and visionary, you must always watch a tendency to be excessive. Sympathetic and idealistic, you may be drawn to the religious life; sometimes offbeat religions attract you. With difficult aspects, you may live in a world of private fantasy, becoming totally escapist.
Filmmakers Cecil DeMille and Federico Fellini.

♃ ♂ ♀ JUPITER CONJUNCT PLUTO

You are determined to enjoy life to the fullest. Dedicated to your ideals, you have a strong drive to achieve your goals. This aspect is often called the kingmaker, as it shows the ability and power of leaders. If misused, you may become totally self-centered and exclude all relationships with others.
Conductor/composer Leonard Bernstein, French revolutionary Maximilien Robespierre.

Squares and Oppositions

♃ □ ♄ JUPITER SQUARE SATURN
♃ ♂ ♄ JUPITER OPPOSITION SATURN

Because you are unable to recognize your limitations, you plod steadily forward in the face of adversity. Success comes late in life, and sometimes you feel that you never get true recognition. Although you are materialistic and conscientious, you lack direction and drive. You must recognize your own self-worth and stop comparing yourself unfavorably to others. You may experience danger from some natural disaster such as flood, earthquake or epidemic.
Actress Suzanne Somers (□), billionaire J. Paul Getty (♂).

♃ □ ♅ JUPITER SQUARE URANUS
♃ ♂ ♅ JUPITER OPPOSITION URANUS

You are critical of accepted codes and try to do something to change them; however, you may bite off more than you can chew. Enthusiastic, independent, outspoken and willful, you want to start at the top, but your success depends upon proper preparation. This aspect suggests that you should not engage in speculation or gambling. You must learn moderation in all things and avoid a tendency to be hypocritical.
President Jimmy Carter (□), aviator Billy Mitchell (♂).

♃ □ ♆ JUPITER SQUARE NEPTUNE
♃ ☍ ♆ JUPITER OPPOSITION NEPTUNE

You are creative and talented, but you must develop self-discipline to channel your energies in a productive direction. You are prone to exaggerate and are careless in monetary and speculative dealings; this can lead to legal or financial problems. You are somewhat revolutionary and may be overemotional in your personal involvements.
Opera singer Cesare Siepi (□), Cuban leader Fidel Castro (☍).

♃ □ ♀ JUPITER SQUARE PLUTO
♃ ☍ ♀ JUPITER OPPOSITION PLUTO

You rarely agree with accepted codes. You set yourself up as a law unto yourself, but then find it hard to accept the consequences. Dogmatic, exaggerating and arrogant, you could be an adventurer and gambler. You seesaw between overconfidence and great self-doubt, and you must learn to profit from your experiences. Be scrupulously careful not to exploit others for your own benefit.
Artist Grandma Moses (□), ambassador Joseph Kennedy (☍).

Trines and Sextiles

♃ △ ♄ JUPITER TRINE SATURN
♃ ⚹ ♄ JUPITER SEXTILE SATURN

This is a fortunate aspect. It indicates constructive power and material success because you are able to set realistic goals for yourself. There is serious purpose to your life, and you are strongly influenced by family tradition. However, you may tend to take the easy way out unless there are also squares and oppositions involving these planets.
Actress Bette Davis (△), comedian Bob Hope (⚹).

♃ △ ♅ JUPITER TRINE URANUS
♃ ✳ ♅ JUPITER SEXTILE URANUS

Original, creative, determined and practical, you can achieve any goal you set for yourself. Your personal liberty is important; you refuse to be tied down to convention and propriety. You are often a mental giant, and you are warm but not at all sentimental.
Industrialist Henry Ford, Sr. (△), singer Sammy Davis, Jr. (✳).

♃ △ ♆ JUPITER TRINE NEPTUNE
♃ ✳ ♆ JUPITER SEXTILE NEPTUNE

You are strongly spiritual and religious, and you like to help others. You would do well in careers involving education, social work, counseling, religion or writing. You are musical and creative, and you have a deep understanding of the mystical and the occult. Often you have psychic ability which you use in a beneficial way.
Mystery writer Agatha Christie (△), poet Arthur Rimbaud (✳).

♃ △ ♇ JUPITER TRINE PLUTO
♃ ✳ ♇ JUPITER SEXTILE PLUTO

You are exuberant, enthusiastic and ambitious, and you encourage others to explore their potentials as much as you do yours. You have great organizational skill, and you are most productive in business, education and politics; however, you are interested in practically everything, so there is no limit to your possibilities.
Artist Michelangelo (△), bandleader Vincent Lopez (✳).

Inconjuncts (Quincunxes)

♃ ⚻ ♄ JUPITER INCONJUNCT SATURN

You must learn timing and proper perspective in your relationships. You alternate between caution and unrealistic expectations and tend to let others expect too much of you. You should avoid any religious prejudice or self-righteous attitudes.
Writer Pearl Buck, Believe-it-or-not Robert Ripley.

♃ ⚻ ♅ JUPITER INCONJUNCT URANUS

Overly optimistic, you seldom give enough attention to details, and your aims are not in line with your capabilities. Learn self-discipline and proper management; this can keep you out of financial and legal difficulties. Don't let people pressure you into situations where they will demand that you prove your friendship.
Psychic Uri Geller, supersalesman Earl C. Anthony.

♃ ⚻ ♆ JUPITER INCONJUNCT NEPTUNE

This aspect shows that an adjustment is needed between your emotions, your intellect and your creative expression. You must learn to distinguish between real and imagined obligations, especially involving serving others. You often intrude into other people's affairs and then feel bitter when you are rejected.
Writers Fannie Hurst and Jean Cocteau.

♃ ⚻ ♀ JUPITER INCONJUNCT PLUTO

You are very assertive and may try to press your ideas and ideals on others without considering whether or not they are interested. Often you must compensate for a lack of educa-

tion, or it may be difficult for you to get ahead professionally. You can be forceful and self-important, or you may imagine that others are keeping you from fulfillment.
President Jimmy Carter, conductor Zubin Mehta.

Lesson 14: Saturn

Important Comments

Did you enjoy delineating Jupiter? We hope so. The more you practice interpretation, the easier it will become.

Before you delve into the realms of Saturn, here are a few more thoughts that seem to help our students to understand the basic principles of astrology.

A very important factor in a chart is the *sign* a planet is posited in. The Moon in Sagittarius will work quite differently from the Moon in Cancer or Capricorn. An equally important facet is the *house* that a planet falls in. The Moon in Sagittarius in the sixth house is quite different from the Moon in Sagittarius in the fifth house. Third in importance are the *aspects*. The Moon square the Sun will work differently from the Moon trine the Sun.

After you truly understand the keywords and key phrases

for the signs, planets, houses and aspects, they will become second nature to you. Delineating will be easy, and the only thing that will keep you from being bored is the wonderful realization that no two people are alike.

Keep up the good work, study our notes on Saturn, and then delineate Judy Garland's Saturn. Our interpretation is in the Appendix on page 296.

Saturn represents the *learning principle*. A lesson learned through Saturn is a lesson you will never forget.

Saturn in the Signs

♄ ♈ SATURN IN ARIES
keyword *ingenious*   fall

It is up to you to develop your many resources to strengthen your character. This is a difficult placement because Saturn imposes delays on the drive and energy of Aries. You are egocentric, and you find it difficult to recognize the rights of others. If you channel this energy properly, you will combine initiative with discipline and be very persistent. Then you will use your inventiveness to great advantage by taking charge in a positive way. Your many subconscious fears give you a strong desire for security. This position can indicate a father complex, or in a woman's chart, a jealous mate. Although your sense of timing is not the best, you have strong reasoning power and love a debate. With difficult aspects, you may be superficial, defensive, impatient and may constantly feel a need to justify yourself. You should learn tact and cooperation with others. Physical exercise is recommended.
Dancer Rudolf Nureyev, dictator Joseph Stalin, physicist Albert Einstein, religious leader Mary Baker Eddy, Governor Edmund G. (Jerry) Brown.

♄ ♉ SATURN IN TAURUS
keyword *trustworthy*

You have a strong need for financial and emotional security and feel happiest when your daily affairs are in order. Your nature is characterized by patience, discipline, determination, practicality and adherence to principles. You approach life with a matter-of-fact attitude. You may lack spontaneity but are willing to work hard for success. Big business, politics and the arts are fields that appeal to you. Thrifty, you acquire material goods for their useful qualities. Your stamina is great, and so is your stubbornness. You are possessive of your loved ones. You will only find inner peace when your sense of values becomes more evolved or when you learn to use your creative potential. Challenging aspects may lead to miserliness, excessive materialism or lack of response to love and beauty.

Composer Igor Stravinsky, Senator Henry Jackson, artist Pablo Picasso, singer Joan Baez, ex-First Lady Pat Nixon.

♄ ♊ SATURN IN GEMINI
keyword *scientific*

You are adaptable, systematic and logical because you can detach yourself and approach matters coolly and rationally. You have great capacity for reasoning, solving problems and writing. This position of Saturn is excellent for mental, intellectual, scientific or mathematical fields. Teaching, research, engineering and secretarial work are good career possibilities. You like to study and will continue to learn throughout your life. It is important that you develop an honest approach to relationships. Saturn adds discipline to Gemini, making the mental functions more practical. Physically, your weak point is your lungs, and you should not smoke. You may experience nervous tension if you overtax your endurance. Difficult aspects can make you doubtful, too critical, and at times even suspicious. On the other hand, you might be shy, have trouble expressing yourself or be a slow thinker.

Writers Franz Kafka and Dante Alighieri, First Lady Eleanor Roosevelt, psychoanalyst Sigmund Freud, singer Paul Mc-Cartney.

♄ ♋ SATURN IN CANCER
keyword *security-conscious*   detriment

Inhibited in your show of love and emotions, you may feel isolated and shy. Your early family life could have lacked tenderness or been somehow troublesome; perhaps this has left you scarred. In spite of this, you are clannish and feel responsible toward your family. In order to preserve an aura of dignity, you hide your inner thoughts and feelings. Although you cry a lot, you cry in private; all people see is your melancholy. Although you need approval and love, your home life is often unstable. Your feelings are easily hurt, yet you lack understanding of others; as much as you would like to help others, you often fail. To achieve material goals, you can be very shrewd and able. You are subject to nervous strain and should guard against gaining weight because of water retention. Challenging aspects can produce hypersensitivity, withdrawal from close involvements and a defensive attitude. *Artist Marc Chagall, playwright William Shakespeare, General George Patton, actress Mia Farrow, comedian Jackie Gleason.*

♄ ♌ SATURN IN LEO
keyword *self-assured*

You have a tremendous drive for personal recognition and control and seek leadership at all costs. You require attention and respect from others, and you are stubborn. As a parent you will be a strict disciplinarian. You should develop better attitudes in dealing with love, romance, children and matters of creative expression. At times, you may lack humor, but you have mental vitality and excellent ability for fields such as education, management and entertainment. Sometimes you are so cautious and reserved that you forget to enjoy life, especially if the aspects to Saturn are difficult. This could lead to disappointments in your love life, problems with your children, losses through speculation or back problems. *Dictator Adolf Hitler, actor Charlie Chaplin, Prime Minister Indira Gandi, pianist Liberace, musician Greg Allman.*

♄♍ SATURN IN VIRGO
keyword ***prudent***

You are practical, careful and hardworking, with a moral and conscientious attitude. You operate with efficiency, accuracy and precision; you will drive yourself and others. You work well in medicine, research, strategy and record-keeping. People sometimes resent that you pay so much attention to detail, punctuality and trivia; this may make you appear quite austere. You must develop a good sense of humor and try to overcome the tendency to worry. When you learn to discriminate between what is important and what is not, you will go far. You have much to offer the world. Difficult aspects can lead to a tendency to nag, a fear of the unknown and digestive problems.
Chief Justice Earl Warren, President Dwight D. Eisenhower, Governor George Wallace, Field Marshall Erwin Rommel, would-be assassin Arthur Bremer.

♄♎ SATURN IN LIBRA
keyword ***reasonable***   exaltation

Although your attitude is disciplined, responsible and serious, you are pleasant, philosophical and have a great sense of justice and fairness. This is a good placement for lawyers, judges and mediators; it is also good for organizational planning, business arrangements and government work. It can indicate a late marriage or partnership with a serious person. Marriage requires a need for patience and hard work; relating to others is one of the lessons to learn with Saturn in Libra. Socially aware, you often attain positions of honor and wealth. Diplomatic and tactful, you work well with others as you prefer cooperating to competing. Difficult aspects can make you demanding, intolerant, lacking in forgiveness and even insincere. You may have kidney problems.
Secretary of State Henry Kissinger, billionaire J. Paul Getty, Congressman Maurice Udall, comedian Jack Benny, astronaut Walter Schirra.

♄♏ SATURN IN SCORPIO
keyword *purposeful*

Your personality is magnetic, and your humor is stinging. You can do well in finance, the occult or any area which requires good repartee. You demand much of yourself and others, and your perfectionist nature has little patience with laziness or unwillingness to work. You have tremendous willpower, energy and intensity, but need to learn to react more calmly to life and its problems. Your approach is subtle, thorough, persistent and determined. You have a great drive for success and a strong ego. You are proud and resourceful, but you carry a deep resentment when you feel that someone has been unjust with you. Your desires are very strong, you can love and hate deeply. With challenging aspects you can be scheming, jealous and revengeful. If you have a poor mental attitude you can be unforgiving, secretive and afraid of dependency. This position can lead to gallstones, constipation or arthritic conditions.
Philosopher Krishnamurti, actors Richard Burton and Marlon Brando, comedian Jonathan Winters, writer Rod Serling.

♄♐ SATURN IN SAGITTARIUS
keyword *dignified*

You have a serious approach to religion, philosophy and higher education and try to adhere to honorable and strict moral codes. Independent and capable, you search for truth and justice. You are intellectually disciplined and have good powers of concentration. You earn what you achieve through hard work and application. You are interested in the occult, both spiritually and philosophically. Your reputation is very important to you; you are proud of your intellectual prowess and hurt when accused unjustly. You are outspoken, and your keen intuition and good scientific ability indicate that you can work well with those afflicted or limited. You could be a good teacher, preacher or political leader. Physical exercise to promote your circulation is important for you. With difficult aspects you could be self-righteous, indecisive, rebellious or resentful, and could try to impose your religious fervor on others.

Indian Leader Mohandas Gandhi, civil rights leader Martin Luther King, artist Henri Matisse, clown Emmett Kelly, ice skater Dick Button.

♄♑ SATURN IN CAPRICORN
keyword **organizing**   dignity

You are ambitious for power, prestige and authority. This is a good position for politics, business, science or any career that involves public acclaim. Since you are persistent, calculating, careful, practical and a good organizer you could easily fulfill your great need to achieve. You may appear cold and austere because you surround yourself with an aura of dignity. Able to accept orders from those above you, you expect the same from those below. You probably had to struggle in your early life to attain security. You are willing to work hard and feel that everyone should achieve through their own effort. With your good background, you value family, pride and honor. Depending on the aspects, you can achieve either a height of evolution and understanding or else the depth of materialism and selfishness. You tend to lack sensitivity and need to develop tolerance and a sense of humor. Your outlook is practical, serious and dutiful, but try to avoid becoming a lone wolf or being too rigid in your attitudes and beliefs. With challenging aspects, you may be unscrupulous in attaining your goals and lack confidence in yourself. You may also be selfish, dictatorial, lonely or overbearing. Physically you must take care of your bones and joints.

Aviator Charles Lindbergh, TV personality Ed Sullivan, U.N. Ambassador Adlai Stevenson, actress Anne Bancroft, anthropologist Margaret Mead.

♄♒ SATURN IN AQUARIUS
keyword **just**

You have strong powers of concentration, and your thinking is democratic and scientific. Inventive and original approaches come easily to you, as well as abstract mathematics and symbolism. You are ambitious, hard working and impartial. Your attitude toward people and relationships is responsible, and you are loyal in friendship. You work well in groups or organizations, as long as you can preserve a feeling of freedom and independence in all you do. Social relationships are important to you, but others may misunderstand your level-headed ways, and interpret them as too cool and collected. With difficult aspects, you may be selfish and resent doing anything that does not please you. You have too much intellectual pride and may lack gratitude or become a total loner. To overcome these tendencies you need time for deep reflection. Physically, you should keep your vital forces and circulation functioning well.

Psychoanalyst Carl Jung, attorney F. Lee Bailey, actress Greta Garbo, singer Pat Boone, writer Thomas Mann.

♄ ♓ SATURN IN PISCES
keyword *accepting*

Imaginative, in fact sometimes too imaginative, you tend to live in the past and may have difficulties dealing with the present. You have great emotional understanding and humility and a willingness to work with and for the underdog. Your perception of others is well developed, but you lack insight into yourself tending to underestimate your own worth. You need quiet and solitude to discover your many abilities; you would especially do well in the fields of literature, research or metaphysics. You may enjoy working behind the scenes, or you could find yourself in a large institution like a hospital, university or government agency. You take life too seriously and react emotionally. Guard against self-pity which can lead to depression, and try to practice emotional detachment. Difficult aspects can lead to excessive worry, psychosomatic illnesses and neurotic tendencies.

Psychic Edgar Cayce, writer Francoise Sagan, actress Jane Fonda, poet Anne Morrow Lindbergh, TV personality Tom Snyder.

Saturn in the Houses

SATURN IN THE FIRST HOUSE
keyword *inhibited*

You are reserved, serious, conscientious, patient and aristocratic. You desire power because you may have had limitations imposed on you during your childhood; possibly you were very shy, but now you want to go forward. You have a feeling of personal insecurity or inadequacy, but this feeling spurs you to great achievements. You have extensive responsibilities, and often this position indicates that you went to work early in life. You were very mature as a youngster, but will get younger as life goes on. If Saturn is very close to the Ascendant, it may indicate that your birth was difficult for your mother. With poor aspects, you may go through life feeling unloved; you can be selfish and suffer from depression.
General George Patton, consumer advocate Ralph Nader, educator Maria Montessori, White House aide Bill Moyers.

SATURN IN THE SECOND HOUSE
keyword *thrifty*

You have anxieties over money, which you earn by the sweat of your brow. You are sensible and orderly in all your financial matters, and although Saturn in this house does not deny money, your success comes slowly. You may be born to great wealth and be stingy in parting with it, or you may come from a background of poverty and overcompensate by making material goods your sole aim. You need to learn a lesson in values; peace of mind comes from the inside and not the outside. However, if Saturn is well aspected, this is a good placement for real estate investments.
Singer Barbra Streisand, President Gerald Ford, Queen Elizabeth II, Senator Birch Bayh.

SATURN IN THE THIRD HOUSE
keyword *careful*

You are patient, tactful and matter-of-fact. You probably had some difficulties with your siblings and grew up feeling lonely. This position of Saturn may indicate a lack of good early education or a lack of love in your childhood home. An able correspondent, you speak well with a mind that is penetrating and capable of good concentration. Your lungs are not strong, and you have many ungrounded fears toward anything that is new. Hard aspects make you feel picked on, or lead to a feeling of inadequacy or depression.

Heiress/revolutionary Patty Hearst, actresses Mia Farrow and Merle Oberon, playwright William Inge.

SATURN IN THE FOURTH HOUSE
keyword *conventional*

Anxious about old age, you have many responsibilities in your home; this could even include taking care of elderly relatives. There is a possibility of the early loss of a parent or difficulties with one of them. You are very attached to your family, and may cling too much to the past. Although you seem independent, you are afraid of leaving your parents; yet you will be much happier once you are away from your place of birth. You feel inadequate and insecure, but these feelings make you try doubly hard at anything you do; this can lead to great achievements. You take great pride in your family ancestry, love antiques and are successful in dealing with land or real estate. Poor aspects can lead to digestive problems due to excessive worry and emotionalism. A good spiritual attitude can help you overcome many of these restricting feelings.

Actress Judy Garland, physicist Albert Einstein, writer Ernest Hemingway, singer Peggy Lee.

SATURN IN THE FIFTH HOUSE
keyword *distant*

You tend to be cold and inhibited, which can lead to rejections in love or problems with children; these problems are mainly due to your inability to understand them. Your creative expression can be hampered unless you learn to give of yourself and take care of others. If you speculate, you will do it wisely and well. You can be a good teacher and disciplinarian. You are attracted to older people, and to those who have a serious and purposeful outlook in life. With challenging aspects to Saturn, you may experience timidity, psychological and sexual hangups or the frittering away of talents and potentials. Yet if you use this position well it can lead to deep love, loyalty, creativity and great scientific achievements.

Writer Zelda Fitzgerald, scientist Marie Curie, columnist Hedda Hopper, Governor Ronald Reagan, singer Mick Jagger.

SATURN IN THE SIXTH HOUSE
keyword *efficient*

Exacting, careful, efficient and reliable, you take your job seriously. You can excel in government work, writing or fields involving mathematics or science. You sometimes feel that you are indispensable and push yourself at the cost of your health. Chronic illness may plague you. Although you seem quiet and unsure of yourself, you do know your own worth. You must learn to blow your own horn and assert yourself. Your basic outlook is conservative, yet it is not necessarily reflected in your appearance or dress. With difficult aspects, you tend to worry and fret too much.

Vice President Nelson Rockefeller, actor Bob Crane, composer Johannes Brahms, writer Thomas Mann.

SATURN IN THE SEVENTH HOUSE
keyword *faithful*   accidental
                                      exaltation

You might experience difficulties or disappointments in marriage or partnerships, or you may have an age disparity with your partner. You have problems relating to others. It would be unwise to marry before you have come to grips with yourself and the outside world. You are cautious in your attitude toward the opposite sex—not without reason since you may have been rejected by the one of your choice. Responsible and adult in your attitudes, you often direct your desire to achieve into areas involving the public. With challenging aspects, a reversal or downfall may follow success and acceptance. Although you are outgoing and gregarious, you also need time to yourself to recharge your batteries. Your health might suffer if you don't take time to be alone. Difficult aspects may make you a loner.

Governor George Wallace, Cornelia Wallace (his wife), astronauts Buzz Aldrin and Neil Armstrong.

SATURN IN THE EIGHTH HOUSE
keyword *solicitous*

Always ready to accept the responsibility of handling your mate's money, you might even handle other people's finances, perhaps in banking or investment. Money does not come easily to you, but you are a hard worker, and when you earn it you know how to keep it. You have a serious approach to sex and are also interested in psychic and psychological matters. Life after death arouses your curiosity, and you will have many years to ponder this because you will probably live to a ripe old age. You have a good mind for legal matters, inheritances, taxes and politics. With difficult aspects, you may be inhibited and have bizarre sexual attitudes and appetites.

Pianist Liberace, Field Marshall Erwin Rommel, Chief Justice Earl Warren, Canadian Prime Minister Joe Clark.

SATURN IN THE NINTH HOUSE
keyword *thoughtful*

Orthodox in your approach, you distrust new ideas, yet you are earnest and desire to know everything thoroughly. Saturn here stabilizes your superconscious faculties; you can be a good teacher, professor, scientist or metaphysician. You could also be successful in publishing, politics, public speaking or preaching. Although foreign countries and foreigners fascinate you, your relationships with them might not be good. In youth your philosophies are dogmatic, but with age you become wiser and more tolerant. You have a whimsical sense of humor, and your mind is deep, meditative and reflective. With challenging aspects, you may be fanatic, intolerant and have a poor relationship with your in-laws. You may either avoid foreign travel, or overdo it and make too many long distance trips or moves.

Presidents Richard Nixon and Franklin D. Roosevelt, comedian Jack Benny, Governor Edmund G. (Jerry) Brown.

SATURN IN THE TENTH HOUSE
keyword *proper*   accidental dignity

You like, need and accept responsibility. Ambitious, demanding respect and determined to succeed, you have excellent business ability. You are also self-reliant, organized and persevering. Perhaps you lack a father image in your life, or maybe you had problems with one of your parents. You feel responsible toward your family and take on obligations unflinchingly. With difficult aspects, you may be arrogant and ruthless in achieving your aims. You may even suffer from a napoleonic complex or lose your position through scandal.

Dictator Adolf Hitler, artist Pablo Picasso, actor Sir Lawrence Olivier, TV personality Zsa Zsa Gabor.

SATURN IN THE ELEVENTH HOUSE
keyword *constant*

You may have many older friends for whom you feel a great sense of responsibility. You are so sensible and reserved that you may find it hard to get close to anyone. Your need for respect from your peers is even greater than your need for love. You compensate for your inner insecurities by hard work and constant involvements. However, your loyalty to friends and causes is unwavering. Poor aspects may thwart many of your wishes and cause you to suffer from loneliness. Or you may become a show-off. You give affection, but you cannot graciously accept it; often you withdraw into a shell.

Attorney F. Lee Bailey, conductor Arturo Toscanini, evangelist Billy Sunday.

SATURN IN THE TWELFTH HOUSE
keyword *circumspect*

Morbidly sensitive, you are inclined to isolate yourself or else to live with a constant wish to retreat. You enjoy solitude; your creativity flows when you work by yourself, but too much isolation will lead to loneliness and fear. Because you are tied down to respectability and accepted mores, you tend to keep your problems locked up within yourself. This can lead to a life-is-against-me attitude. You must cultivate an optimistic outlook and a hope for the future. You should get away from self-centered attitudes and learn to serve humanity or those close to you. With difficult aspects, your father may have faded out of your life early.
Prime Minister Indira Gandhi, writers Ralph Waldo Emerson, Erich Maria Remarque and Mark Twain.

Saturn in Aspect

Any aspect to Saturn indicates *a lesson to learn;* these aspects involve the abilities to *concentrate,* to *become disciplined* and to *give form and substance* to your life.

The conjunction *emphasizes* these principles.

The square and opposition challenge you to *succeed* or to *become aware of the need to accept responsibility.*

The trine and sextile give you the flow and opportunity to *learn and concentrate.*

The inconjunct teaches you to *adjust to limitations and delays.*

Conjunctions

♄ ☌ ♅ SATURN CONJUNCT URANUS

Your motto is, "I'll do my own thing." You are self-willed and self-reliant. If Saturn is the stronger of the planets, you are self-disciplined; if Uranus is stronger, you may be flighty. You might have difficulties in the house where the conjunction takes place, but with persistence you can work them out. You understand and respect tradition but are open to the future. You are impatient with average minds and superficial people, and you look up to those who have achieved success. Because of your nervous tension, it is important that you learn to relax. *Boxer Muhammad Ali, writer Erich Maria Remarque.*

♄ ☌ ♆ SATURN CONJUNCT NEPTUNE

You are a good planner, have excellent business sense and mathematical and political ability. With your aptitude for giving creative form to your ideas, you can be very artistic, particularly if Neptune is the stronger. This conjunction can provide inspiration and make you a practical idealist, especially if you learn to channel your intuition and imagination. This often is the aspect of the magician. Distrustful of others, no one can deceive you for long. You question everything and you always operate with your own logic and reason. Negatively used, you may develop a divided nature, mental distress or involvements with impractical projects.
Artist Pablo Picasso, inventor Thomas Edison.

♄ ☌ ♀ SATURN CONJUNCT PLUTO

You are ambitious for power and status. Your dedication to control can either be for good or for evil. You are willing to endure a lot to reach your goals. You understand others intuitively and can use them for your own benefit. Effective in all you undertake, you gain respect and admiration easily. You are secretive about your plans and can become frustrated or suffer from deep obsessions, unless you are actively engaged in a project.
Senator Eugene McCarthy, dictator Benito Mussolini.

Square and Oppositions

♄ □ ♅ SATURN SQUARE URANUS
♄ ☍ ♅ SATURN OPPOSITION URANUS

Very much an individual, you can be radical, a bit drastic and have a know-it-all attitude. Yet you are also apprehensive about making decisions; you look for approval before you assert yourself. You become aggressive toward those in authority in order to hide your real feelings of insecurity. Once you learn the art of compromise, you will be a hard and progressive worker and will do particularly well in large groups or organizations. You can even make positive use of your lack of tact; it can be a refreshing approach to the public.
Governor Ronald Reagan (□), Governor George Wallace (☍).

♄ □ ♆ SATURN SQUARE NEPTUNE
♄ ☍ ♆ SATURN OPPOSITION NEPTUNE

You can be either crafty and designing or the complete opposite, lacking all ambition. You may assume other people's guilt; instead you should overcome your fear of failure, face competition and learn to like yourself. You are capable and multi-talented in finance, business and the arts. You may find it difficult to distinguish between your real friends and those who would take advantage of you. You search for the ideal partner; sometimes you prefer to stay alone forever rather than give up your ideals. You have quite a bit of emotional strain and inhibition to work out. It is wise to stay away from psychic influences.
Actress Marilyn Monroe (□), singer Bobby Darin (☍).

♄ □ ♀ SATURN SQUARE PLUTO
♄ ☍ ♀ SATURN OPPOSITION PLUTO

Once you learn to plan, you have the ability to succeed as an executive, but your emotional insecurity makes you loath to admit that others know more than you do. Therefore you often appear dictatorial. You can be a poor loser, and may have unpredictable behavior patterns. Because you fear poverty, status is important to you. You may be too hasty in your efforts to reach the top and need to cultivate patience.
Writer Thomas Mann (□), writer Ernest Hemingway (☍).

Trines and Sextiles

♄ △ ♅ SATURN TRINE URANUS
♄ ✶ ♅ SATURN SEXTILE URANUS

You have initiative, willpower and endless determination. Practical and intuitive, you need freedom but are willing to work for it. Your keen judgment and insight into others will bring you many accomplishments. You respect money but are not attached to it. You have a lot of common sense, good administrative ability, and you respect knowledge and are bored by those who don't use their minds; you are a born fact finder. *Scientist Louis Pasteur (△), consumer advocate Ralph Nader (✶).*

♄ △ ♆ SATURN TRINE NEPTUNE
♄ ✶ ♆ SATURN SEXTILE NEPTUNE

Your parents established good morals and ethics in your early years. You have much foresight and tactical ability. Because your sense of self-preservation is strong, you always protect your own interests. You are methodical, organized, imaginative, inspirational, business-like and able to take on a lot of responsibility. You are aware of your obligations and live up to them. You learn things through experience, are ambitious and don't like to be surpassed by others. *Financier Bernard Baruch (△), Vice President Hubert Humphrey (✶).*

♄ △ ♀ SATURN TRINE PLUTO
♄ ✶ ♀ SATURN SEXTILE PLUTO

With your great tolerance of others, you are able to overcome many of the frustrations and limitations of other aspects. You are powerful, energetic and able to concentrate; your aims are realistic. You know and are able to objectively evaluate your own shortcomings. Because you can arouse enthusiasm in others, you can get much accomplished. Because your foundation is strong, you do not fear competition.

Actor Dustin Hoffman (△), record executive Neil Bogart (✶).

Inconjuncts (Quincunxes)

♄ ⚻ ♅ SATURN INCONJUNCT URANUS

You need approval and are willing to go far in order to get it. Often you are torn between tradition and your upbringing on the one hand and new modern concepts on the other. After you overcome your insecurities, you will do well with your inventive ideas and your ability to give form to abstract thought. Success in your chosen field is often more important to you than love or marriage. This can lead to stressful relationships.
TV personality Steve Allen, dancer Cyd Charisse.

♄ ⚻ ♆ SATURN INCONJUNCT NEPTUNE

You are disturbed by any suffering and injustice around you; although you desire to bring about changes, you feel very guilty when you have neither the energy nor willpower to do so. Motivated in spiritual, intuitive areas, you have poetic and philosophical qualities. When there are more obligations than you can handle, you tend to escape from reality. That escape can take a physical or psychological form such as exhaustion, hard-to-diagnose illnesses or a fairy-tale sense of reality.
Writer Rabindranath Tagore, singer Judy Collins.

♄ ⚻ ♀ SATURN INCONJUNCT PLUTO

A stickler when it comes to living up to obligations, you often take on more than your share. You also remind others of what you think their duties are; this is not always well received. If you are without a cause to fight for, you may indulge in sexual excesses. You are a perfectionist in anything you undertake, and like careers that put you in charge of many people or their resources. Politics or investment are natural fields for you. In personal relationships you let your partner dominate you or use you; learning your own self-worth is one of the most important adjustments that you need to make.

Vice President Walter Mondale, actress Brigitte Bardot.

Lesson 15: Uranus

Some General Comments

Our students never fail to ask us about challenging or flowing aspects. Why do we say that neither is bad or good, yet then say "With difficult aspects this position might do such and such"? A very good question!

In order to be a total person, you need some areas that are difficult to spur you on to achievement and some areas that are easy so you can enjoy life. If a planet has only challenging aspects, it is difficult to express the energies of that planet. It poses a challenge for you to overcome the stumbling block of the aspect and transform it into a stepping-stone.

If a planet has only easy or flowing aspects, you may take everything for granted and exert no effort. This is because you don't experience any stress which would require effort on your part. In this case you may not use many of your potentials, and they may be ignored or forgotten.

Ideally we look for easy and hard aspects to compensate each other.

Let's look at Judy Garland's horoscope as an example. Her Sun opposes her Mars; this is a challenging aspect, but also one that can give awareness if used positively. How can she use it positively? Through which channel? She has a sextile from her Sun to Neptune. This gives her the opportunity to use her creative talents. The drive and action of Mars can be used through the sextile of the Sun to Neptune. Without this opposition, she might squander that talent because there would be no stress or tension to push her into creativity.

To summarize, the challenges or tensions of the more difficult aspects should be channeled through the flow of the easier aspects.

Now, please familiarize yourself with the material in this lesson on Uranus; then delineate Judy Garland's Uranus. Our delineation is on page 298 in the Appendix.

Uranus represents the *freedom urge.* It is the planet of individualism, originality, awakening and breaking with tradition. It is the first of the so-called *transcendental* planets. Uranus stays in a sign for approximately seven years. Because it appears in the same sign for so many people, its house position is more important in describing attitudes and traits than its sign position.

Uranus in the Signs

♅ ♈ URANUS IN ARIES
keyword *impetuous*

You are a pioneer in any field you engage in. Self-willed, independent and resourceful, you often make breaks and start anew. You are assertive, at times even vehement and hostile, and have your own sense of morals. This allows you to feel free to act as you please. You have good mechanical ability and an unusual amount of nervous energy. If you use this position harmoniously, you will put all of your inventiveness and ideas into constructive channels; if you use this position inharmoniously, you can be rebellious, tactless, lacking in self-control and fanatic; you may violently reject all traditions of the past. Uranus was last in the sign of Aries from 1928 to 1934.

Playwright John Osborne, murder cult leader Charles Manson, actress Audrey Hepburn, baseball player Hank Aaron, astronaut Neil Armstrong.

♅ ♉ URANUS IN TAURUS
keyword *improvising*   fall

Determined to find new ways to be practical, you are bursting with new ideas in fields such as finance, earth resources and economic reforms. You may be limited in your expression if you place too much emphasis on materialism. Used positively, your many musical and artistic talents will come to the fore. Your creativity is strong, and you have a magnetic appeal to others. Difficult aspects to Uranus can produce marital upsets, unexpected troubles in love affairs, jealousy and stubbornness. Uranus was last in Taurus from 1935 to 1942.

Pianist Van Cliburn, playwright George Bernard Shaw, actress Jane Fonda, baseball player Sandy Koufax, singer Graham Nash.

♅ ♊ URANUS IN GEMINI
keyword *innovative*

Brilliant, inventive and original, you take a different approach to fields such as literature, education, communications media and electronics. Because you are restless, it is difficult for you to follow an idea through to the end. However, you are able to grasp new concepts and you favor reforms, especially in education, where you may promote ideas such as free universities. Flowing aspects to Uranus may give you flashes of genius; difficult aspects may give abrupt speech, impractical and even uncoordinated thinking, little thought for other people's feelings, problems with siblings or relatives, or an unfinished education. Uranus was last in Gemini from 1942 to 1949.

Musician George Harrison, Julie Nixon Eisenhower (daughter of President Nixon), psychic Uri Geller, movement leader Angela Davis, singer David Bowie.

♅ ♋ URANUS IN CANCER
keyword *restive*

You seek your freedom by adopting a different attitude toward home and marriage. You acept your parents as peers rather than authority figures, or you may disregard them totally. You may not like the lifestyle your family has established and feel more at home in communal living or you could go on a back-to-nature kick. If you do choose a traditional home, you will fill it with gadgets and electronic items, or you may do most of the building with your own hands. You love to travel and roam and you have a different concept of what patriotism means. Sensitive and intutive, you are able to accept the metaphysical and occult. Challenging aspects may bring emotional ups and downs; your feelings may be erratic, and your temperament irrational. Uranus was last in Cancer from 1949 to 1956, and previously from 1865 to 1872.

Writer Andre Gide, heiress/revolutionary Patty Hearst, would-be assassin Arthur Bremer, tennis player Chris Evert, rock star Peter Frampton.

♅ ♌ URANUS IN LEO
keyword *liberated*   detriment

New artistic expressions and a liberated approach to love are typical of those born with Uranus in Leo. Some manifestations of this are: discotheques, new rhythms like disco and rock-and-roll, new educational tools and different techniques and subjects in literature. You are sure of your ideas and stubbornly adhere to them. Your ego is prominent; you enjoy being unconventional and different and may have deep insights into humanity. You have boundless determination and are willing to overthrow those things which do not suit you. You must learn self-discipline, or else you can be quite destructive. Uranus was last in Leo from 1956 to 1962; before that from 1871 to 1877.

Caroline Kennedy (daughter of President John F.), Prime Minister Winston Churchill, psychic Edgar Cayce, writer Hermann Hesse, TV actor Shawn Cassidy.

♅ ♍ URANUS IN VIRGO
keyword *inquiring*

Your approach to work is original, and you have enough practicality to gain most people's acceptance. This is the age of computers; technical advances will be right up your alley. Those born when Uranus was last in Virgo (from 1962 to 1968) are still too young to have proven themselves and revealed their potential, but Uranus's entrance into this sign brought on renewed interest in ecology, natural foods and so on. Your nature is studious, inventive and humane; you are a good teacher. Your down-to-earth approach and ability to analyze and discriminate are helpful in bringing about needed changes. Those born during this time period are builders. With difficult aspects you may tend to get involved in too many cults, or you may have unusual health problems. Uranus was also in Virgo from 1877 to 1884.
Presidents Harry S. Truman and Franklin D. Roosevelt, physicist Albert Einstein, First Lady Eleanor Roosevelt, artist Pablo Picasso.

♅ ♎ URANUS IN LIBRA
keyword *reforming*

Uranus in Libra brought about and will bring again new approaches to marriage and social conduct, where a meaningful relationship is more important than the legal contract that goes with it. You pay attention to people's motives, and you have new concepts regarding justice. You enjoy all new forms of architecture, music and the arts. With your tremendous charm and personal magnetism, you can get away with the wildest and oddest notions without being offensive. With challenging aspects, you might not be willing to accept responsibilities; you might be too independent, self-willed and have marital problems. Uranus was last in Libra from 1968 to 1975; before that from 1884 to 1891.

Playwright Eugene O'Neill, dictator Adolf Hitler, architect Charles Le Corbusier, writer Ralph Waldo Emerson, dancer Vaslav Nijinsky.

♅ ♏ URANUS IN SCORPIO
keyword ***indomitable***   exaltation

Your emotions are intense, and your approach is daring, original and leans toward the occult. Fascinating and dynamic, you exude sex appeal. You need to make many adjustments from childhood on, but you accept these challenges and are in control of your body and mind. You are decisive in your actions and have little understanding of laziness. You like to probe deeply, and you have scientific and mechanical ingenuity. You can find new approaches to surgery or do research into strange and unknown illnesses. You must try to overcome your jealousy, possessiveness and inability to cater to another's wishes. Difficult aspects may bring out a revengeful and rebellious attitude, a violent temper or an intense desire to change what you don't like. Uranus was last in Scorpio in 1891 to 1898 and is transiting Scorpio again from 1975 to 1981.

Philosopher Krishnamurti, composer Richard Wagner, Nazi leader Hermann Goering, Field Marshall Erwin Rommel, baseball player Babe Ruth.

♅ ♐ URANUS IN SAGITTARIUS
keyword ***progressive***

Free expression of any kind is very important to you. You embrace new religious concepts and tend toward fields such as parapsychology and metaphysics and will approach them with a scientific and objective attitude. You have a good sense of humor and an optimistic outlook, and you are compassionate and liberal. You love to travel and will do so at a moment's notice. You like to expand your horizons and do not want to be bound by dogma or orthodoxy. With challenging aspects, you can be skeptical, agnostic, excitable and even rebellious. Uranus was last in Sagittarius from 1898 to 1904 and will return again to this sign from 1981 to 1988.

Singer Ethel Waters, nutritionist Adelle Davis, clown Emmett Kelly, playwright Noel Coward, pianist Vladimir Horowitz.

♅ ♑ URANUS IN CAPRICORN
keyword *constructive*

You like to bring changes to areas such as government, politics and legislation for the purpose of creating a better future. Although you preach tomorrow, you are reluctant to let go of yesterday. Your brilliant ideas make you a magnetic and exciting leader. Your hunches and insights are good; you are able to take old traditions and view them in new and different ways. Interested in land, resources and livestock, you can relate to these fields scientifically. Yet there is a basic conflict between Capricorn, which likes and adheres to tradition, and Uranus, the planet of change. If you cannot reconcile this conflict, you may become restless, nervous and overextended. Uranus was last in Capricorn from 1905 through 1912, and will return again to this sign from 1988 through 1995.

Governor Ronald Reagan, Vice President Hubert Humphrey, Senator Barry Goldwater, President Lyndon B. Johnson, religious leader Mary Baker Eddy.

♅ ♒ URANUS IN AQUARIUS
keyword *humanitarian*   dignity

In its own sign Uranus is very strong, penetrating, inventive, scientific and occult. You have a deep desire to change everything for the betterment of humanity, but your approach to this might be eccentric and is definitely going to be individual. Your leadership ability is unquestionable. A free thinker and open to all new ideas, you are intellectual, detached and at times too independent for your own good. You enjoy working with people and for people. With difficult aspects, you may be unconventional, impractical and even revolutionary. Uranus was last in Aquarius from 1912 to 1919 and will be there again from 1995 to 2002.

Ex-First Lady Lady Bird Johnson, evangelist Billy Graham, writer Mary McCarthy, baseball player Joe DiMaggio, Prime Minister Indira Gandhi.

♅ ♓ URANUS IN PISCES
keyword *visionary*

You are very changeable, but in your heart, you always have good intentions. Intuitive, idealistic and imaginative, you have mystical tendencies and are interested in meditation, yoga and eastern philosophies. Artistic and aesthetic, this is an excellent position for acting, because you like to escape into different worlds. You can be self-sacrificing and may experience a spiritual struggle to overcome materialistic tendencies and seek other, more evolved achievements. Overly sensitive, your nervous system is touchy; you need to know your limits and learn to relax both physically and emotionally. With challenging aspects, you might have a wish to escape with the help of alcohol, drugs or sex. Uranus was last in Pisces from 1919 through 1927.

Actress Marilyn Monroe, TV personality Merv Griffin, comedian Jonathan Winters, actor Richard Burton, singer Sammy Davis, Jr.

Uranus in the Houses

URANUS IN THE FIRST HOUSE
keyword *eccentric*

You are original, scientific, independent and high-strung; you can either make or break laws. Your breadth of vision and insight make you a leader ahead of your time, or you can be abrupt, tactless, dictatorial or perverse. You follow your own intuition, for better or worse, and believe in and live up to your own code of ethics. You receive a lot of attention, at times because of your magnetic appeal and at times because of your screwball approach. Direct, outspoken and restless, you are a nonconformist.

Strongman Arnold Schwarznegger, Governor George Wallace, attorney F. Lee Bailey, astrologer Isabel Hickey.

✓ URANUS IN THE SECOND HOUSE
keyword *kaleidoscopic*

You experience many financial ups and downs, receive unexpected windfalls and rarely have what would be considered a steady income. You tend to find original methods of earning money. With your great desire for independence, you would do better in your own business than in a nine to five work situation. You ignore the accepted value systems and usually substitute your own. You are strong willed and try to dominate your loved ones. You might receive money through either inheritance or partners. With difficult aspects, this is not a good position for speculation.

Singer Barbra Streisand, playwright Noel Coward, Governor Ronald Reagan, psychometrist Kenny Kingston.

URANUS IN THE THIRD HOUSE
keyword *inventive*

You can be a genius, in tune with your times and very inventive and scientific. Your unconventional way of communicating is good for writing and speaking of any kind. Your keen and alert mind makes this a good position for research. Though unpredictable in your behavior, you have an open mind and love new ideas. With challenging aspects, you might be cranky, willful, rebellious and abusive in your manner of speaking. You may also experience sudden and unexpected separations from brothers and sisters.

Senator Edward M. Kennedy, Vice President Spiro Agnew, actors Clark Gable, Cary Grant and Marlon Brando.

URANUS IN THE FOURTH HOUSE
keyword *unsettled*

You may experience changes in residence and ups and downs in your home life. Perhaps your mother was quite original, or maybe one of your parents misunderstood you. Anyway, your background is unusual; you may have been separated from your family at an early age, or lived under unusual circumstances. Unless Uranus is in a fixed sign, you don't like a settled life for yourself, and you prefer to change jobs, homes and partners frequently; yet you also fear being alone. In your later years, you may become interested in astrology and the occult.

Writers A.J. Cronin, Zelda Fitzgerald and Ernest Hemingway, actresses Brigitte Bardot and Marlene Dietrich.

URANUS IN THE FIFTH HOUSE
keyword *outré*

Romantic and attracted to the unusual, you will have many strange love affairs. Although you are fond of speculation and gambling, this is not the best placement for these activities. Your children may be unusual, you may have an illegitimate child or give a child up for adoption. Your excellent physical coordination is good for sports, and you are also very creative. You can be reckless, even foolhardy and may flaunt convention and disdain anything trite and ordinary. You always want to be the chief, never the indian.

Tennis player Billie Jean King, actor Robert Taylor, baseball player Babe Ruth, producer David Selznick.

URANUS IN THE SIXTH HOUSE
keyword *erratic*

You are nervous and high-strung and like to operate in your own way. You need a job where you can move around. You tend to drive yourself mercilessly, to the point of exhaustion. You do not like to accept the authority of others and can

become irritable and impatient when things don't go your way. You have excellent scientific abilities, good coordination and a sense of timing, beat and rhythm. With challenging aspects, you are prone to sudden health upsets or mysterious illnesses.
Baseball player Jackie Robinson, conductor Arturo Toscanini, President Jimmy Carter, actress Deborah Kerr.

URANUS IN THE SEVENTH HOUSE
keyword *unpredictable*

You would like an unusual partner or an original and different type of partnership. Or perhaps you may marry on the spur of the moment and then divorce just as suddenly; or you could marry while too young or immature, then realize your mistake and start all over again. In other words, there is a lack of permanence in your relationships with others. You are very independent. Your chosen partner may be eccentric, exasperating and a law unto himself or herself, or you may place very little importance on your mate, treating him or her as an appendage. You may make the public or your clients the important people in your life. This position indicates literary and artistic pursuits.
Actress Elizabeth Taylor, columnist Hedda Hopper, Ambassador Adlai Stevenson, ventriloquist Shari Lewis.

URANUS IN THE EIGHTH HOUSE
keyword *experimental*   accidental exaltation

There may be a few upsets concerning someone else's money, and you should exercise caution in business partnerships. You might find unusual ways of handling or investing other people's money and could benefit by unexpected legacies. You have psychic intuition and are interested in the occult and afterlife. You tend to fall in love with those who cannot reciprocate or gratify your needs. You usually keep your rather unconventional ideas about sex to yourself. You have a satirical sense of humor and might have strange dreams and premonitions. If Uranus is in challenging aspect to Mars, your death will likely be quick and sudden.

Cornelia Wallace (wife of Governor George F.), psychic Uri Geller, yippie leader Jerry Rubin, baseball player Vida Blue.

URANUS IN THE NINTH HOUSE
keyword **unorthodox**

Inventive, resourceful, independent and adventurous, you enjoy long trips to exotic places and might have strange experiences during your travels. Unorthodox in your religious views, you have an intuitive, socialistic and utopian outlook. With difficult aspects, you could be a zealot. Your legal matters can take unexpected turns; you would be wise to avoid lawsuits. Teaching, publishing and foreign affairs are good careers for you. You would also be a good political leader, since you can be a talented social reformer.

Indian leader Mohandas Gandhi, Field Marshall Erwin Rommel, Congressman Maurice Udall, tennis player Chris Evert.

URANUS IN THE TENTH HOUSE
keyword **distinctive**

When you have a cause you are a great fighter. With your vision you could be a splendid leader of world affairs with the ability to change old ways. However, with challenging aspects you may rebel and attack authority of any kind. You are very original, imaginative, altruistic and humanitarian. Since you are an awkward follower, you strive to be in charge. You may experience many sudden career changes and disappointments; or you may feel misunderstood, especially by others in positions of authority. However, an unusual or different kind of career will always appeal to you. With aspects to the Sun, you will probably be interested in the occult and astrology.

First Lady Eleanor Roosevelt, dictator Benito Mussolini, atheist Madelyn Murray O'Hair, football commissioner Pete Rozelle.

URANUS IN THE ELEVENTH HOUSE
keyword *unemotional*   accidental dignity

Your friends may be strange and original, and you want to help humanity in some unusual way. You have interesting aims in life and are a non-conformist. You make friends and new acquaintances quickly but shy away from close relationships. Although you may appear arrogant and snobbish, you like to surround yourself with people and you like to be admired. You'll probably have two different sets of friends: artistic or bohemian (Uranian) friends and more conventional traditional (Saturnian) friends. Your approach to sex is unusual and you may have some sexual problems or hangups.
Writer Thomas Mann, Senator Robert Kennedy, writer Erich Maria Remarque, astronaut Neil Armstrong.

URANUS IN THE TWELFTH HOUSE
keyword *psychic*

You desire to break through convention and restraint and have a tremendous need to free yourself from society's demands. Enchanted by the mysterious and the romantic, you may have several secret love affairs. You are intellectual, mystical and secretive and work in unusual ways. This is a good position for research or any behind-the-scenes activity. With challenging aspects, you may be eccentric. Unresolved conflicts in the unconscious may make your life difficult. Unless you exert self-control, you can be your own worst enemy and may go through life alone.
Murder cult leader Charles Manson, western actor Roy Rogers, dictator Adolf Hitler, actor Charlie Chaplin.

Uranus in Aspect

Any aspect to Uranus should be interpreted as *awakening, freeing* and *unexpected*.
   The conjunction emphasizes the *creative will*.
   The square and opposition awaken your *individualism*.

The trine and sextile free your *inventive flow* and make it easy for you to do the unusual.

The inconjunct demands *compromise between acceptance and rebellion.*

Conjunctions

♅ ♂ ♆ URANUS CONJUNCT NEPTUNE

The last time this conjunction took place was from 1821 to 1824. This aspect will not occur again until 1992. You have tremendous artistic talents, often in the category of genius. You are kind and eccentric with good intentions and a keen imagination. You identify yourself with the masses and will fight for freedom. This aspect indicates research into some unusual field.

Scientist Louis Pasteur, poet Charles Baudelaire.

♅ ♂ ♀ URANUS CONJUNCT PLUTO

This aspect occurred from 1963 to 1968 and before that in the 1850's. You go to extremes to be different or to preserve freedom. You respect all life, whether it is human, animal or plant. You have great stamina and regenerative ability; you can also be a revolutionary.

Botanist Luther Burbank, artist Vincent Van Gogh.

Squares and Oppositions

♅ □ ♆ URANUS SQUARE NEPTUNE
♅ ☍ ♆ URANUS OPPOSITION NEPTUNE

You are high-strung, intense and easily upset, but you know your limits. You need a positive emotional outlet. Your idealism is at times confused or impractical, and you can be rebellious or else apathetic and ostrich-like. You might get involved in unusual groups or indulge in drugs or alcohol; or you may have deep inner fears that your security will be taken away.

Heiress/revolutionary Patty Hearst (□), writer Jean Paul Sartre (♌).

♅ □ ♀ URANUS SQUARE PLUTO
♅ ♌ ♀ URANUS OPPOSITION PLUTO

You can be a political idealist, fighting injustice, or you can be the procrastinator who lets Johnny do it. Your nature is rather thoughtless, impatient and combative. You have an intense sense of self-preservation and an inability to compromise. Women with this position tend to resent the inferior role they feel is allotted to them.

Senator Edward M. Kennedy (□), TV personality Ed Sullivan (♌).

Trines and Sextiles

♅ △ ♆ URANUS TRINE NEPTUNE
♅ ✶ ♆ URANUS SEXTILE NEPTUNE

You like to find your own means of expression, even if it disregards accepted standards. A revolutionary thinker, you are very suspicious of government. You are attracted to mysticism, the occult and the esoteric. Your great creative imagination can be inspirational. Depending on the aspects, you can have great appeal to the masses.

Playwright George Bernard Shaw (△), singer Wayne Newton (✶).

♅ △ ♀ URANUS TRINE PLUTO
♅ ✶ ♀ URANUS SEXTILE PLUTO

Pluto's spiritual energy and Uranus's awakening power operate together either to build or to separate. This position

gives you endurance and strength, and it enables you to accept the new, especially if you believe it is for the betterment of the world. You are appalled by injustice and alert to the dangers of dictators. You are a true idealist.
Atheist Madeline Murray O'Hair (△), scientist Marie Curie (✳).

Inconjuncts (Quincunxes)

♅ ⚻ ♆ URANUS INCONJUNCT NEPTUNE

You are an avid protector of the underdog and will try to fight any injustice. You often feel that you haven't done enough and may become a rebel or turn off completely and be self-centered. However, you could be a good social worker. This aspect indicates creative originality. It last occurred between 1922 and 1928.
Congresswoman Shirley Chisholm, Vice President Walter Mondale.

♅ ⚻ ♇ URANUS INCONJUNCT PLUTO

Because you are often subjected to circumstances beyond your control, you frequently feel frustrated. You are in awe of those who have achieved, kowtow to them and then become resentful. Once you overcome your feeling of futility, you will experience your creative talents in research and literature and will realize you are a very able leader.
Writer Ralph Waldo Emerson, Vice President Hubert Humphrey.

Lesson 16: Neptune
More Important Comments

In lesson 3 we gave you a few keywords for the Moon's nodes; why haven't we mentioned them since? There is a reason, of course. We want you to know as much about astrology as possible, so that when you pick up another astrology book, you at least will know what the symbols ☊ and ☋ mean. But we are dealing with an astrological refinement; the nodes are like icing on the cake. It is not that the nodes are unimportant; they are helpful in deeper and more detailed interpretations, but they are beyond the scope of basic astrology, and in this book we are only dealing with basics. Once you are familiar with the basics, you will be ready for the refinements. When you are more advanced, you will learn about the Moon's nodes and their interpretation by sign and house.

The same goes for the Midheaven. In our delineation we

mentioned briefly that the Midheaven represents your career and in lesson 5 we gave you a few keywords for the tenth house. At this point that is really all you need to know. When you are more advanced you will learn about the Midheaven in greater detail and how it may indicate career possibilities.

In the meantime, we hope you realize how much information you can determine with the knowledge that you have already acquired.

Now, on to this lesson and a detailed study of Neptune. After you have absorbed the information in this lesson, please interpret Judy Garland's Neptune. For our delineation please refer to page 299.

Some General Remarks Regarding Neptune

Neptune is the second of the transcendental planets. It is called a *generational* planet, because it stays in each sign of the zodiac for approximately fourteen years. Everyone born during this time has Neptune in the same sign; therefore, for a personal reading, the house position is the important factor. Because Neptune spends fourteen years in a sign, its properties leave an imprint on that time; thus we have two descriptions for Neptune, the major historical happenings of the era and the personal characteristics shared by people born during that time.

Neptune represents both the *spiritual urge* and the *escapist urge;* it represents your *wish to fool yourself* and your *creative and intuitive capacity.*

Neptune in the Signs

♆ ♈ NEPTUNE IN ARIES
keyword *radical*

Neptune was last in Aries from 1861 to 1874. This transit brought with it the invention of dynamite, the machine gun and the typewriter. During this period the U.S. Civil War and the Franco-Prussian War took place and the first Women's Suffrage Law was passed in the state of Wyoming. Genetics were discovered and the great Chicago fire occurred.

People born when Neptune was last in Aries pioneered

many new religious and philosophical concepts. They shared a great sense of a mission to be fulfilled. They expressed strong imagination, creativity and self-awareness. An afflicted Neptune produced schemes filled with false pride and egotism and people who craved notoriety.
Revolutionary Sun Yat Sen, Swami Vivekananda, Statesman Benjamin Franklin, writer H.G. Wells, modern bluebeard Henri Landru.

♆ ♉ NEPTUNE IN TAURUS
keyword *artistic*

Neptune was last in Taurus from 1874 to 1887. It was the era of the first experimental cars, the Daimler-Benz engine, the bicycle, Edison's incandescent lamp and phonograph and the telephone. It brought the first Woolworth five-and-ten-cent store, as well as a financial panic.

If you were born with Neptune in Taurus, you have an aesthetic approach to the sciences and the arts; you respond to music and beauty, yet you also have innate business sense, a great need for security and can be easily misled by others. With aspects to Pluto you might have healing powers. Difficult aspects to Neptune may lead to a preoccupation with material assets or self-deception and carelessness in your handling of money.
Industrialist Walter P. Chrysler, medical missionary Albert Schweitzer, Muslim leader Aga Khan, dancer Isadora Duncan, President Herbert Hoover.

♆ ♊ NEPTUNE IN GEMINI
keyword *perceptive*

Neptune was last in Gemini from 1887 to 1901. This was the era of the steam automobile, the diesel engine, the first airplane, photographic film, electronics, Marconi's wireless and radio signals, the submarine, the zipper, X-rays, psychoanalysis and the building of the Eiffel Tower.

If you were born during this transit, you have many new

theories about trade, commerce, travel and communications. Alert, inquiring and restless, you have a desire for new and varied experiences and have difficulty putting down roots. With difficult aspects, you may be preoccupied with superficial values, susceptible to outside influences, argumentative, crafty, narrow-minded and gossipy.

Secretary of State John Foster Dulles, aviator Billy Mitchell, fighter pilot Eddie Rickenbacker, publisher Henry Luce, actor Charlie Chaplin.

♆ ♋ NEPTUNE IN CANCER
keyword *protective*

Neptune was last in Cancer from 1901 to 1915. This transit was the time of uprisings in Mexico and China, World War I, the San Francisco earthquake, the founding of the Boy Scouts of America, the Pure Food and Drug Law, the discovery of vitamins and Einstein's theory of relativity.

If you were born with Neptune in Cancer, you have strong ties to the earth and to your home and family. You are idealistic, emotionally sensitive and protective of others. Staunchly patriotic, open to mystical and religious ideas, you are willing to sacrifice for others. With challenging aspects, you may become self-indulgent, pessimistic and live too much in a dream world, or you may have difficulties at home, perhaps linked to your mother.

Filmmaker Walt Disney, pediatrician Benjamin Spock, TV French Chef Julia Child, Maharishi Mahesh Yogi, Saint Joan of Arc.

♆ ♌ NEPTUNE IN LEO
keyword *speculative*

Neptune was last in Leo from 1915 to 1929. It was the era of the signing of the Versailles Peace Treaty, the Russian Revolution, the start of the League of Nations, the Beer Hall Putsch in Germany signaling the rise of Nazism, prohibition in the United States, the Scopes affair where a teacher was tried for teaching evolution, Stalin's first Five Year Plan, Lindbergh's solo trans-Atlantic flight, the invention of the rocket, the first films with sound and the discovery of penicillin.

If you were born during this transit, your basic inclinations are romantic, idealistic and artistic. You have an aptitude for entertainment, a flair for the dramatic, a tendency to exaggerate and a willingness to try anything once. Speculation is right up your alley. You idealize love and enjoy courtship; you desire power but don't like to accept authority. If Neptune is afflicted, you could be dictatorial, subversive, and extravagant in your pursuit of pleasure. You could suffer through love affairs or your children.

Conductor Leonard Bernstein, Senator Robert Kennedy, singer Maria Callas, Cuban leader Fidel Castro, TV personality Johnny Carson.

♆ ♍ NEPTUNE IN VIRGO
keyword *technical*   detriment

Neptune last transited Virgo from 1929 to 1943. During this era the world experienced the Teapot Dome scandal over U.S. oilfields, the Stock Market Crash, the repeal of prohibition, entry into the atomic age, the dropping of the gold standard, the passing of the Social Security Act, World War II and race riots. The aerosol spray, computers, electric shavers, FM broadcasting and radar were invented during this period. The depression of the 1930's thwarted some of the creative and imaginative faculties of people born during this transit.

If you were born with Neptune in Virgo you have new concepts about health and conditions of employment. You are among the first generation to accept psychiatry as part of your daily life. You probably experience a strong pull between reason and emotion, and may have trouble accepting responsibilities, which may lead to escape through drugs or other psychedelic means. With difficult aspects, you may have breakdowns and neuroses. You are critical and may be quick to tear down the old without having something new to replace it with. However, you may also be a great humanitarian and fight for worthwhile causes.

Actress Jane Fonda, musician John Lennon, conductor Zubin Mehta, artist Andy Warhol, filmmaker Peter Bogdanovich.

♆ ♎ NEPTUNE IN LIBRA
keyword *dependent*

Neptune was in Libra from 1943 to 1956 and previously from 1778 to 1792. This period brought the end of World War II, the forming of the United Nations, the Taft-Hartley Labor Act, the Marshall Plan, the state of Israel, Senator Joe McCarthy's pursuit of supposed communists in government, U.S. Supreme Court decision on the unconstitutionality of racial segregation in schools, the Mau-Mau uprising in Africa, discovery of high-frequency masers, the first hydrogen bomb and television for everybody.

If you were born in the 1940's, the 1950's or in the eighteenth century, you are interested in new concepts regarding relationships and laws, and uncertainties about obligations and needs.

You take new and subtle approaches to the arts. You want to be humanitarian, altruistic, compassionate and peace-loving, but you may end up being impractical, drug-oriented, lazy and without willpower. "Doing your own thing" has often caused more divorces than marriages, more rift than cohesion, which is typical of Libra working through the veil of Neptune.

Musician George Harrison, movement leader Angela Davis, assassin Sirhan Sirhan, religious reformer Savonarola, philosopher Arthur Schopenhauer.

♆ ♏ NEPTUNE IN SCORPIO
keyword *subtle*

Neptune was in Scorpio from 1956 to 1970 and previously from 1792 to 1806. This is the generation of the Berlin Wall, Sputnik, the first man on the Moon, Castro, the first sit-ins, the Vietnam War, civil rights marches, heart transplants, polio vaccines, the laser beam, quasars, hippies and the drug culture.

If you were born with Neptune in Scorpio, you are investigative, magnetic, emotional and possessed of great regenerative powers. The intensity with which you attack anything leads to new approaches in painting, literature, religion, politics and all facets of life. If Neptune is afflicted, it may produce black magic, obsessions, treachery and peculiar sex practices, especially if you have challenging aspects to Venus or Mars.

Artist Michelangelo, poet Heinrich Heine, writer George Sand, religious leader Brigham Young, runaway slave Dred Scott.

♆ ♐ NEPTUNE IN SAGITTARIUS
keyword *prophetic*

Neptune is in Sagittarius from 1970 to 1984 and previously was there from 1806 to 1820. Sagittarius is the sign of openness, frankness and idealism; Neptune in this position is bound to bring out many hidden things, such as the Watergate revelations, similar incidents in England, France and Germany (the Willy Brandt scandal). Discoveries of big business bribes in foreign countries and the unethical conduct of big business or of American legislators are not surprising either. At the turn of the nineteenth century, Aaron Burr was tried for treason; Napoleon was exiled; electro-magnetism was discovered and the theory of advanced numbers was presented.

People born then and now feel a need for higher religious and philosophical values. You can explore the powers of the mind, revise existing laws and search for the deeper meaning of life. You have new ideas about education; you are interested in foreign cultures and feel easy with a concept of universal religion. If Neptune is afflicted, you may wander aimlessly, lack judgment, distrust others and believe in false prophets.

Political philosopher Karl Marx, Chief Justice Oliver Wendell Holmes, physicist Issac Newton, editor Horace Greeley, poet Walt Whitman.

♆ ♑ NEPTUNE IN CAPRICORN
keyword ***earthbound***

Neptune was last in Capricorn from 1820 to 1834 and this transit will occur again from 1984 to 1998. This was the era of the Monroe Doctrine, the slave rebellion, the Erie Canal and the railroads. It brought the blast furnace, Braille printing, cement, the friction match, the reaper and the tractor.

People of that era were under a strong parental influence and they were traditional, conventional and conscientious. They had a deep sense of responsibility and self-discipline, and they tried to put all creative feelings into practical and tangible application. When Neptunian forces were stronger than the Capricornian ones, they incorporated spiritual and poetic imagination into their daily lives.

We presume that when Neptune enters Capricorn in 1984 there will again be many practical discoveries; maybe people will tap the oceans for food, or new forms of government and political concepts may emerge.
Scientist Louis Pasteur, industrialist Alfred Nobel, engineer Alexandre Eiffel, philosopher Herbert Spencer, Cardinal Wolsey.

♆ ♒ NEPTUNE IN AQUARIUS
keyword ***theoretical***

Neptune was in Aquarius from 1834 to 1847 and this transit will occur again from 1998 to 2012. This was the era of the Alamo, the Mexican War, Livingston's exploration of Africa, the first use of anesthetics, the potato famine in Ireland, the Opium War in China, the laws of thermodynamics, the discovery of uranium, the streetcar, the stereoscope and the pneumatic tire.

The combination of Neptune and Aquarius produced people of social, philosophical and political orientation. Their detached attitudes, combined with the ability to understand the abstract, resulted in many new approaches to the arts and many new inventions. When Neptune again transits Aquarius, many astrologers feel that it might be the beginning of the one thousand years of peace predicted in the Book of Revelations in the Bible and that universal harmony may become a reality. We hope that they are right.

Inventor Thomas Edison, physicist Wilhelm Roentgen, philosopher Jean-Jacques Rousseau, writer Mark Twain, philosopher Friedrich W. Nietzsche.

♆ ♓ NEPTUNE IN PISCES
keyword *mystical*   dignity

Neptune was last in Pisces from 1847 to 1861. Brigham Young settled in Utah with his Mormon followers; John Sutter started the California Gold Rush and Marx and Engels wrote *The Communist Manifesto*. It was the time of the Pony Express, the Suez Canal, the first commerical oil well, Darwin's theory of evolution, the beginning of oceanography, the Bunsen burner, the glider and the safety pin.

Neptune is in its own sign in Pisces; this transit is inspirational, spiritual, sensitive and even prophetic. This placement indicates a talent for poetry and music, an understanding of those in need, medical discoveries and new cultural concepts. *Physician Walter Reed, chemist Paul Ehrlich, botanist Luther Burbank, pianist Ignace Paderewski, attorney Clarence Darrow.*

Neptune in the Houses

NEPTUNE IN THE FIRST HOUSE
keyword *dreamy*

Refined, gentle, vague and imaginative, you may be a dreamer who changes plans and ideas according to your mood and who lives in a world of fantasy. You do not see yourself clearly, nor do others see you as you really are. You appear to be glamorous, mysterious, magnetic and charismatic. With good aspects you will use your strong imagination in artistic pursuits. With difficult aspects your imagination may sap your energies, make you subject to strange experiences and bring on hard-to-diagnose illnesses.

Actress Marilyn Monroe, writers Victor Hugo and Robert Louis Stevenson, Ambassador Adlai Stevenson.

NEPTUNE IN THE SECOND HOUSE
keyword *impractical*

You must be very honest, or you may experience money problems. Your financial judgment is not always good, and you should avoid complicated money situations or too much credit buying, because cash tends to flow through your fingers. You love luxury yet are idealistic about material possessions. With difficult aspects you are an easy prey for money-making schemes and may be very impractical.

Queen Marie Antoinette, physicist Isaac Newton, singer Judy Collins, football commissioner Pete Rozelle.

NEPTUNE IN THE THIRD HOUSE
keyword *persuasive*

You are very intuitive and imaginative and you tend to daydream and need to learn concentration. Art or literature would be excellent outlets for you; you sometimes use a pseudonym or an alias. Insecurities early in life can lead to nervousness later. You might live with a relative because of problems in your parental home, or you may have stepbrothers and stepsisters. With a strong Mercury or Uranus, you will be productive and can either be a supersalesperson or a con artist. With difficult aspects, your mind may be vague and you may not be very academic; or your relatives might misunderstand you.

Psychoanalyst Carl G. Jung, writer Ralph Waldo Emerson, comedienne Lily Tomlin, Happy Rockefeller (Mrs. Nelson).

NEPTUNE IN THE FOURTH HOUSE
keyword *searching*

Your sense of home and background is religious, and your attitude toward your parents, idealistic, yet you may change your residence a lot or experience confusion about your identity; perhaps you were adopted or grew up with foster parents. You are artistic and musical; you don't mind self-sacrifice and you need time by yourself to find your path. With challenging aspects, you can be the wanderer of the world and not feel at home anywhere, until you realize that inner peace of mind is the answer to your problems. You may have an alcoholic or disappearing parent.

Opera singer Joan Sutherland, artist Toulouse Lautrec, President Gerald Ford, writer Max Schulman.

✓ NEPTUNE IN THE FIFTH HOUSE
keyword *creative*

Romantic, speculative and rich in creative potential, you tend to over-dramatize situations and over-idealize your loved ones. This is a great position for actors, musicians and painters. Your approach to life is youthful, even childlike, and romances or affairs are important to you. You may love someone who is not free. With difficult aspects you may make sacrifices for your children or may experience an unwanted pregnancy and give a child up for adoption or have an abortion. Because you do not see your children clearly, it is easy for them to take advantage of you.

Senator Robert Kennedy, actor Farley Granger, composer Frederick Chopin, murder cult leader Charles Manson.

NEPTUNE IN THE SIXTH HOUSE
keyword *inspirational*

Unless Mars is strong, you may tend to idleness or drifting. With Neptune here, your illnesses may be difficult to diagnose. You are extremely sensitive, and you should be careful with all medicines and drugs. Strong aspects to Saturn will help balance your work and life and will help you cultivate good habits. This is a good placement for doctors, nurses, psychiatrists and humanitarians; it endows you with a poetic humor. You love solitude.

Philosopher Emannuel Kant, religious reformer Savonarola, comedian Jack Benny, actress Carol Burnett.

NEPTUNE IN THE SEVENTH HOUSE
keyword *unrealistic*

Because you are vulnerable to the influences of others, your choice of a partner is very important. You and your mate don't see each other clearly. You may form socially unacceptable attachments or you may fall madly in love and elope. With Neptune in this house, you need to take off your rose-colored glasses and learn to face reality; you must also learn to give without expecting so much in return. If you have difficult aspects, stay away from legal involvements and read the fine print before you sign anything. This position of Neptune sometimes indicates a marriage or partnership to one who is handicapped.

Writers Oscar Wilde and Emile Zola, White House Chief of Staff Hamilton Jordan, entertainer Joel Grey.

NEPTUNE IN THE EIGHTH HOUSE
keyword *soulsearching*

You are receptive, intuitive and possibly psychic. You may experience strange dreams, nightmares, or insomnia. Your death may occur in your sleep or while you are under anesthesia. You may have an extravagant partner and all joint finances must be scrutinized. Be careful of hypnosis because you are too easily put under. Neptune in this house gives you a mysterious charisma that helps you to get support from others, therefore many politicians have this placement. Challenging aspects can lead to depression and easy addiction to drugs or alcohol. Whenever surgery is recommended, be sure to get a second or third medical opinion.

Saint Joan of Arc, Senator Edward M. Kennedy, Governor Ronald Reagan, producer Mike Todd.

NEPTUNE IN THE NINTH HOUSE
keyword *intellectual*

You are tolerant, religious, intuitive and impressionable. Interested in educational programs and social reform, you enjoy any kind of learning and have aptitude for foreign languages. You like to help the underprivileged and love to travel. Your imagination is boundless, and you relate well to foreigners. If Neptune is afflicted, you may be impractical and neglect your education. Use extreme care in experiments with astral projection.

Singer Sarah Vaughan, poet Percy Shelley, Vice President Nelson Rockefeller, President John F. Kennedy.

NEPTUNE IN THE TENTH HOUSE
keyword *aspiring*

Since you like to present an unusual image to the world, this is a good placement for those who serve humanity. You may aspire higher than you can actually reach, or the world may not give you credit for work you have done. This is a perfect position for actors, in films or on TV. The world sees you as glamorous; your disposition is idealistic. Parents are not much help to you; whatever you achieve you have done by yourself. You have a good sense of the feelings and motivations of those around you and could be a diplomat. With challenging aspects, you may have secret goings-on, or you may be full of self-doubt.

TV personalities Johnny Carson and Ed Sullivan, filmmaker Walt Disney, labor leader Caesar Chavez.

NEPTUNE IN THE ELEVENTH HOUSE
keyword *quixotic*

You range from a non-discriminating sociability to total anti-social behavior. You associate with all kinds of oddballs or are the perfect no-strings-attached friend. You can be a generous person or else a schemer and plotter. You dream big dreams, and your hunches are nearly always correct. With difficult aspects, you don't reason well and may suffer disappointments through friends and associates.

Writer Zelda Fitzgerald, writer Edgar Allan Poe, actress Elizabeth Taylor, President Richard Nixon, actress Ellen Burstyn.

NEPTUNE IN THE TWELFTH HOUSE
keyword ***aesthetic***   accidental dignity

Sensitive to your subconscious and your psyche, you may at times suffer from a feeling of confinement. You are artistic with a talent for dancing. You can be a source of wisdom and intuitive insight as long as you face reality and do not deceive yourself. Despite your need to help others you suffer from a deep-seated loneliness. This placement is excellent for doctors, nurses and work in hospitals, large institutions, or with the handicapped.

General George Patton, reformer Annie Besant, writer George du Maurier, Prime Minister Benjamin Disraeli, Juan Carlos I of Spain.

Neptune in Aspect

Neptune has made few aspects to Pluto in the last two hundred years. The conjunction took place at the end of the nineteenth century and the square at the beginning of the nineteenth century. The only aspect it made in the twentieth century is the sextile.

Conjunction

♆ ☌ ♇ NEPTUNE CONJUNCT PLUTO

This was a very subtle aspect affecting fundamental attitudes in human society. It brought turning points and new ideas through service to all of humanity.

Philosopher Krishnamurti, Chief Justice Earl Warren.

Square

♆ □ ♇ NEPTUNE SQUARE PLUTO

This aspect brought social and political upheaval. People were victims of, or took part in, corruption. Used positively, it made them probing, digging and inventive; used negatively, they became obsessive.

Shorthand inventor Isaac Pitman, philosopher Herbert Spencer.

Sextile

♆ ⚹ ♇ NEPTUNE SEXTILE PLUTO

This is a creative and artistic aspect. It also indicates fights against human injustice and changes in the court and legislative systems. This aspect can bring open government, freedom of expression and the positive use of mystical or occult talents. Negatively, it can indicate dropping out of society.

Chief Justice Oliver Wendell Holmes, actress Mia Farrow.

Lesson 17: Pluto

General Comments

There is only one planet left to learn about, small but powerful Pluto.

Pluto is the farthest planet from the Sun. First found in 1930, it is the last planet discovered so far. It is too small to be seen with the naked eye, and it is even difficult to photograph with powerful modern telescopes.

Pluto's orbit is the most eccentric in our solar system and its motion is the slowest of any of the planets. It takes approximately 248 years to travel through the zodiac; it stays in each sign anywhere from twelve to thirty-two years. Strangely enough, it stays thirty-two years in Taurus, the sign of its detriment, and twelve years in Scorpio, the sign of its dignity.

Pluto is the third of the transcendental planets. Since its motion is so slow and it is so far away from the Earth, its influence is abstract and not immediately felt by the individual. But, as with anything that takes time to develop, Pluto's eventual impact is deep and far reaching. The entrance of Pluto into a new sign leaves an imprint on an entire generation. We shall briefly describe some of the historical events of Pluto in each sign and then give you an idea of the characteristics of people born then. However, since Pluto is truly the generational planet, and its movement from one sign to the next signifies the beginning of a new generation, Pluto's house position is more personal; it indicates and gives insight into the role you may be destined to play.

Pluto represents both the *reforming and the destroying urges*. It rules our deepest subconscious and because it embodies the *principle of transformation and regeneration*, it can bridge the spiritual and material worlds.

After you study this lesson, please delineate Judy Garland's Pluto and check our answers in the Appendix on page 300.

Pluto in the Signs

♀ ♈ PLUTO IN ARIES
keyword *initiative*

Pluto was last in Aries from 1823 to 1851. This was the era of the American pioneer, the exploration of the Wild West, the California Gold Rush and the invention of the Colt revolver. During this period, the first college degree was given to a woman, the first postage stamp was issued and ether was used as an anesthetic for the first time.

Individuals born with Pluto in Aries have a tremendous desire to reform, an obsessive need for power or revenge if they feel attacked, great daring and much vigor. Their imagination knows few bounds, but they need self-discipline or they can deplete themselves physically.

Writer Jules Verne, billionaire John D. Rockefeller, writer Horatio Alger, artist Paul Cezanne, outlaw Jesse James.

♀ ♉ PLUTO IN TAURUS
keyword ***utilitarian***   detriment

Pluto was last in Taurus from 1851 to 1883. This was the time of the first transcontinental railroad, the first commercial oil well, the building of the Gotthard Tunnel and the Suez Canal, the beginning of corporate organizations and the invention of the stock ticker. There was a growth of materialism and the blossoming of the Victorian era.

People born with Pluto in Taurus show endurance, stubbornness, sensuality, artistic ability and obsessive needs for wealth and permanence. This was exploited by the rich while the working classes endured great hardship.

Newspaper publisher William Randolph Hearst, President William Howard Taft, revolutionary Nicolai Lenin, psychoanalyst Alfred Adler, artist Vincent Van Gogh.

♀ ♊ PLUTO IN GEMINI
keyword ***sweeping change***

Pluto was last in Gemini from 1883 to 1913. This era brought changes and inventions that have altered our way of life. The discoveries of electricity, airplanes and automobiles brought about new ways of communication and transportation. It was also a time of delving into the human mind through psychoanalysis and the first intelligence tests. It was an era of firsts: the first subway, the first newsreel, the first camera and the first fountain pen.

If you were born with Pluto in Gemini, you are family-oriented, but also restless and impetuous. You search for new ways to express yourself and to expand your intellect, but you can also be sarcastic and critical. After the repression of the Victorian Era, the pendulum swung into almost compulsive candor.

Columnist Walter Lippmann, broadcaster Edward R. Murrow, writer Franz Kafka, cartoonist Rube Goldberg, statesman David Ben Gurion.

♀ ♋ PLUTO IN CANCER
keyword **upheaval**

Pluto was last in Cancer from 1913 to 1938. During this period the patriotic love of country innate in Cancer developed into chauvinism and pride, which finally led to World War II. It was a time of new concepts in government, from our own New Deal to fascism, nazism and communism. It was the time of the emancipation of women, the first woman cabinet member, the baring of legs and knees, new approaches to child rearing and new methods of food preparation.

If you were born with Pluto in Cancer, you probably have a great need for security, as well as a need to achieve emotional maturity. This position indicates social awareness. Pluto in Cancer works very intuitively and instinctively, and it loves to break with tradition. However, it could also make you resentful and even morbid.

Abigail "Dear Abby" Van Buren, designer Pierre Cardin, TV producer Jack Webb, singer Lena Horne, musician Ray Coniff.

♀ ♌ PLUTO IN LEO
keyword **power**

Pluto was last in Leo from 1938 to 1957. It was the time of World War II, the explosion of the first atomic bomb (Pluto rules atomic power), dictatorships in many corners of the world, teenagers coming into their own and TV available for all.

On the individual level, if you were born with Pluto in Leo you have self-confidence and a great sense of authority. You have good business ability and you may promote mass interests. It can also lead to sexual exploitation or the enjoyment of perverse pleasures, and it may bring about a desire to rule or to dominate.

Football player Joe Namath, singers Cher and Jose Feliciano, skier Jean Claude Killy, actor Peter Fonda.

♀ ♍ PLUTO IN VIRGO
keyword *technical development*

Pluto was last in Virgo from 1957 to 1971 and previously from 1708 to 1723. These periods marked tremendous changes in labor and industrialization. Computers came into their own, which totally changed work patterns. New medical discoveries revolutionized the practice of medicine; the birth control pill changed our attitudes toward sex. The realization of dangers inherent in food additives brought a return to natural nourishment, home gardens and vitamins. This was the time of teacher and student strikes and the demands of racial minorities for equal opportunity. This period also brought the first manned space flights. When Pluto was last in Virgo, Reaumur and Fahrenheit invented the thermometer, a very Virgoan invention.

On the personal level, this placement makes you analytical, inventive, technical and perfectionist. You have ability in medicine, psychiatry and business. You can also be puritanical and overly critical.

Writer Samuel Johnson, cabinetmaker Thomas Chippendale, poet Thomas Gray, writer Horace Walpole, philosopher Jean-Jacques Rousseau.

♀ ♎ PLUTO IN LIBRA
keyword *social instincts*

Pluto entered Libra in 1971 and will remain in this sign until 1983; previously Pluto was in Libra from 1723 to 1737. This position brings new approaches to marriage, justice, prison reform, the arts and international relations. In its previous passage through Libra it brought freedom of the press, the first public library and the discovery of the chronometer.

If you were born with Pluto in Libra, you have a love of beauty and a need for harmony. Your sense of justice and social instincts are well developed. You are adaptable and might experience a conflict between opposing viewpoints. You may feel a great sense of responsibility toward other people but you could be fickle in your one-to-one relationships.

President George Washington, philosopher Immanuel Kant, hypnotist Franz Mesmer, adventurer Giovanni Casanova, revolutionary Patrick Henry.

♀ ♏ PLUTO IN SCORPIO
keyword *redemption*   dignity

Pluto will be in Scorpio from 1983 to 1995; Pluto was also in Scorpio from 1737 to 1749. As far as we know, few things happened when Pluto was last in Scorpio; there were no great discoveries or any important wars or revolutions; and there was no great new wave in the arts. However, there were some interesting explorations, and Bering discovered Alaska.

Yet most astrologers feel that Pluto's re-entry into Scorpio will bring tremendous changes and upheavals. It might be the true beginning of the Aquarian Age; it might also signal the Armageddon predicted in the Bible. We are neither psychics nor seers, but our logic tells us that there may be many business and monetary reforms, new insights into the workings of nature, innovative medical approaches (maybe a resurgence of natural healing) and a better understanding of the subconscious.

People with this placement will be sensitive to their environment, emotionally intense, intrigued with the mysterious, penetrating in all they undertake and at times even ruthless. *Industrialist Pierre Dupont, traitor Benedict Arnold, General Charles Cornwallis, astronomer William Herschel, artist Francisco Goya.*

♀ ♐ PLUTO IN SAGITTARIUS
keyword *reformation*

Pluto was last in Sagittarius from 1749 to 1762. This was the era of the publication of the first encyclopedia, Benjamin Franklin's lightning rod, the beginning of the Industrial Revolution and the beginning of the British Empire in India. It was a period of great learning. Many rugged individualists were born during these years. When Pluto enters Sagittarius in

1995, we hope it will bring with it spiritual regeneration, a new approach to religion and a return to the more fundamental laws of nature.

Individuals with this placement have a great need for personal freedom. Their approach is philosophical and humane. They are enthusiastic and versatile, and they have great faith in human nature.

Writer Johannes von Goethe, Secretary of the Treasury Alexander Hamilton, writer Horatio Alger, Prime Minister William Pitt, revolutionary Marquis de Lafayette.

♀ ♑ PLUTO IN CAPRICORN
keyword *evolution*

Pluto was last in Capricorn from 1762 to 1778. This was the time of the American Declaration of Independence, the Boston Tea Party, Watt's invention of the steam engine and the reign of Louis XVI and Marie Antoinette. The Industrial Revolution was in full swing. The rigidity of many governments of the time led to rebellions and uprisings in later years.

On a personal level, this position gives perseverence, ambition, efficiency in organizing and managerial ability. Those who have Pluto in Capricorn are conservative, materialistic and spirtually strong.

Millionaire John J. Astor, inventor John Fulton, writer Madame de Stael, composer Ludwig van Beethoven, Emperor Napoleon Bonaparte.

♀ ♒ PLUTO IN AQUARIUS
keyword *revelation*

Pluto was last in Aquarius from 1778 to 1798. This was the time of the American Revolution, the Constitution and the Bill of Rights, the French Revolution, the discoveries of the cotton gin, the first balloon and the first parachute. The first banks were opened and Herschel discovered Uranus.

Individuals with this position are intellectual, humanitarian, ingenious, unconventional, and they love freedom. They are searchers for truth, and they know how to communicate their dreams and ideas.

Statesman Daniel Webster, poet Lord Byron, philosopher Arthur Schopenhauer, composer Gioacchino Rossini, fairy tale recorders the Brothers Grimm.

♀ ♓ PLUTO IN PISCES
keyword *enlightenment*

Pluto was last in Pisces from 1798 to 1823. In art and literature this era was known as the Romantic period, and it saw the beginning of socialism in Europe, the adoption of the Napoleonic code of law and the fight for Mexican independence. Mesmer made his first experiments into the realm of psychic phenomena; Fulton invented the steamboat, and dark lines were discovered in the solar spectrum.

On the personal level, this position produces people who are easily impressed, compassionate, sensitive, imaginative and charitable. Their personalities are magnetic, but they can also be self-sacrificing and at times even morbid.

Composer Franz Schubert, writers Honoré de Balzac, Hans Christian Andersen and the Brontë sisters, political philosopher Friedrich Engels.

Pluto in the Houses

PLUTO IN THE FIRST HOUSE
keyword *striving*

This is a strong placement, and you are someone to be reckoned with. You are creative, but you may have a dual personality, and do nothing half-way. Strong, resilient and robust, and although somewhat prone to infection, you generally recover quickly. You are intense; your personality is magnetic, and you often crave power. Your ego is strong and you show many faces to the world: brooding, restless, energetic, passionate. With difficult aspects you may experience a lack of direction and you may appear argumentative, uncooperative and disagreeable.

TV personalities Dinah Shore and David Frost, Secretary of State Henry Kissinger, writer Johannes von Goethe, actor/producer Orson Welles.

PLUTO IN THE SECOND HOUSE
keyword *indefatigable*

You are able to turn liabilities into assets; you may have several different sources of income. Wealth often comes to you in a sensational manner and, with your astute financial ability, you handle it well. Because you have a desire to acquire material things, you must guard against treating your loved ones as possessions. This is a good placement for tax dealings, monopolies, corporate finance and banking. Pluto in the second house is often found in the charts of millionaires. If improperly used, you can be grasping and avaricious, and you may stoop to any level for financial or political gain.

Billionaire J. Paul Getty, Secretary of State George Marshall, writer Henry Miller, actor John Travolta.

PLUTO IN THE THIRD HOUSE
keyword *futuristic*

You are never lukewarm in your mental attitudes and have a need to cry out and be heard, by speaking, by writing or by ranting and raving. This may give you an unusual relationship with your brothers or sisters. Though this placement appears frequently in the charts of school drop-outs, education is important to you, and you achieve it at any cost. You are often forced to take note of your failures or shortcomings and may have to make drastic changes at some time in your life. With extreme aspects you may experience the loss of siblings, problems with neighbors or mental difficulties.

Psychoanalyst Carl Jung, playwright Tennessee Williams, filmmaker Alfred Hitchcock, actor Burt Reynolds.

PLUTO IN THE FOURTH HOUSE
keyword *complex*

With Pluto in the fourth, you can surely change or transform yourself. Your home is a focal point in your life, and you need to have your authority recognized there. Due to childhood circumstances, you often have a chip on your shoulder. There is probably something unusual about your family background: the early loss of a parent, a dictatorial parent or a family scandal. Wealth may come in your later years, possibly through the earth sciences, research, real estate or scientific endeavors. With difficult aspects, you may feel deeply rebellious of established values, and you may isolate yourself from society. *Attorney F. Lee Bailey, murder/cult leader Charles Manson, pianist Oscar Levant, anthropologist Margaret Mead.*

PLUTO IN THE FIFTH HOUSE
keyword *risk-taking*

You have an inborn love of gambling and are willing to take many risks emotionally and financially. Often you may make great gains because of your daring. With your strong eroticism, sex can be a motivating force in your life, or else you can turn in the opposite direction and be completely asexual or celibate. Pluto in this position complicates your emotional balance; you need to develop a creative outlet. With challenging aspects, there can be troubled pregnancies, and you can be extremely possessive of your loved ones. *Ventriloquist Edgar Bergen, Chief Justice Earl Warren, actor Spencer Tracy, FBI director J. Edgar Hoover.*

PLUTO IN THE SIXTH HOUSE
keyword *researching*

An extreme individualist, you are not afraid to stick your neck out to help others and are often engaged in the healing arts or nutrition. You may feel that you have a preordained mission in life. You have a deep need to serve humanity, do research or

pursue scientific objectives. Pluto here will sometimes complicate your health by causing blockage, constipation, abnormal growths or tumors; in the teen years it can give problems with acne. Unless you channel your energies properly, you could become a hypochondriac and run from one doctor to the next. You could become the victim of your own pent-up energies and must face and overcome any bad habits.
Astrologer Doris Chase Doane, nutritionist Adelle Davis, writer Mark Twain, inventor Thomas Edison.

PLUTO IN THE SEVENTH HOUSE
keyword *circumstantial*

You are dynamic, magnetic and temperamental. Your activities affect other people as greatly as they affect you. Your partner may be of a different religious or cultural background; this will require many adjustments in your partnership. Sometimes you may marry for necessity, or you may experience divorce, elopement or the disappearance of a partner. When used properly, you can be a trail blazer and establish world opinion in your field. You may receive public acclaim and prominence, but it must often be shared with a partner. When used improperly, this placement can lead to legal problems; a lack of diplomacy can make many enemies.
Aviator Charles Lindbergh, Senator Edward M. Kennedy, Indian Leader Mohandas Gandhi, Egyptian Prime Minister Gamal Nasser.

PLUTO IN THE EIGHTH HOUSE
keyword *investigative*   accidental dignity

Since this is Pluto's natural house, the other world may occupy your thoughts. Religion has real meaning to you, and you investigate all occult things deeply. Because your body is able to regenerate itself, this placement often indicates a long life. You are analytical , have good money sense and can wield a lot of financial power. Research, medicine or science could appeal to you. You may earn money through matters relating to death, e.g., as a mortician. With challenging aspects you could be a religious fanatic or overly sensual. You could also be one who will stop at nothing to promote your obsessions on unsuspecting victims.

Dictator Adolf Hitler, President Charles de Gaulle, artist Francisco Goya, actor Tyrone Power.

PLUTO IN THE NINTH HOUSE
keyword *pioneering*

Restless, eager and adventurous, you are willing to try anything and to experience all. You may aspire to an impossible dream. You must travel; foreign lands may beckon you, and you could be a space traveler. You might take a foreign spouse, or you may be a refugee. You have an insatiable need for learning and can be a good writer of occult, mystery or sex novels. You may change your culture or religion. With difficult aspects, you may be bigoted, opinionated and unwilling to listen to another's viewpoint. You may have legal problems with authorities, often in foreign lands, or problems with your in-laws.

Vice President Nelson Rockefeller, writer Thomas Mann, explorer Robert Peary, Greek shipping magnate Stavros Niarchos.

PLUTO IN THE TENTH HOUSE
keyword *political*

You are self-assertive and determined and willing to fight authority if necessary in order to achieve your goals. Strong, courageous and tenacious, you can be a dictator, an innovator, a planner or an inventor. With difficult aspects, your insistence on self-determination can border on megalomania. You are a leader in your own circle or profession, and you may be either loved or hated, but you will never be ignored. You have an obsessive need to be the best and to outshine those around you. A perfectionist, you drive yourself relentlessly. You can present your ideas lucidly and eloquent-

ly. With difficult aspects, you can be cunning, vindictive, sadistic and cheating.
President Richard Nixon, political philosopher Karl Marx, artist Pablo Picasso, writer Ernest Hemingway.

PLUTO IN THE ELEVENTH HOUSE
keyword *fulfilling*

You are intensely loyal, have a strong communal sense, an urge to reform and a wealth of plans. Interested in worldly affairs, you may participate in reform movements or social improvements. Your friends are important to you, and you are helpful to them; however you must take care that they do not influence your life too strongly. With challenging aspects you must learn to discriminate in your choice of associates, because you may be attracted to those who will lead you astray. This placement often indicates a loner.
President Lyndon Johnson, writer Zelda Fitzgerald, actress Marilyn Monroe, baseball player Jackie Robinson.

PLUTO IN THE TWELFTH HOUSE
keyword *isolating*

Pluto in the twelfth house can bring you face to face with temptation. You must gently uncover your fears and frustrations and bring them out of your subconscious with patience and understanding. You need to change your inner attitudes; this is difficult because you are reluctant to change the course of your life. You work best behind the scenes, and you understand others' limitations. With challenging aspects, you may have some psychological problems, perhaps even be confined. You may feel pain, both physical and mental, from obscure or unidentified sources.
Physician Charles Mayo, heiress/revolutionary Patricia Hearst, chess player Bobbie Fischer, boxer George Foreman.

Summary

This brings us to the end of this introductory manual. We hope that you enjoyed our book, we hope that you learned a lot, but most of all, we hope that astrology will help you lead a fuller and happier life.

Here's one more chart for you, the horoscope of Muhammad Ali, so you can practice all you've learned so far. While you delineate Ali's chart review all the lessons once more.

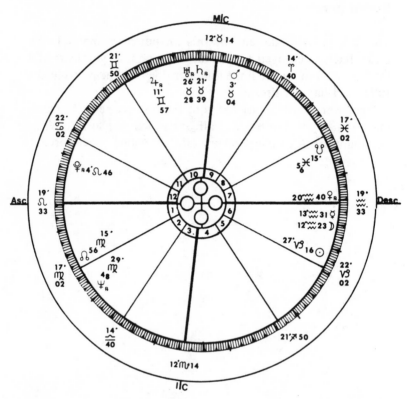

Figure 12: The Natal Horoscope of Muhammad Ali Born January 17, 1942 at 6:35 p.m. Central Standard Time in Louisville, Kentucky. Longitude 38° N 15′, latitude 85° W 45′.

longitude	☽	☿	♀	☉	♂	♃	♄	♅	♆	♇

cardinal:			
fixed:			
mutable:			
fire:			
earth:			
air:			
water:			
angular:			
succedent:			
cadent:			
dignity:			
exaltation:			
detriment:			
fall:			
L:	S:	R:	E:

Appendix

Lesson 2: Quiz 1

1. William Shakespeare—B. Sun in Taurus, ruler Venus in Gemini, the sign identified with writing.
2. Florence Nightingale—A. Sun in Taurus, ruler Venus in Cancer, the sign that signifies nurturing and caring for others.
3. Robert Peary—D. Sun in Taurus, ruler Venus in Aries, the sign of pioneering and exploring.
4. Leonardo da Vinci—C. Sun in Taurus, ruler Venus in Taurus, the sign that signifies the arts, love of beauty and color.

Figure 13: Natural or Flat Wheel This is the completed chart from lesson 1. Each house of the flat wheel shows the glyph of the sign natural to that house, the glyph of the ruling planet, the element of each sign, the quality of each sign, the quality of each house, the keywords for each house and the division of the signs according to the positive/negative principle.

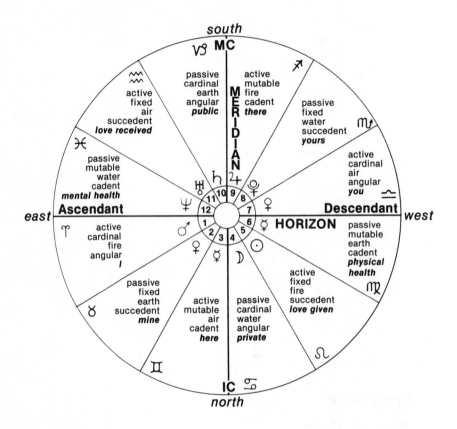

Lesson 2: Quiz 2 (page 19)

1. false	13. true	25. false
2. false	14. true	26. true
3. true	15. true	27. false
4. true	16. true	28. true
5. false	17. false	29. false
6. false	18. false	30. false
7. true	19. true	31. false
8. false	20. false	32. true
9. false	21. false	33. false
10. true	22. true	34. false
11. true	23. false	35. true
12. true	24. false	

Correct answers:
 1. I am
 2. ruled by the Moon
 5. twelfth sign
 6. I have
 8. I will
 9. rules the breasts and stomach
17. imagination
18. ruled by Venus
20. I think
21. I balance
23. rules the head
24. ambition
25. imagination
27. eighth sign
29. I understand
30. ruled by Neptune
31. ruled by Mars
33. rules the intestines
34. opposite of Aries

Lesson 3: Quiz (page 30)

1. ☽ ☿ ♀ ☉ ♂ ♃ ♄ ♅ ♆ ♇

2. a. ♉   3. i. ♅   3. t. ☉
    b. ♋   j. ♄ ♀   u. ♃
    c. ♋   k. ♃   v. ♀
3. a. ☿   l. ☽   w. ☉
    b. ☉   m. ☉   x. ☿
    c. ♃   n. ♇   y. ♅
    d. ☽   o. ♀   4. ♅ ♆ ♇
    e. ♃   p. ☽
    f. ♂   q. ♇
    g. ♄   r. ♆
    h. ♆   s. ♅

Lesson 4: Quiz (page 44)

1. ♈ ♌ ♐
2. ♉ ♍ ♑
3. ♊ ♎ ♒
4. ♋ ♏ ♓
5. first, fourth, seventh, tenth
6. second, fifth, eighth, eleventh
7. third, sixth, ninth, twelfth
8. ♈ ♋ ♎ ♑
9. ♉ ♌ ♏ ♒
10. ♊ ♍ ♐ ♓
11. Scorpio
12. fifth house
13. Capricorn
14. Scorpio
15. Scorpio; Mars
16. Aquarius, Pisces; Saturn, Jupiter
17. Gemini
18. Libra
19. twelfth house
20. first, fifth, ninth
21. second, sixth, tenth
22. fourth house cusp

23. first house cusp
24. Gemini, Virgo
25. Venus; Taurus, Libra

Lesson 5: Quiz (page 53)

Venus in Aquarius in the fifth house (Ruler Uranus in Virgo in the twelfth house.) Venus represents the affections, the social urge, the sense of values and how you show any of these qualities.

With Venus in Aquarius, Roosevelt showed his affections in a cool fashion; his feelings were ruled more by intellect than emotion. His social urges were often individualistic and at times unpredictable. His sense of values leaned more towards the humane and the progressive. With the ruler Uranus in the practical sign Virgo, he expressed these qualities in a down-to-earth way.

Adding some Leo overtones, since Leo is the natural sign of the fifth house, we find him romantic, idealistic, self-assured and generous, but only as far as the intellect of Aquarius and the earthiness of Virgo will allow.

The fifth house position shows that his affections, values and social urges were directed toward his children, love affairs and pleasurable sports; most of his creativity was channelled into a practical area, work—in his case politics.

Mars in Gemini in the tenth house (Ruler Mercury in Aquarius in the sixth house.) Mars represents energy, action, the aggressive urge, initiative and how you expend them.

Mars in Gemini shows versatility; thus he expressed his energies in many different ways. Since Gemini is an air sign, we can say that Roosevelt needed to involve his mind in whatever he did.

With the ruler Mercury in Aquarius in the sixth house, we add more of the air quality, the quick wit, the independent way of thinking and the love and talent for communication. Much of this was shown through work since the ruler is in the sixth house.

The tenth house position of Mars adds a nuance of Capricorn; this helps to ground the changeable Gemini nature

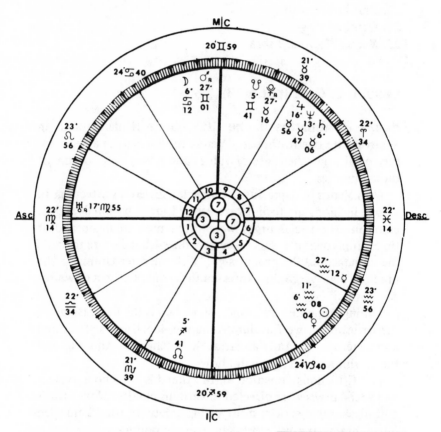

Figure 14: The Natal Horoscope of Franklin Delano Roosevelt This is the completed chart from page 73 in lesson 7.

longitude										
6 ♋ 12	☽									
27 ♒ 12		☿								
6 ♒ 04	⊼		♀							
11 ♒ 08	⊼		♂	☉						
27 ♊ 01			△		♂ᴿ					
16 ♉ 56				□		♃				
6 ♉ 06	✳		□	□			♄			
17 ♍ 55					△			♅ᴿ		
13 ♉ 47			□	□		♂	♂	△	♆	
27 ♉ 16		□								♀ᴿ

cardinal:	☽
fixed:	♄ ♆ ♃ ♀ ♀ ☉ ☿
mutable:	♂ ♅ M A
fire:	none
earth:	♄ ♆ ♃ ♀ ♅ A
air:	♂ ♀ ☉ ☿ M
water:	☽
angular:	♂ ☽
succedent:	♀ ☉ ♄ ♆ ♃
cadent:	☿ ♀ ♅
dignity:	☽
exaltation:	☿
detriment:	☉
fall:	

L: 3	S: 3	R: 0	E: 4

and to direct it into responsible and serious avenues. Instead of being restless and scatterbrained, he appeared businesslike and hardworking.

Since the tenth house stands for profession, career, honor, ambition and so on, we now realize that most of his energies were to further these personal aims.

Jupiter in Taurus in the eighth house (Ruler Venus in Aquarius in the fifth house.) Jupiter represents the ability to expand and grow, the protective urge and philosophical aspirations.

In Taurus this growth progressed in a stable way. He had the patience to work his way up; his ideals stayed in practical realms, and he showed thoroughness in all his endeavors. Since the ruler Venus is in Aquarius in the fifth house, again his aims and expansion pattern were based on reasoning and his mental processes were creative and inventive.

Scorpio, the natural sign of the eighth house, produces resourcefulness and gave him good probing and investigative ability. The eighth house shows the support we receive from other people, and Roosevelt has not only Jupiter but Saturn and Neptune in this house as well. You will find that most politicians have strong eighth houses. No wonder, since support from other people is the basis of politics.

Saturn in Taurus in the eighth house (Ruler Venus in Aquarius in the fifth house.) As you see, Saturn is in the same sign and house as Jupiter. Whereas Jupiter represents the ability to expand and to grow, Saturn represents the security and the safety urge. It shows the capacity for a career and the discipline and responsibilities required. It is the teacher and taskmaster of the horoscope.

With Saturn in the earth sign Taurus, Roosevelt readily accepted responsibility and discipline. This placement also indicates a great need for security, and most earth signs seek it in material areas. But with the ruler in Aquarius he found much of this security in his own intellectual ability; his career was based on his capacity to communicate well. This is something that we often encounter in charts that have a predominance of air signs.

The Scorpio overtone of the eighth house would add depth to the Taurus Saturn, reinforcing his determination and

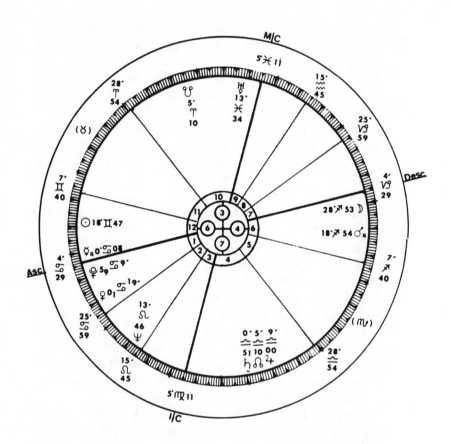

Figure 15: The Natal Horoscope of Judy Garland This is the completed chart from page 76 in lesson 7.

longitude									
28 ♐ 53	☽								
0 ♋ 08	☌	☿ᴿ							
19 ♋ 01			♀						
18 ♊ 47				☉					
18 ♐ 54				☍	☌	♂ᴿ			
9 ♎ 00							♃		
0 ♎ 51	□	□						♄	
13 ♓ 34			△	□	□	☌			♅
13 ♌ 46				✳	△	✳	☌		♆
9 ♋ 59							□		△	♀

cardinal:	☿ ♀ ♀ ♄ ♃ A
fixed:	♆
mutable:	☉ ♂ ☽ ♅ M
fire:	♆ ♂ ☽
earth:	none
air:	☉ ♄ ♃
water:	☿ ♀ ♀ ♅ A M
angular:	♀ ♀ ♄ ♃ ♅
succedent:	♆
cadent:	♂ ☽ ☉ ☿
dignity:	
exaltation:	♄
detriment:	
fall:	

L: 2	S: 4	R: 0	E: 4

motivation. Scorpio is passionate, Taurus is sensual, and the eighth house is the house of sex. Because the planet Saturn indicates insecurity, we can presume that Roosevelt had some sexual hangups.

Lesson 8: The Sun (page 80)

If you have delineated Judy Garland's chart and are just checking in the Appendix to see how you did, congratulations! You are on your way to becoming an astrologer. If you did not, keep in mind that our entire delineation of this horoscope is based on keywords and phrases taken from this book. Your learning experience is to check back to see which words we did or did not use and why.

The Sun in Gemini in the twelfth house We find Judy Garland's inner self or basic personality in Gemini. Her nature was dual, adaptable (reinforced by many mutable planets), talkative (reinforced by the Moon in Sagittarius), sympathetic (reinforced by ruler Mercury in Cancer) and restless (reinforced by many cadent and mutable planets). Because the ruler of Gemini is in Cancer, some of the scatterbrained or idle-chatter qualities will be toned down, and we can say that she was more tenacious, conscientious and emotional than if Mercury were also in Gemini. Communication is important, though, especially since the third house of communication has Leo on the cusp, which is ruled by the Sun in Gemini. She was irresponsible at times and needed changes of scenery (substantiated by Sun square Uranus, which we will deal with later).

We've already discussed some of the Cancerian overtones added by the ruler Mercury in Cancer; we also must add a Pisces nuance because the Sun in the twelfth house takes on the Pisces qualities of compassion, sympathy and emotion. (This fits with the overview which we have already established.) We can say that she was musical, not because we know that this is Judy Garland the singer, but because Pisces and Taurus are musical signs. Neptune rules the Midheaven (her career), and Venus, the ruler of Taurus, is strong in this chart because it is angular in the first house.

Judy Garland's Sun is in the twelfth house; in this position the Sun shines behind the scenes, and we must assume that she would have preferred a less public life. Yet a twelfth house Sun is often the position of actors and actresses; instead of revealing themselves, they can hide behind a role. Although she did not work in an institution but in a big movie studio, according to her descriptions it often felt like an institution. She did not do research (another twelfth house occupation); the rest of the chart does not reinforce that inclination, but with all the Cancer in her chart she could have done some charitable work had she decided to go in that direction.

Because Judy Garland's Sun has many difficult aspects, we can say that she was her own worst enemy.

Sun Opposition Mars Judy Garland's Sun is in nearly exact opposition to Mars; this made her a fighter, gave her enthusiasm and indicates that she was quite outspoken. She did not come on too forcefully though, because neither Gemini nor Cancer act that way, but she did speak before she thought and perhaps put her foot into her mouth or hurt people unwillingly. Once the see-saw motion of an opposition becomes balanced and the awareness of the polarity has been learned, oppositions become helpful and positive. We don't feel that Judy Garland ever learned this.

Sun square Uranus Sun square Uranus made Judy Garland impulsive, rash and eccentric; she did her own thing without concern for what it did to others. However, this square gave her tremendous magnetism, especially in her career, since Uranus is near her Midheaven. It also made her nervous and accident-prone, and she certainly did attract upsetting conditions and events.

Sun sextile Neptune Sun sextile Neptune provides imagination and creativity. We will fully delineate Neptune when we come to lesson 16. This aspect made her tender (Cancer is strong in her chart) and romantic because Neptune is in the romantic sign Leo. This aspect also showed that she was devoted to her mate and family.

Lesson 9: The Moon (page 104)

The Moon in Sagittarius in the sixth house We are now discussing Judy Garland's emotional makeup; the Moon shows moods, instincts, desires and needs. When we look at the description of the Moon in Sagittarius, we have to keep in mind that Garland's Moon is ruled by Jupiter in Libra in the fourth house and also that her Moon is in the sixth house adding Virgo overtones. We must also look at the aspects in order to understand the potential uses of this placement of the Moon.

The Moon in Sagittarius indicates that Judy Garland was socially accepting, naive, but also not unaware of class consciousness because the ruler Jupiter is in Libra, and Libra is refined at times to the point of being snobbish. She was open and friendly but this showed up more in her work (sixth house) than in her private life because of the twelfth house Sun. She was searching, inspirational and restless; these qualities have already been established in our overview and in our delineation of her Sun. When we look at the Moon's aspects, we see that she had only squares and oppositions which are challenging and tension-producing. We can deduce from this that she had many problems keeping her emotions under control. This fact needs to be kept in mind when delineating the Moon. For this reason we have picked some of the less positive keywords and phrases to describe this placement of the Moon.

We can say that she was unsettled in both mind and body, that she required a lot of activity and that she needed to roam. She was actually more sensitive than her free and breezy attitude revealed. Religion, poetry, philosophy and music were important to her, and she liked to help others. She loved freedom and independence, but only to a certain point because her Cancer stellium made her somewhat dependent. She was careless and sometimes reckless. All tension-producing aspects challenge a person to great activity and achievement. In talking about the Moon we are dealing with emotional challenges; if there are too many of these challenges, life can become extremely difficult and often overwhelming.

The Libra overtones (the ruler of Sagittarius is Jupiter in Libra) add charm, a desire to please and to be liked, and an indecisiveness. This Libra influence also reinforced her fondness for the arts.

The sixth house position of the Moon shows Virgo nuances; Garland responded well to appreciation and encouragement, but she tended to be over-eager emotionally (also seen in the aspects). The Virgo feeling added industriousness and a desire for perfection.

With the Moon in her sixth house we see changeability, not only in her emotional makeup but in her work as well. Wherever we find the Moon in a chart is where there are ups and downs; Judy Garland's work reflected this flux. We can also assume that she liked to mother people, and that when she took the time she was a good cook. We can also say that many of her illnesses were psychosomatic, brought on by her nervousness and emotionalism.

Moon opposition Mercury The Moon is in nearly exact opposition to Mercury (1° orb). This made her unreasonable, overly sensitive (seen in previous aspects), but also loyal to friends and causes. Highstrung and excitable, she needed to learn about compromise and self-control.

Moon square Saturn. The Moon is in a close square to Saturn (less than a 2° orb). This is a difficult aspect since it indicates an insecurity that nearly always dates back to childhood and difficulties with one of the parents—in her case the mother. This square made Judy Garland work very hard trying to prove herself, and it also shows a lack of self-confidence.

Lesson 10: Mercury (page 135)

Mercury in Cancer in the twelfth house Mercury represents mental capacity, reasoning ability and the means of communication. Judy Garland's Mercury is in Cancer, ruled by the Moon in Sagittarius in the sixth house. Again we interpret the Cancer feeling with certain Sagittarian overtones, and then we add some Piscean feeling because of the house position.

Judy Garland's mental qualities were emotional, and she was swayed by her senses instead of reasoning in a detached and objective way. Although tenacious, she was also influenced by her environment; this made her moody and changeable. (These are all factors which we have already seen and which we are now confirming.) Kindness and praise would be the most effective way to reach Judy Garland. She was creative and intuitive with empathy for the suffering of others, but she also tended to feel sorry for herself. Since Mercury has few but mostly challenging aspects we can say that she was mentally evasive, and with the twelfth house position of the Sun we can also say that she found it difficult to face the truth or herself—two factors which go hand in hand. Home and family were important to her, but again, with the ruler Moon in Sagittarius in the sixth house, the emphasis is more on work than it would be were the Moon in another sign or house.

Sagittarius adds sincerity, a good sense of humor, impulsiveness and a multitude of interests (which she had anyway with the Sun in Gemini). The twelfth house position adds Piscean overtones; this re-emphasizes her intuition and the romantic inclination of her thinking process; again it shows that she kept her innermost thoughts well under cover.

Mercury in the twelfth house indicates that her mind worked in subtle ways, that she lacked confidence (seen before), but that she hid this fact. She needed to face reality rather than live in a dream world. Mercury in this house again substantiates that her decisions were based on feeling rather than reason.

Mercury square Saturn This shows that she was traditional, shy and reserved, but also hardworking, responsible and ambitious. This aspect again indicates childhood difficulties, this time relating more to her father. Mercury square Saturn also indicates insecurity and defensiveness that could easily lead to depression. We would not call her suspicious because neither Sagittarius, where the ruler of Mercury is placed, nor Gemini (her Sun sign) support that fact.

Lesson 11: Venus (page 158)

Venus in Cancer in the first house Judy Garland's Venus is also in Cancer, and again the ruler is in Sagittarius in the sixth house. Venus is angular in the first house, which adds an Aries overtone. Venus in Cancer indicates that Garland was sensitive, idealistic and self-indulgent. Since Venus represents affections, values and social urges, we can say that Garland was looking for an ideal mate to love and to be loved by, a romantic person who would protect her and not hurt her.

Fearful of being hurt, she did not show this, but rather she kept busy or put on an "I don't care" act. Venus in Cancer also indicates gentleness and charm, and again we note that she liked to care for her loved ones.

With the ruler of her Venus in Sagittarius we see idealism and also flirtatiousness. The first house Aries overtone again shows her magnetic appeal and her restlessness. It also adds a certain ardor to her style and love nature.

Venus in the first house indicates beauty, personal grace and a happy disposition. She liked to be spoiled and enjoyed social occasions and lovely surroundings. Her personality was outgoing and acting was easy for her; she liked flirting and music and had a sweet tooth. Her ego was healthy, and she could be quite self-indulgent. These are all traits that we have noted previously in her chart. There is one sentence in our delineation of Venus in the first house that does not fit Judy Garland: "Early life is usually pleasant." In the delineations of the Sun, the Moon and Mercury, that we saw the Sun/Mars opposition, the Moon/Saturn square and the Mercury/Saturn square all indicate parental problems. Since the parents represent the early life we have to conclude that her youth could not have been easy, although it might have had its pleasant moments and rewards.

Venus inconjunct Mars This gave Judy Garland difficulties in satisfying her desires. She needed to overcome a negative attitude towards herself. Often taken advantage of, her drive to succeed was usually at the cost of love and affection.

Venus trine Uranus This again shows her magnetic personality and also her tendency to fall in love quickly and often. She relished life and had an abundance of creativity which we know that she used. She needed an adequate outlet for her emotions. This aspect again substantiates the fact that she might have had more than one marriage and certainly more than one partner.

Lesson 12: Mars (page 179)

Mars in Sagittarius in the sixth house Mars shows drive, energy and sexual inclinations. Garland's Mars in Sagittarius in the sixth house had Virgo overtones. Jupiter, the ruler of Sagittarius, is in Libra.

Mars in Sagittarius indicates that she operated with great bursts of energy but that she did not have much endurance. With her love of change she often embraced new ideas without investigating them first. She had great natural vitality, rhythm, tempo and harmony. Cheerful and socially popular, she was sexually exploratory; this is substantiated by Aquarius on the cusp of the eighth house, the house of sex. She lacked follow-through because Mars has difficult aspects, but the Libra nuance would add charm, cooperation and sociability to this placement. The Virgo overtone shows her enjoyment and enthusiasm for work, as well as a certain discipline. Mars in the sixth house again substantiates that she was a hard worker; it also indicates that she could drive herself unmercifully, even to the point of illness; in fact, her co-workers may have found her pace difficult to keep up with. She had a hot temper which she needed to control, and since she was ambitious to get ahead in life, she probably learned this fairly early.

Mars square Uranus This indicates a strong will; it also indicates a leader who can go far once self-restraint has been learned. She needed to recognize her limitations, or else she would overwork or have accidents. Again we see reckless love affairs and quick marriages. This is not a chart that indicates what we might call an orderly or well regulated life.

Mars trine Neptune This is the easiest and most flowing aspect that Mars makes. This flow should be used to develop positive expressions of drive and energy. It shows talent in musical or literary areas which should be fully developed. We know that she used her musical talent, but she never developed her writing ability. She was sympathetic, inspirational, loving and emotional—tendencies that we have already seen in many other areas in her chart.

Lesson 13: Jupiter (page 198)

Jupiter in Libra in the fourth house Jupiter shows the area of expansion; in Libra it expresses itself in an artistic, sociable, cooperative and refined way. Venus, the ruler of Libra, is in Cancer in the first house; therefore we must add some

Cancerian overtones, both because of the ruler and because of the fourth house position.

However, it was hard to keep an emotional balance and there was occasional indecision. Judy Garland's Jupiter has three aspects: one flowing and two challenging. With this in mind, we feel that it was easy for her to expand artistically, to be popular and to be a good conversationalist, especially since we have had confirmation of these abilities by other aspects in the chart. The Cancer overtone adds generosity, the ability to relate well to the public, graciousness and maybe a weight problem. Because Jupiter is exalted in Cancer, this overtone is a beneficial one.

Jupiter inconjunct Uranus This made her overly optimistic, lacking in attention to details and not very self-disciplined. Yet this aspect also indicates that she had to learn inner discipline to avoid financial difficulties. She also had to learn not to be pressured into proving herself again and again, both to her friends (Uranus is the natural ruler of the eleventh house of friendship) and in her career (Uranus is near the Midheaven, signifying career).

Jupiter sextile Neptune This again shows her musical and creative ability, but also indicates that she could have used this energy in a religious or spritual way had she wanted to. This aspect again shows that the areas of writing, charity and social work could have been good areas for her.

Jupiter square Pluto This re-emphasizes the feelings of inadequacy which we have seen before in this chart. This aspect left her torn between supreme self-confidence and self-doubt. In hindsight we know that she used both the negative and positive approaches in her lifetime. At times she would be arrogant, exaggerate, take big gambles and jump into adventures. She was not likely to set herself up as a law unto herself because of the strong Cancer influence in the chart; Cancer prefers to please and to adhere to existing laws whenever possible.

Lesson 14: Saturn (page 216)

Saturn in Libra in the fourth house Saturn is well placed in Libra, the sign of its exaltation. However, the only aspects

Saturn makes in Judy Garland's chart are squares to the Moon and Mercury, which we delineated in lessons 9 and 10. Both of these squares are nearly exact; therefore they form a basic part of her character. We also note that Saturn in the fourth house and the ruler Venus in Cancer add strong Cancerian overtones; in the fourth house the planet Saturn is not comfortable, nor working at its best. All of these factors have to be kept in mind when looking at this horoscope. Because of Saturn's difficult aspects, Judy Garland was not as disciplined and responsible as one might assume under other circumstances, nor was she very good at organizational planning or business. The learning lessons of Saturn would all apply since squares in a chart all indicate the need to learn or to achieve something. Because her Saturn rules the seventh house, marriage required patience and hard work. Relating to others was also one of the lessons to learn. She was demanding, both of others and herself, and sometimes intolerant.

Adding some Cancer feeling reinforces traits that we have already noticed, such as that her early family life was difficult and probably left scars, the sense of responsibility she felt toward her family, the hiding of her inner thoughts and feelings to preserve an aura of dignity, her need for love and approval, a troubled home life, hypersensitivity and a tendency to gain weight.

The fourth house position of Saturn again shows difficulties with one of the parents and a strong attachment to the family. She did better away from her home or place of birth; her innate feeling of inadequacy and insecurity spurred her to great achievement and made her try doubly hard at anything she undertook. She was prone to digestive problems, mainly brought on by worry and emotionalism. A good spiritual attitude would have helped to overcome many of these problems.

Saturn is the teacher, the taskmaster. It can bring delays and impose limitations. But Saturn is totally just and fair; what you sow is what you reap. If you accept Saturn's lessons positively, you will reap your rewards. Garland's lessons were difficult because her emotional insecurity was deeply ingrained. She was easily depressed, and we know that for her the quickest way to overcome these feelings was through her work, where she received applause and acclaim. But her career kept her too busy to really look within herself, to overcome her problems from the inside out instead of from the outside in. Had she taken the time to do this, she might have matured differently and been a much happier person. But she did not choose that course, and we see how her free will ultimately determined the way she lived.

Lesson 15: Uranus (page 235)

Uranus in Pisces in the tenth house Uranus is the most elevated planet in Judy Garland's horoscope, and therefore very important. Because Uranus stays in each sign for about seven years, millions of people have Uranus there. Therefore, the house position becomes more important than the sign. All of the people with Uranus in Pisces are intuitive, but Judy Garland, with many planets in water signs, was especially intuitive. All people born within these seven years would reflect some of the changeability of Uranus in Pisces, but Garland, with many mutable planets, reflected this trait much more. We have already established her artistic abilities and acting talents, and this placement of Uranus and the ruler Neptune in Leo emphasized these. Uranus also confirms other characteristics which we have previously seen: oversensitivity, nervousness, the need to learn her limits and the need to relax. She had both challenging and flowing aspects to Uranus and it was up to her to choose which ones she would use most. This placement also indicates the wish to escape with the help of drugs, alcohol or sex.

The Capricorn nuance added to Uranus in the tenth house showed a forward-looking attitude, yet also a reluctance to let go of yesterday. This also confirms her sense of restlessness and her nervous temperament.

Uranus in the tenth house indicated that she could be a fighter for a cause or a rebel against any kind of authority. Since there are both flowing and challenging aspects, it was up to her how she was going to use these energies. We know by hindsight that she chose the latter course. This position also helped to bring on the many disappointments and career changes she experienced, and it also explains why she was so often misunderstood. We don't know if she had any interest in astrology or occult matters, but she could have been so inclined.

Uranus inconjunct (quincunx) Neptune This indicates that she was a great protector of the underdog, that she abhorred injustice, but that she also felt guilty for not doing enough in any of these areas. As a result, she often chose not to do any of it, becoming self-centered or self-absorbed instead. Again we see that Garland and the many others who have this aspect are creative and original. In this chart though, because Uranus is in the tenth house conjunct the Midheaven and the ruler Neptune in the second house, part of this originality provided her with inner and outer resources, that is, inner talent and the ability to earn money with that talent.

Uranus trine Pluto. This gave her endurance and strength, and it enabled her to accept new concepts. It also provided her with an idealistic outlook. Again we realize that since Uranus is so close to her Midheaven (her career), and Pluto is so close to her Ascendant (her outer personality) that much of that strength, endurance and idealism was applied to her career.

Lesson 16: Neptune (page 251)

Neptune in Leo in the second house Veiled Neptune, the planet of illusion and delusion, dreams, deception, spiritual enlightenment, artistic talent and creativity, is placed in dramatic Leo and the ruler Sun in Gemini.

As we explained in lesson 16, Neptune remains in each sign for fourteen years; it is a generational planet. All people born with Neptune in Leo have romantic inclinations with an inborn idealism and artistic ability. In Garland's chart we have seen her talents and potentials in the field of entertainment; this would only serve to reinforce what we have previously determined, including the Gemini versatility of being able to act, dance, sing and more.

Neptune in the second house relates to Taurus. This adds an aesthetic approach to the arts and a need for security, which we have already seen in many other areas. Neptune in the second house indicates that her financial judgment was weak and that she needed to be honest and avoid any monetary schemes; this position of Neptune indicates that money flowed through her fingers. Because Neptune is the ruler of Pisces and Pisces is the sign on her Midheaven, we can see that she could earn money through whatever career she chose. Since most of Neptune's aspects are easy and flowing, we feel that earning money was not hard for her, but keeping and managing it was difficult.

All of the aspects to Neptune have already been delineated, when we discussed the aspects for the Sun, Mars, Jupiter and Uranus.

Lesson 17: Pluto (page 266)

Pluto in Cancer in the first house Pluto remained in Cancer for twenty-five years. As we pointed out in lesson 17, it brought about many generational changes. In the personal chart it shows a great need for security—a quality always associated with Cancer. In Garland's case we know by now that security was one of her basic needs, as was the need to achieve emotional maturity. Her Pluto in Cancer is ruled by the Moon in Sagittarius, which added optimism and much enthusiasm and gave her a bubbly quality, which was quite noticeable since Pluto is positioned close to her Ascendant. Because of this proximity we know that Pluto had much influence on her personality.

Pluto in the first house indicated intensity, a craving for power and a tremendous ambition. Her personality was magnetic, yet she showed many faces to the world—sometimes brooding, sometimes energetic, sometimes passionate and at other times restless.

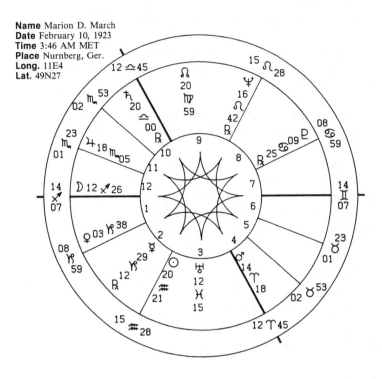

Name Marion D. March
Date February 10, 1923
Time 3:46 AM MET
Place Nurnberg, Ger.
Long. 11E4
Lat. 49N27

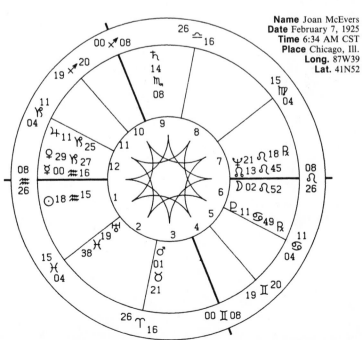

Name Joan McEvers
Date February 7, 1925
Time 6:34 AM CST
Place Chicago, Ill.
Long. 87W39
Lat. 41N52

RECOMMENDED READING

Other books you may enjoy at this learning level are:

Cosmic Combinations by Joan Negus which provides 99 exercises to help you expand your ability to apply what you have learned from these books.

12 Times 12 by Joan McEvers which shows you how to combine Sun positions with the rising sign and discusses house positions as well.

The Gold Mine in Your Files by Anna Kria King which suggests a practical way to catalogue your charts so that you can learn more about astrology (on a personalized level).

The best value in everything you need
to calculate and interpret charts
from
ACS Publications, Inc.
P.O. Box 16430, San Diego, CA 92116

We calculate... You delineate!

CHART CALCULATIONS

Natal Chart wheel with planet/sign glyphs. Choice of house system: Placidus (standard), Equal, Koch, Campanus, Meridian, Porphyry, Regiomontanus, Topocentric, or Alcabitius. Choice of tropical (standard) or sidereal zodiac. Aspects, elements, planetary nodes, declinations, midpoints, etc. 2.00
Arabic Parts All traditional parts and more 1.00
Asteroids ⚳ ⚴ ⚵ ⚶ in wheel + aspects/midpoints ... .50
Asteroids ⚳ ⚴ ⚵ ⚶ + 15 new ones for 20th century only 1.00
Astrodynes Power, harmony and discord with summaries for easy comparison 2.00
Chiron, Transpluto (only one) in wheel .... N/C
Concentric Wheels Any 3 charts available in wheel format may be combined into a '3 wheeler' 3.00
Deduct $1.00 for each chart ordered as a separate wheel.
Fixed Stars Robson's 110 fixed stars with aspects to natal chart 1.00
Fortune Finder more Arabic Parts — 97 ancient (Al Biruni) and 99 modern (Robert Hurzt Granite) 2.00
Graphic Midpoint Sort Proportional spacing highlights midpt. groupings. **Specify integer divisions of 360°** (1=360°, 4=90°, etc.) 1.00
Harmonic Chart John Addey type. Wheel format, harmonic asc. eq. houses. **Specify harmonic number** . 2.00
Harmonic Positions 30 consecutive sets of positions **Specify starting harmonic number** 1.00
Heliocentric Charts Sun-centered positions 2.00
House Systems Comparison for 9 systems......... .50
Local Space Planet compass directions (azimuth & altitude) plus Campanus Mundoscope .... .50
Locality Map USA, World, Europe, S. Amer., Far East, Austl., Mid East and Africa map — choice of rise, set, and culmination lines or Asc., Desc., MC, IC lines for each map 6.00
Midpoint Structures Midpoint aspects + midpoints in 45° and 90° sequence 1.00
Rectification Assist 10 same-day charts. **Specify starting time, time increment, e.g. 6 am, every 20 minutes** 10.00
Relocation Chart for current location. **Specify original birth data and new location** 2.00
Uranian Planets + halfsums..................... .50
Uranian Sensitive Points (includes Uranian Planets). 3.50

HUMAN RELATIONSHIPS

Chart Comparison (Synastry) All aspects between the two sets of planets plus house positions of one in the other..................... 1.50
Composite Chart Rob Hand-type. Created from midpoints between 2 charts. **Specify location** 2.00
Relationship Chart Chart erected for space-time midpoint between two births 2.00
Interpretive Comparison Report Specify natal data for 2 births 8.00

COLOR CHARTS

4-Color Wheel any chart we offer in new, aesthetic format with color coded aspect lines............ 2.00
Local Space Map 4-color on 360° circle 2.00
Custom 6" Disk for any harmonic (laminated, you cut out) overlays on our color wheel charts 4.00
Plotted Natal Dial for use with custom 6" Disk 2.00
Specify harmonic #
Custom Graphic Ephemeris in 4 colors. **Specify harmonic, zodiac, starting date.**
1 or 5 YR TRANSITS with or without natal positions 5.00
1 or 5 YR TRANSITS, NATAL & PROGRESSED 7.00
85 YR PROGRESSIONS with natal positions 10.00
NATAL LINES ONLY (plus transparency) 4.00
additional natal (same graph) 1.00
additional person's progressions (same graph) 2.00

FUTURE TRENDS

Progressed Chart in wheel format. **Specify progressed day, month and year** 2.00
Secondary Progressions Day-by-day progressed aspects to natal and progressed planets, ingresses and parallels by month, day and year. **Specify starting year, MC by solar arc (standard) or RA of mean Sun** ....5 years 3.00
10 years 5.00
85 years 15.00
Minor or Tertiary Progressions Minor based on lunar-month-for-a-year, tertiary on day-for-a-lunar-month. **Specify year, MC by solar arc (standard) or RA of mean sun** ....1 year 2.00
Progressed Lifetime Lunar Phases a la Dane Rudhyar..................... 5.00
Solar Arc Directions Day-by-day solar arc directed aspects to the natal planets, house and sign ingresses by month, day and year. **Specify starting year.** Asc. and Vertex arc directions available at same prices ....1st 5 years 1.00
Each add'l 5 years .50
Primary Arc Directions (Includes speculum) . . 5 years 1.50
Specify starting year Each add'l 5 years .50
Transits by all planets except Moon. Date and time of transiting aspects/ingresses to natal chart. **Specify starting month.** Moon-only transits available at same prices. .... 6 mos. 7.00
OR 12 mos. 12.00
summary only 6 mos. 3.50
summary only 12 mos. 6.00
calendar (9 planets OR Moon only) 6 mos. 7.00
calendar (9 planets OR Moon only) 12 mos. 12.00
calendar (Moon & planets) 6 mos. 12.00
calendar (Moon & planets) 12 mos. 20.00
Interpretive Transits. SPECIFY STARTING MONTH
Outer Planets ♃♄♅♆♇..........12 mos. 8.00
Hard Aspects Only ☌☍□∠⚼
Outer Planets ♃♄♅♆♇..........12 mos. 10.00
Soft & Hard Aspects △⚹⚻☌☍□∠⚼
9 Planets ☉☿♀♂♃♄♅♆♇ ....6 mos. 15.00
Hard Aspects Only ☌☍□∠⚼ 12 mos. 25.00
9 Planets ☉☿♀♂♃♄♅♆♇ ....6 mos. 18.00
Soft & Hard Aspects △⚹⚻☌☍□∠⚼ 12 mos. 30.00
Returns in wheel format. All returns can be precession corrected. **Specify place, Sun-return year, Moon-return month, planet-return month/year.** Solar, Lunar or Planet 2.00
13 Lunar 15.00

POTPOURRI

Winning!! Timing for gamblers, exact planet and transiting house cusps based on Joyce Wehrman's system. 1-7 days (per day) 3.00
8 or more days (per day) 2.00
Biorhythms Chart the 23-day, 28-day and 33-day cycles in .... Printed { per mo. .50 / 12 mos. 4.00 } black/white graph format.
4-Color Graph on our plotter .... Color 6 mos. 2.00
Custom House Cusps Table for each minute of sidereal time. **Specify latitude ° ′ ″** 10.00
Custom American Ephemeris Page Any month, 2500BC-AD2500. **Specify zodiac (Sidereal includes RA & dec.)**
One mo. geocentric or two mos. heliocentric 5.00
One year ephemeris (**specify beginning mo. yr.**) ... 50.00
One year heliocentric ephemeris 25.00
Fertility Report The Jonas method with Sun/Moon-squares/oppositions to the planets, for 1 year 3.00
Specify starting month.
Lamination of 1 or 2 sheets 1.00
Transparency (B/W) of any chart or map.
Ordered at same time..................... 1.00
Handling charge per order..................... 2.00

SAME DAY SERVICE — Ask for Free Catalog

ASTRO COMPUTING SERVICES, Inc.
P.O. BOX 16430
SAN DIEGO, CA 92116-0430
NEIL F. MICHELSEN

(Prices Subject to Change)